CAROLINA'S LOST COLONY

CAROLINA'S LOST COLONY

Stuarts Town and the
STRUGGLE FOR SURVIVAL
in Early South Carolina

Peter N. Moore

THE UNIVERSITY OF
SOUTH CAROLINA PRESS

© 2022 University of South Carolina

Published by the University of South Carolina Press
Columbia, South Carolina 29208

www.uscpress.com

Manufactured in the United States of America

31 30 29 28 27 26 25 24 23 22
10 9 8 7 6 5 4 3 2 1

Library of Congress Cataloging-in-Publication Data
can be found at http://catalog.loc.gov/.

ISBN 978-1-64336-360-8 (hardcover)
ISBN 978-1-64336-361-5 (paperback)
ISBN 978-1-64336-362-2 (ebook)

To Nathaniel,
Shaila, and Matthew

Contents

Illustrations and Maps

Acknowledgments

Writing this book has given me great joy, but it would not have been possible without the generous help of colleagues and the financial support of my university. I owe a debt of gratitude to Alex Moore, who offered much encouragement and read the entire manuscript before it went to press. Michael Winship made numerous suggestions for clarifying and strengthening my work on Scottish Covenanters; and Carla Pestana, Claudio Saunt, and Peter Hoffer read portions of the manuscript and shared their insights. Thanks also to my colleagues at Texas A&M University–Corpus Christi who reviewed grant proposals, wrote letters of support, and helped me refine my approach at critical junctures in the project: David Blanke, Robert Wooster, Sandrine Sanos, Dan Riechers, Colleen Fitzgerald, and especially Pat Carroll, who gave invaluable advice on reading seventeenth-century Spanish archival documents. Students from my undergraduate class on colonial America kindly agreed to join a focus group that read and critiqued my prologue to make it more accessible to nonspecialists. Thank you, Will Steagall, Alyssa Aguilar, Gabby Bazan, Sarah Serna, David Cardenas, and Benjamin Lugo. Discussing this chapter with you was one of the highlights of the project, as was my work with a promising young graphic design student, Amanda Espericueta, who drew the maps for the book.

South Texas is far away from the archives in Florida, South Carolina, and Scotland, and my archival research would not have been possible without the financial support of Texas A&M University–Corpus Christi. Awards from the Office of Research and Innovation and the College of Liberal Arts, combined with funds from my department's Joe B. Frantz Endowment, paid for multiple archival visits, and a semester of research leave from the Center for Faculty Excellence gave me time to write. Through the Employee Betterment Program, I was able to take coursework to improve my Spanish reading skills. As always, Brenton Day provided excellent interlibrary loan service, which was absolutely essential for the timely completion of this book.

Much of my research took place during the pandemic, and I am grateful to the archivists who persevered through shutdowns, furloughs, and backlogs to make their collections available. Virginia Ellison at the South Carolina Historical Society; Bryan Collars and Steve Tuttle at the South Carolina Department of

Archives and History; Michele Wilbanks and James Cusick at the P. K. Yonge Library; Lynsey Nairn at the Mount Stuart Archives on the Isle of Bute; Charles Brown at the St. Louis Mercantile Library; and the staff at the Clements Library, the Hollings Special Collections Library, the Special Collections Library at the University of Glasgow, the Centre for Research Collections at Edinburgh University Library, the National Records of Scotland, and the National Library of Scotland patiently answered queries, scanned documents, and accommodated my visits.

I made several new acquaintances over the course of this project, all of whom made crucial contributions to my understanding of the peoples and places featured in this book. Many thanks to Chester DePratter, Eric Graham, Lou Roper, and Greg Waselkov for pointing me in the right direction. A family friend, Julia Rúbies Subirós, provided much-needed help in translating a Spanish letter. An old acquaintance, Randolph Scully, kindly shared his work in progress on seventeenth-century slavery reform, and another, Lorri Glover, offered advice and encouragement. I was also delighted to meet a group of local history enthusiasts from Beaufort, South Carolina, who were kind enough to meet with me to discuss the project and show me the lay of the land in Port Royal. Larry Koolkin, Alexis Bomar, Mary Lou Brewton, Tom Wilson, Phil Cromer, Stephen Murray, Chris Allen, and the encyclopedic Larry Rowland made my visit to Beaufort both educational and entertaining.

Once again, I am fortunate to publish with the University of South Carolina Press. I am grateful for the professionalism, wisdom, and support of my editor, Ehren Foley, who never failed to appreciate this project and carefully shepherded it through the publication process. The Press's anonymous reviewers gave the manuscript a thorough critique, which saved me from multiple embarrassing mistakes and vastly improved the final product. Portions of chapters 2–4 were previously published in the article "Scotland's Lost Colony Found: Rediscovering Stuarts Town, 1682–1688" (*The Scottish Historical Review*, volume XCIX, issue 1, no. 249 [April 2020], 26–50). Parts of the prologue and chapter 1 were published in the article "Indigenous Power and Collapse on the Lower South Carolina Coast, Precontact–1684," (*South Carolina Historical Magazine*, volume 120, no. 1 [January 2019], 4–29). A portion of the epilogue was published as "An Enslaver's Guide to Slavery Reform: William Dunlop's 1690 Proposals to Christianize Slaves in the British Atlantic" (*Church History*, 91, no. 2 [June 2022], 264–85).

I have been blessed to have a lifelong friend, partner, and companion who never fails to love and support me. Thanks, Kim, for listening patiently as I processed this project on our morning walks. This book is dedicated to our three children, Nathaniel, Shaila, and Matthew, who are all grown up now. The world is as broken now as it ever was, but your compassion, acceptance, curiosity, and gentleness give me hope for its future.

Introduction

CAROLINA'S LOST COLONY FOUND

Early in the morning of March 7, 1685, while it was still dark, sixty Yamasee slave raiders attacked the village of Santa Catalina de Afuica, a Spanish mission town in central Florida's Timucua province. For nearly two weeks, the Yamasees had traveled undetected across 250 miles of forest and swamp, following half-remembered paths and crossing rivers swollen by the spring rains. This was their first foray into slaving, and they had chosen their victims well: Santa Catalina de Afuica was a small village on Florida's exposed northern frontier, and it was far from the provincial garrison, making it an easy target. Still, the Timucuans were old and bitter enemies, and the Yamasees knew they would mount a fierce defense. The attackers would need to catch them by surprise, using the darkness and their newly acquired firearms—supplied by their Scottish partners at Stuarts Town, a newly established colony on the Carolina coast (at present-day Beaufort)—to sow fear and confusion. Approaching Santa Catalina from two directions, the Yamasees took the town by storm while its people slept, shouting war cries and firing their weapons as they swept through the village. Dazed and disoriented, many villagers fled into the woods to save themselves. For four hours, the Yamasees sacked, burned, and plundered Santa Catalina. They murdered eighteen Timucuans, torched their homes, and looted and burned the mission house and chapel. They stole the silver communion plate, the friar's robes, and, oddly, some Spanish prayer books. They also took twenty-eight women and boys captive. By eight o'clock, they were on the road again, going first to Tama, their ancient ancestral homeland in central Georgia, then to Yamacraw at the mouth of the Savannah River, not far from their new home on the Carolina coast, where they would deliver the "great booty" to their Scottish friends.[1]

This little-known raid on Santa Catalina de Afuica, and, more generally, the Scottish–Yamasee partnership that made it possible, marked a turning point in the history of the colonial southeast. The story begins in 1684, when Scots and Yamasees, with no coordination and completely by accident, colonized a cluster of sea islands known as Port Royal, which was located on the contested borders of Spanish Florida and English Carolina. Instead of competition and conflict, their dual colonization of Port Royal led to collaboration.[2] Together, the Scots and Yamasees stood to make their joint settlement into a regional power center that threatened the security of St. Augustine and the commercial ambitions of Charles Town. The raid on Santa Catalina was a bold assertion of their power. It signaled their intention to exploit Florida's weaknesses and occupy its receding frontier and to control the lucrative trade in Indian slaves and animal hides with the Native peoples of the interior. For a brief moment in 1685, all eyes turned to Port Royal, which, months earlier, had been little more than a sleepy backwater of sparsely peopled Indian towns on the forgotten edge of two empires. Its colonization set in motion a chain of hostilities, realignments, coalescences, displacement, and destruction that transformed the region. The full story of this dual colonization has been lost. Recovering it is key to understanding the colonial southeast at a pivotal moment in its history.

In broad terms, this regional transformation, which took place between 1660 and 1690, can best be described as a shift from a Spanish colonial world to a British colonial world, although these labels do not do justice to the Native peoples who co-created these worlds. In the mid-seventeenth century, relations between southeastern Natives and Europeans were framed by Florida's mission system. Within this system, Natives lived in missionized towns and were similar to medieval peasants, exchanging their labor and much of their cultural and political autonomy for Spanish goods and protection. Outside of this mission system, on the frontiers of La Florida in what is now Georgia and South Carolina, Indigenous people lived in independent but interconnected towns, some of them quite populous and powerful, and they had little or no contact with Europeans.

By the early eighteenth century, this had changed dramatically. Relations between Natives and Europeans were now framed by a commercial system built mainly around the Indian slave and deer skin trade. Within this system, some Indigenous peoples were trade partners; that is, enslavers who supplied English traders with Indian captives. Others, especially those within the Spanish missions, were commodities who were torn from their communities and families and sold as slaves, mostly to the West Indies. The commercial market for these Indian slaves rapidly transformed the region. The Spanish mission towns retreated, and Florida's Indigenous population collapsed. To capitalize on the slave trade and protect themselves from enslavement, Native people on the borderlands of Florida and Carolina consolidated their autonomous towns and reorganized into powerful confederations, such as the Creek, Chickasaw, and Catawba. This transformation was well under way by 1690, although its full implications would not be known until the first decades of the eighteenth century, when the Indian slave trade consumed the enslavers themselves.[3]

It is tempting to see this transformation as somehow inevitable, as part of an unstoppable transition to capitalism and modernity. Southeastern Indians enslaved one another long before the Europeans arrived, thus creating the conditions for a more destructive slave trade fueled by global demand for labor. In the same way that Native populations declined when they encountered Old World diseases, ancient Indian practices of captive-taking exploded when mixed with capitalist labor markets and the English demand for slaves. It was just the nature of things, like a chemical reaction. As unregulated capitalism marched on, modern market-based relationships displaced medieval feudal societies. English ruthlessness and luxury goods tapped into human greed and bent everything to the will of the market, and the British way prevailed.

It is hard for us to imagine a past where Native populations are not decimated and where Anglo-America doesn't win. From the vantage point of the seventeenth century, however, the direction of historical change did not lead inevitably to the commercial Indian slave trade and the British colonial world. In the early 1680s, commercial Indian slavers were outliers, and the Indian slave trade was contested on both sides of the Atlantic. Powerful people pushed back against Indian slavery. Others, including even some of the enslavers themselves, imagined intercultural communities based on Christian as opposed to market relationships. Moreover, the English were just one "tribe" among many. Charles Town's security was just as precarious as St. Augustine's, and both were more precarious than that of the powerful Native towns of the interior. Preoccupied with problems of their own, both were also hamstrung in relation to the small Scottish colony of Stuarts Town and the much larger Yamasee settlement, and they could do nothing to prevent the Scots and Yamasees from acting in their own interest. In short, there were moments when alternative futures were possible and other moments when these alternatives were closed off. The Scottish–Yamasee colonization of Port Royal was one of these pivotal moments.

This book unpacks this moment. Instead of global forces, it stresses contingency. It gives attention to local circumstances, personal rivalries, unexpected opportunities, and shifting conditions. This ever-changing context informed decisions on the ground and shaped the course of events. It shows how the colonization of Port Royal in 1684 destabilized an already unstable region, which now stood on the edge of a knife. Although neither the Scots nor the Yamasees came to Port Royal to become slavers—indeed, far from it—they did just that, joining hands to raid Santa Catalina and sell the Timucuan captives abroad. In so doing, they revived Carolina's dormant Indian slave trade, with catastrophic consequences. How this happened and the fallout from it are the subject of this book.

I have tried to tell this story from all sides, incorporating the perspectives of Scots, English, Spaniards, and a variety of Indigenous peoples.[4] Of all these groups, Natives were easily the most powerful force in the region, far more so than the European colonizers who were hustling around its edges to score Indian souls, labor, or trade deals. Like many recent histories of the colonial southeast, this one places Indian power at the center of the story.[5] It begins with the long backstory of the original Native towns of coastal Carolina. In the sixteenth century, these peoples frustrated Spanish attempts to impose a colonial order on their world and forced Spain to abandon its colony, Santa Elena, along with its dreams of a vast continental empire anchored at Port Royal. The story continues with the migration of Westo slavers into the region in 1660, who "ruinated" the coastal towns and thereby removed the main obstacle to England's colonization of Carolina in the 1670s.[6] Finally, it concludes with the Yamasees, who occupied lands claimed by the English and Scots—who were powerless to stop them—and controlled access to trade between the British and Apalachicola peoples of the interior. During the first century and more after European colonization of Carolina, Indigenous coastal peoples, Westos, Yamasees, and Apalachicolas were pulling the levers of regional power, whereas the Spaniards, English, and Scots were struggling to penetrate the region and get a piece of the action. These Indigenous power brokers, moreover, kept their eyes mostly on other Natives. They were guided more by internal political concerns and diplomatic relations with other Indigenous groups than by relations with Europeans.

When I started doing research for this book, I did not expect to find Native people at the center of it. I had done considerable work on the social and religious history of colonial South Carolina, focusing especially on Scottish and Scots Irish Presbyterians, and I was mainly interested in the story of the Scottish colony of Stuarts Town. During the Restoration era, the Scots were excluded by English law from trading in the English empire and forced by King Charles II to conform to his rule over their national church. As persecution intensified in the early 1680s, they sought to make Stuarts Town a religious refuge as well as a profitable commercial enterprise. Once they settled into Port Royal, however, the Scots became much more interested in building an empire than creating a religious safe haven. This brought them into their pivotal alliance with the Yamasees, and this dual colonization, not merely the Stuarts Town settlement, became the subject of the book. Unlike the Yamasees, the Scots had very little power, although they failed to realize it at the time. They were passionate colonizers, but their meager resources did not match their lofty ideals and imperial aspirations, and their story ended tragically.

The tension between the Scots' religious and economic motives makes up a secondary thread in the narrative of this book. The Stuarts Town colonizers were Covenanters, radical Presbyterians who had sworn an oath to resist all attempts by state actors, up to and including the king, to control the Church of Scotland. They·launched their colonial project at the height of persecution, driven in part by a dream to create a religious haven and convert Native people to Protestant Reformed Christianity. Instead, they enslaved Christian Indians and exploited a variety of other people to support their colonial enterprise. Their persecution did not make the Scots more tolerant—certainly not toward Roman Catholics and their Anglican cousins in England—nor did suffering for their principles make them more empathetic toward other unfree people. Seeing themselves as warriors in a cosmic struggle between Christ and Antichrist, they wanted religious power, not just religious freedom. This included the power to impose uniform belief and practice on others, and they considered themselves obligated by their sacred oaths to God to seek and use such power at all cost. These ironies should not surprise us. The Scots were not the only refugees who came to America seeking religious freedom but who ended up enslaving, dispossessing, and displacing others. Their story is another reminder that America's founding myth of religious freedom is fraught with contradictions.

Besides its implications for the history of the colonial southeast, centering this story around Native people and Port Royal brings a new perspective to the early history of South Carolina. Historians have depicted this history as an unfolding struggle between the Lords Proprietors, who governed the Carolinas from afar in London, and colonial officials who ruled it on the ground in Charles Town. However, from the vantage point of Port Royal, the real centers of power in Carolina were in Indian country, and Native peoples created the conditions in which European colonizers operated. In the sixteenth century, Indigenous peoples at the three chief lowcountry towns—Escamaçu, Orista, and Coçapoy—controlled Spanish access to the Carolina coast and set the terms of trade and missionization. In 1680, it was the Westos' attempt to draw English-allied Indians into their own orbit, rather than the power struggles between English traders in Charles Town, that brought about war between the Westos and English. That same decade, Yamasee and Apalachicola headmen, not Charles Town traders, Goose Creek planters, or Lords Proprietors, made key decisions about the Indian slave trade and which Europeans would be given access to it. Instead of pulling the strings, European colonizers were the supplicants who responded to Indian initiatives. They sat on the margins of Indigenous power centers in Yamasee Port Royal and the Chattahoochee River Valley.[7]

And yet, the reopening of the commercial slave trade did not end well for Indigenous people. For all their power, in the end, Natives were victims as well as agents of the slave trade. The triumph of the British colonial system devoured southeastern Indians and shattered their world. It smothered the Yamasees in debt to English traders, which imperiled their liberty and ultimately engulfed the region in war. Despite their confederations, southeastern Natives could not control the monster they had helped to create, and it consumed them.

Although the tragic events of the 1680s may seem remote to us, the seventeenth century was not as different from our time as we might like to think. Today, we would call the raid on Santa Catalina de Afuica a crime against humanity. We would recognize it as a form of human trafficking or one of the many modern-day slaveries familiar to poor and developed societies alike. Carolina's Lords Proprietors, the English noblemen who governed the colony from London, agreed. They railed against the "pernicious Inhumane barbarous practice" of buying and selling Indian captives, and they repeatedly tried to discipline the "dealers in Indians" at Charles Town who engaged in it (although they did not bat an eye at enslaving Africans). Provincial officials and traders resisted them at every turn. Indeed, few colonial societies were so lawless and unruly, so factious and self-serving, or so ruthless, greedy, and inured to violence as seventeenth-century South Carolina. Long before its rice plantations and Black majority, the "bloody butchers" of Carolina, as one exiled Presbyterian prisoner called them, created a slaving society built around the brutal exploitation and sale of stolen Indians, Africans, and Europeans. In 1684, however, as Yamasees and Scots were flooding into Port Royal, this future was far from certain. The proprietors did not know that they were fighting a losing battle, nor did they believe that Carolina was rotten at its core. Along with the Scots and Yamasees, they hoped for a better world.[8]

Prologue

THE INDIGENOUS WORLD OF
THE LOWER CAROLINA COAST

The only surviving origin story of South Carolina's Indigenous coastal people comes from the southernmost tribe, the Escamaçu. It tells of a great flood that killed all but two people who had taken refuge in a cave, where they found a dead bird. As they plucked its red feathers and blew them into the wind, each feather became a different tribe with its own language. The two beings gave names to the tribes. The singing of another red bird told them the flood waters had receded, and in the same way, their people, even if deep in the woods and far from the rivers, could tell if the tide was ebbing or flowing by the notes of the birdsong.

Through this story, the Escamaçus understood their place in the Indigenous world of the southern coastal plain. Birds were beings of great spiritual power in southeastern Indian culture, and feathers symbolized that power. Plucked from the same source, the Escamaçus shared a common, sacred origin with their neighbors, but as different feathers from the same bird, they were differentiated by language, name, and place. They were all, however, placed by the sea as people of the water. Born out of a destructive flood, created to ply the creeks and rivers of the coastal islands and get their sustenance from the marshes and inlets, able to read the changing tide in the call of birds, they were connected with the water, and their lives ebbed and flowed with the seasonal rhythms of the coastal plain.[1]

At the center of the coastal Indians' world was the autonomous town.[2] The town was a social, political, and sacred place, not just a physical one. It was made up of small family groups or bands that broke off in winter to hunt and gather in the forests of the interior coastal plain and then reunited in the spring to fish, plant corn, and gather oysters and other foods from the inlets and estuaries. Towns were democratic, led by *caciques* or *cacicas* (headmen or head-women) who governed with the consent of tribal councils made up of the heads of families and lineages.[3] Towns also hosted feasts led by shamans or *iawas*, who used elaborate rituals to summon and petition the powerful gods who sustained them as separate and independent people. Separateness was at the core of coastal Indians' identity. It was sustained not only by their gods but also by their languages, subsistence economies, political autonomy, and cultural choices; yet they were separate together. They had no common name, identifying instead with their towns—Escamaçu, Orista, Combahee, Stono, Coçapoy, and Cayagua —but they shared a common culture. Grounded in their local identities but having similar practices, values, and customs, the coastal people understood their towns to be parts of an organic whole. Theirs was an Indian world of small and distinct but interconnected peoples of great collective power—like feathers from the same bird—and together they dominated Carolina's lower coastal plain.[4]

The Spanish colonizers who came to the southeast in the sixteenth century disrupted but did not shatter these coastal Indian communities. Instead of seeing them as conquerors or colonizers imposing a Spanish imperial order on Indigenous people, Natives saw them as yet another small, autonomous tribe in an Indian world, and they tried to integrate the Spanish colony, Santa Elena, into their world order. Although they had a healthy respect for Spanish firearms and valued Spanish trade goods, Indians never viewed the colonizers as more than coequals. They did not recognize Spanish political pretensions or claims over their territory, and they frustrated Jesuit and Franciscan missionaries' attempts to "reduce" them through the mission system. When Spaniards forgot their place or failed to abide by Indian social norms, the colonizers incited violence. The Spaniards called this violence "rebellion," and historians have called it "resistance," but both of these terms rest on the false assumption that the Spaniards were dominant, which they never were. Instead, they were dependent, and in the end, their power rested solely on superior military technology and brute force. However, Spain did not need a military outpost on the Carolina coast, just as coastal Indians did not need a Spanish garrison with no ability to form trade relationships. As a result, military force was no basis for a successful colony on the Carolina coast, a land devoid of mineral wealth, nor did it give Indians any space for incorporating the Spaniards into their world. Ultimately unable to either integrate or expel the Spaniards, the coastal people simply outlasted them. Their history, both before and after contact, is a story of Indigenous power, not conquest or decline.[5]

THE INDIAN WORLD ORDER

Escamaçu was one of seven distinct polities that made up the coastal zone in the contact era. Its territory lay between Port Royal and the Savannah River, making it the southernmost of Carolina's coastal peoples. Escamaçu was bordered

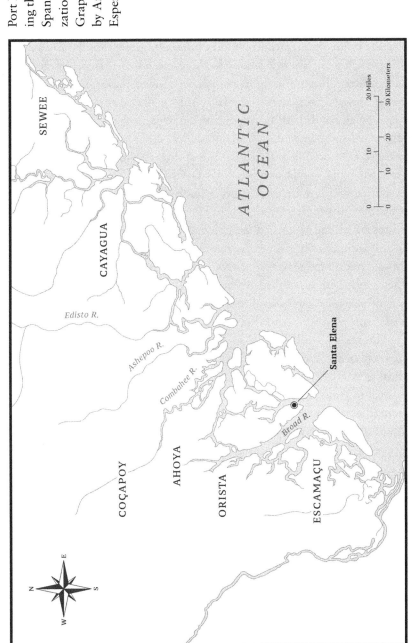

Port Royal during the Era of Spanish Colonization, ca. 1570. Graphic design by Amanda Espericueta.

on the north by Orista, a strategically significant cluster of towns at Port Royal. Further inland, some fifty miles up either the Salkehatchie or the Santee River, lay Caçao (or Coçapoy), one of the most populous towns in the region. Among the remaining towns, most of which make only fleeting appearances in the historical record, the most significant was Cayagua, which was near present-day Charleston.[6]

Like the origin myth, archaeological evidence suggests that the Escamaçus and their neighbors were indigenous to the coast rather than recent arrivals. Hunter–gatherers began using the Sea Islands around present-day Port Royal as sites of seasonal migration in the Late Archaic period some four thousand years ago. Small bands lived inland during the winter, where they subsisted on nuts and roots and hunted deer, bear, and turkey, all of which were plentiful in the resource-rich interior coastal plain. In spring, they migrated to the coast and gathered in places such as present-day Daws Island on the Port Royal River, where marine and estuarine resources were concentrated and could support large numbers of people at once. These annual "family reunions" were social gatherings of extended kinship groups, and they provided opportunities to marry and socialize. Over time, the number and size of these sites increased. By the late precontact period, some Natives were occupying them year-round, and they evolved from seasonal base camps to something more like the semi-permanent villages of Woodland farmers who lived in the interior. After 1400 the coastal peoples began growing maize there, though they did not produce enough surpluses to feed themselves year-round and continued to migrate inland in small bands during winter. This archaeological evidence agrees with the historical record. The Jesuit missionary Juan Rogel described this same pattern of seasonal mobility among the Oristas in 1570, adding that the Indians had practiced these economic strategies "for thousands of years." Later, Spanish and English observers also commented on the coastal tribes' preference for hunting and gathering over full-time farming.[7]

Coastal Natives were only marginally influenced by the Mississippian economic, social, and cultural innovations that penetrated the southeast after 1000 C.E. Unlike traditional Woodland communities that blended small-scale farming with hunting and gathering, Mississippian societies were agriculturalists. They grew surpluses of maize to support large, sedentary populations, and they minimized hunting and gathering. The most powerful Mississippian communities were organized as paramount chiefdoms, which were governed by semidivine hereditary rulers who claimed descent from the sun and lived atop platform mounds. These mounds, which also housed temples and served as burial sites for rulers, were the most distinctive architectural feature of Mississippian culture. Unlike Woodland societies, which were divided along gender and age lines but were otherwise egalitarian, chiefdoms were stratified and included classes of nobles, warriors, priests, and commoners. At their height in the middle Mississippian period, the most advanced of these southeastern chiefdoms were expansive, sustaining their large populations by ensnaring outlying towns in debt or subduing them militarily and forcing them to pay tribute in the form of maize.[8]

By the late Mississippian era (1350–1600 C.E.), the greatest of these centralized chiefdoms were breaking apart, and chieftains relied increasingly on their ability to supply prestige trade goods to their neighbors to command warriors and tribute. However, although they were smaller and less stable than their predecessors, the paramount chiefdoms of the Carolina and Georgia interior still exerted power over large swaths of territory, and Mississippian cultural practices pervaded the region. The most prominent chiefdom in South Carolina was at Cofitachequi in the piedmont, some one hundred miles from the coast. When Hernando de Soto came through the region in 1540, Cofitachequi was ruled by a great "Lady," carried on a litter covered with pure white cloth. Its chief town had three temple mounds containing pearls, copper, and deer skins, and its second town, Talimeco, had some five hundred houses and thousands of residents (typical coastal villages had about twenty houses and two hundred residents). Outlying villages, which extended in a fifty-mile radius from the chiefdom's center, supplied these central towns with corn. Another Mississippian chiefdom, Ocute, bordered the interior coastal plain of central Georgia. Mississippian influence was also pronounced among the Guale people of coastal Georgia, just south of Escamaçu, who had revitalized an old burial mound around 1350 and made it into a robust ceremonial center for the next century. The Guales had no single, centralized chieftain, but they cultivated maize intensively, and they had hereditary rulers, or *micos*, with power over small groups of towns (that is, more power than caciques, who were the heads of towns, but less power than paramount chieftains like the Lady of Cofitachequi, whom the Spaniards described as an empress).[9]

Despite their proximity to these Mississippian societies, Carolina's coastal Indians were not subject to these chieftains, and they adopted few Mississippian practices. As already noted, they were not sedentary agriculturalists but chose instead to practice seasonal mobility. This gave them a diverse diet of roots, nuts, wild fruit, game, and seafood, which was supplemented by, but not dependent on, maize. Seasonal food scarcity lowered fertility and kept their populations relatively low, as did their practice of discouraging pregnancy among young women. They had no overarching ruler, or mico, living instead in relatively small, independent towns governed by caciques or cacicas together with tribal councils. Unlike the Guales and other, more fully Mississippianized societies, they practiced monogamy and divided labor along gender lines, not class. Also, they did not build mounds, although their material culture featured some soft Mississippian adaptations, such as round council houses, open plazas for playing ball, and Mississippian style ceramics. They also had some fairly elaborate ceremonial religious practices that reflected Mississippian influence, but at most they borrowed pieces of Mississippian culture, adapting it to their own uses while clinging to their traditional economies and forms of social organization.[10]

The coastal tribes also held fast to their traditional languages. Indeed, one of the most interesting characteristics of these communities is that they spoke two or more different, even mutually unintelligible, languages. Historians and linguists dispute this point, but analysis of tribal names and over one hundred surviving words attributed to the coastal people suggests that they spoke multiple unknown languages unrelated to any of the major linguistic families of the southeast. This linguistic argument is further supported by indirect evidence based on the use of interpreters by the Spaniards. For example, when Francisco Fernández de Ecija sailed up the Carolina coast in 1605 searching for French traders, he asked for three interpreters, one for Escamaçu, one for Cayagua (Kiawah), and a third for Joya. On a second voyage in 1609, Ecija's interpreter was Maria de Miranda, a Native Escamaçu who had married a Spanish soldier and moved to St. Augustine twenty years earlier. Miranda was only able to speak to a Cayagua captain because "he understood something of the (Descamagu) language," indicating that the two languages were otherwise unintelligible to one another. Several cases from the early 1670s also show Spaniards' use of multiple interpreters when interrogating Indians from Escamaçu and Kiawah. Although they inhabited the same coastal zone and shared common cultural practices and forms of social organization, Carolina's coastal Indians spoke languages that were distinct from one another and from those of the Muskogean-speaking groups to their south and west, further reflecting their strong local or town identities and sense of separateness.[11]

Coastal peoples' economic practices, linguistic and cultural choices, and forms of political and social organization were all expressions of their autonomy. This autonomy, moreover, was sacred. Their values and practices, their very separateness itself, had a spiritual source and a religious dimension, and they were reflected in myth and ritual. In the beginning, spiritual beings had placed coastal people by the sea and given them separate names, languages, and identities. Honoring their separateness meant honoring the gods who gave and ultimately sustained that separateness. To neglect their obligations to these gods was to risk abandonment, dependency, and destruction as a people.

Some of the earliest European visitors to Port Royal left wonderful descriptions of coastal Indians' spiritual practices along with hints of their dread and awe of their great god, Toya. In 1562, the French colonizer René Laudonnière witnessed Orista's feast of Toya. The ceremony began when the participants, "painted and trimmed with rich feathers of divers colors," slowly proceeded from the cacique's house to the central plaza, led by three shamans or iawas, shaking timbrels and chanting mournfully. After circling the plaza three times, the men suddenly bolted into the woods "like unbridled horses," and the women, filled with grief and rage, cried and cut the arms of young girls with mussel shells, so that "the blood flowed which they flang into the ayre, crying out three times, *He Toya*." The young men remained in the woods for two days. During this time, the iawas ritually summoned Toya. When he appeared to them, they asked him for "divers strange things." Returning to the village on the third day, the young men danced "with a cheerful courage," gladdening the hearts of the old men who were excluded from the ritual. After concluding these ceremonies, the cacique invited his French guests to join the feast, which the Indians "fell on, eating with a greediness," for they had fasted for three days and were famished.[12]

With its drama, broad participation, multiple shamans, extended duration, communication with the spirit world, elaborate costume, fasting, feasting, and blood rituals, this ceremony clearly reflected Orista's great fear of and respect for Toya, a powerful god who must be properly honored. These were not empty rituals; they defined the Oristas' relationship with Toya, their sustainer. They took this relationship seriously, as a matter of life and death. The rituals were sacred, and when the cacique's French guests laughed at the ceremony, he would not allow them to witness it (the only reason Laudonnière learned the details was because one of his men secretly left the cacique's house and "hid himself behind a very thick bush" to watch the proceedings). Toya's words were also sacred, and the iawas warned their people not to tell the French what Toya had said to them in the woods. Eight years after Laudonnière's visit, the Jesuit missionary Juan Rogel learned a similar lesson about offending Orista's god, whom Rogel called "the Demon." After spending eight months with the Oristas, Rogel had earned their trust but won no converts, so he tried a direct approach, telling them plainly that "to become sons of God, they must become enemies of the Demon, for he is evil and loves all evil things." The Oristas were "greatly displeased" and "very much offended" at these words, and they refused to listen further to Rogel. Insisting that "the Demon was so good that there was nothing better than he," they abandoned Rogel "because [he] spoke evil of the Demon." Whatever benefits coastal Indians derived from their relationship with Spanish missionaries—which came mostly in the form of gifts, mediation with Spanish officials, and limited protection from abusive soldiers—they were not worth risking the displeasure of Toya, the source of all good things.[13]

The spiritual beings who placed them along the water expected them to stay there, and the coastal peoples developed a deep sense of place and rootedness that further distinguished them from the Mississippian peoples of the interior. Faced with the rise and fall of chiefdoms and shifting, unstable power dynamics of the late Mississippian era, some inland peoples adapted by giving up their attachments to local places and embracing mobility; not so for the coastal towns. When facing the prospect of collapse after devastating slave raids by the Westo Indians in the late 1660s, the headmen of Escamaçu and Ahoya, although welcomed by Spanish authorities to resettle under their protection in Guale, decided to remain in their ancestral towns. The coastal peoples were firmly rooted in their place, and even the threat of enslavement and annihilation could not overcome their sense of fixity.[14]

The world of the coastal Indians was constructed to protect their separateness and sacred autonomy. Seasonal mobility enabled them to avoid maize dependency along with dependency on neighboring chieftains in search of tribute. It also kept their populations relatively low. Living in dispersed settlements and decentralized polities, staying beyond the reach of inland chiefdoms, holding onto their local languages, and rejecting Mississippian mobility and the cultural practices that supported chiefdoms were assertions of their independence and values in a Mississippian world. Myth and ritual infused these values and practices with spiritual power. Religion explained their place in the wider world, sacralized their social order and traditional ways, and governed their relations with outsiders. In this Indigenous world, everything worked together to sustain their independence and identities as separate people from a common source.

INTEGRATING SANTA ELENA INTO THE COASTAL INDIANS' WORLD

In the 1560s, the coastal towns permitted both French and Spanish colonizers to settle in their territory. The French colony, Charlesfort, located at the lower end of Port Royal Island, was short-lived (1562–1563). After Laudonnière's departure, the remaining colonists' provisions were destroyed in a fire, and hunger set in. Orista and Escamaçu had no surplus corn to share with them and sent them instead to the more sedentary Guales to the south. The Guales were generous. They gave maize not once but twice to the Frenchmen, but their generosity only prolonged the colony's agony. Soon the colonists mutinied, killed their

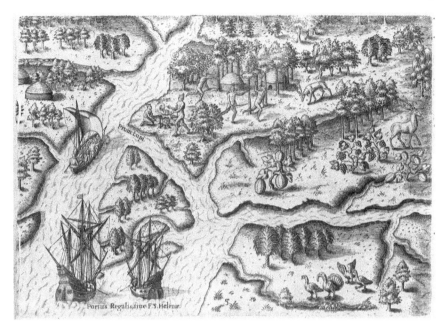

Theodor de Bry and Jacques le Moyne, *They Reach Port Royal,* 1591.
Library of Congress, Prints and Photographs Division,
reproduction number LC-USZ62–380.

commander, and sailed back to Europe on a makeshift boat, thanks in part to local Indians who supplied cordage for the sails. Miraculously the boat was seaworthy, and a handful of sailors were eventually rescued by an English ship. They had survived by eating the corpses of their dead companions.[15]

In contrast, the Spanish colony, Santa Elena, was the centerpiece of Spain's ambitious plan to control the continent. The Spaniards hoped to find a great river or system of roads connecting the Atlantic coast with Spanish silver mines in Zacatecas, Mexico, and they were especially anxious to prevent the French from colonizing the coast and thereby gaining access to Zacatecas. Although Santa Elena was better funded and had a longer life than Charlesfort, it too was plagued by hunger and ended in failure. Natives challenged every Spanish attempt to dominate them, and Spaniards frustrated Indians' efforts to incorporate them into the Indigenous world on Indian terms. As a result, the Santa Elena period of coastal peoples' history, which spanned the years 1566–1587, was marked by tension, general hostility, periodic flashes of violence, and a long and bloody war.[16]

The coastal people had surely heard of the violent exploits of Florida's *adelantado,* or governor, Pedro Menéndez de Aviles, before he came to their country in 1566 to establish a colony. Menéndez had recently slaughtered two groups of French Protestants, or Huguenots, well to their south on the Florida coast. In the 1560s, Protestantism was spreading rapidly in France, posing a threat to its neighbor, Spain, a Roman Catholic power. To Menéndez, the Huguenot colonies at Port Royal and elsewhere on Florida's coast were not only a violation of Spanish sovereignty and a threat to Spain's new world mineral wealth; they were also an attempt by the "false Christians," as Menéndez styled the Protestants, to spread their perfidious anti-Christian religion among the Natives and unite them with his French enemies. His determination to defend Spain's territorial claims thus took on the added dimension of a religious crusade, in which the normal rules of war did not apply. Menéndez destroyed Fort Caroline on the St. Marys River and massacred its one hundred forty French defenders. He executed some two hundred Huguenot prisoners of war who had been cast away south of the Spanish fort at St. Augustine, and he was determined to root out the French refugees rumored to be living among the coastal peoples of Guale and Port Royal. News traveled fast in Indian country, and Menéndez's reputation for ruthlessness surely preceded him when he came to Port Royal the following year. The coastal people gave him a cautious welcome.[17]

However, Menéndez was no run-of-the-mill conquistador. To be sure, he was a forceful leader, and he came to Orista backed by one hundred heavily armed soldiers. His diplomacy was laced with threats to cut off Natives' heads, and his offers of friendship seemed to be conditioned on their willing subordination to him and his king. On the other hand, Menéndez promised to bring families to Santa Elena, not just soldiers for a garrison but farmers and artisans with wives and children to settle a town. This sent a signal to his Indigenous hosts that the Spaniards came in peace and planned to settle, not make war and conquer.[18]

Menéndez was also a skillful negotiator, and he came as a peacemaker. On route to Port Royal, he stopped in Guale on the Georgia coast, where he learned that Guale and Orista were at war with one another. The Guales and some French castaways who lived among them had taken two Orista men captive and planned to execute them. This situation played perfectly into Menéndez's hands. He acquired these captives and returned them to Orista, earning a debt of gratitude from their families, who "caressed him very much and wept for joy." As a result of this gift, the Oristas gladly accepted Menéndez's offer to broker peace with Guale while allying with him against their mutual enemy, the French (although they had befriended the French at Charlesfort, the Oristas turned against them after the Frenchmen joined the Guale raiders in taking the two captives). In addition, the Spaniards brought hatchets, which they exchanged for

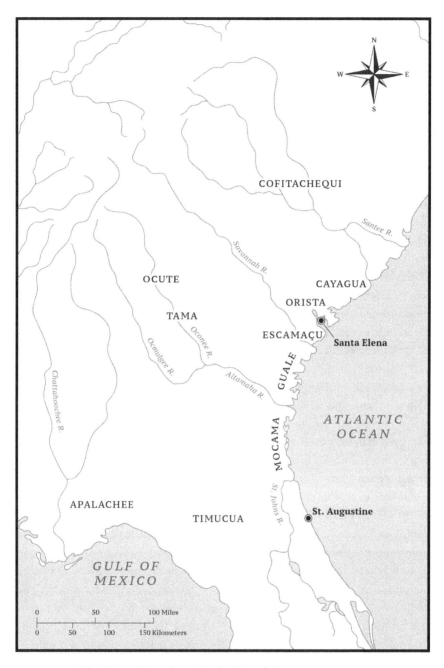

The Coastal Southeast in the Era of Contact, ca. 1570.
Graphic design by Amanda Espericueta.

burned pearls and deer skins, establishing a mutual and reciprocal relationship of exchange that reinforced their friendship and partnership. Thus, from the Natives' perspective, the Spaniards, despite their show of force, might become trusted and valuable neighbors whom the Oristas could integrate into their exchange economy and even use as go-betweens to mediate intertribal disputes.[19]

Integrating outsiders began with kinship, which was the fundamental principle of social and political organization in the coastal peoples' world, as it was for Natives throughout the southeast. Within and between the towns, kinship determined who did and did not belong; who could marry or have sex with whom; how individuals related to those around them and outside their community; and who could be enslaved, tortured, or killed. In general terms, kinship offered personhood and protection to those within the social group; non-kin did not belong, leaving them unprotected and disposable. Kinship was, thus, the door through which outsiders entered into the coastal Indians' world. If not related by blood, they could be admitted to the group through marriage, adoption, or offers of fictive or symbolic kinship. European traders frequently took Indigenous wives to cement their ties to Native communities and create the social context needed for trusting trade relationships. Similarly, Native people often took captives during raids or battles and adopted them to replace loved ones who had recently died. Adoption turned captives into kin. It protected them from execution, exchange, or enslavement, and it enabled the captive-takers to maintain their population.[20]

At Orista, the cacique invited Menéndez to live among them, probably assuming that he would take an Orista wife. When Menéndez declined, the cacique made him an honorary "elder brother," admitting him into Orista's kinship system through this fictive relationship. Either deliberately or by accident, Menéndez misinterpreted the gesture. In southeastern Indians' matrilineal societies, blood kinship or lineage was reckoned through the mother and the women on her side of the family. The most important male figure within this system was not the father but the mother's brother, who had responsibility for the well-being of his sister's children, serving as protector and teacher as well as disciplinarian. One of these brothers would be designated "elder brother" and would have authority as head of the lineage. Among the mother's children, however, brothers were also distinguished by titles of "elder brother" and "younger brother." As children, the older brothers had no authority, but they were expected to care for and defend their younger siblings. The Oristas would have applied this latter meaning of "elder brother" to Menéndez, indicating their desire for good brotherly relations with the Spaniards and protection from their enemies. The Spanish text says as much, noting "that Orista and others had

taken him for their elder brother, to defend them from their enemies." These enemies included the French, but chief among them were the Guales, with whom
Orista was at war. As fictive kin to Orista, the Spaniards automatically became
enemies of Guale. This is why both Native groups insisted on making him an
elder brother—neither wished to be his enemy—and why it was imperative that
Menéndez, who sought friendship with both groups, conclude the peace agreement on both sides. However, Menéndez interpreted his elder brother role in the
other sense, as an acknowledgement of his authority and their subordination.
The Oristas took him as elder brother "in order to do what he should command
them," and he was entitled to "command them at his will." Subsequent events
showed that neither the Oristas nor the Guales had any intention of being commanded by the Spaniards, and the fatal implications of these misunderstandings
would play out as events unfolded.[21]

In addition to setting the terms for the Spaniards' social integration into the
coastal Indians' world, Orista also controlled the process for incorporating the
Spaniards into their settlement system. When Menéndez told the cacique that
"he was going in search of a good site" for his town because "it was not right
that they should live among the Indians, and quarrel afterwards," the cacique
"told him of one, near the place where the vessel was anchored." The site was
at the southern end of Port Royal Island and stood on the same spot of ground
as Charlesfort, where two major rivers converged as they emptied into Port
Royal Sound. To the Spaniards, this was an excellent strategic location that gave
them a deep water port for their large vessels. Pronouncing it "very good and
pleasant," they immediately went to work building their fort, which Menéndez
christened San Felipe. However, the Oristas had their own reasons for steering
Menéndez to this site. It placed the Spaniards safely on the edge of the coastal
Indians' territory, six miles from the closest village and fifteen miles from the
main town.[22] With their backs to the sea and surrounded by water, they were
easier to monitor and contain. The site was unoccupied and possibly undesir-
able. Spanish farmers later complained that the soil was too sandy to grow corn
and produced little forage for cattle. It would not sustain even their relatively
small numbers. They wished to move inland where the soil was more suited to
farming, but the Natives would not allow it, and they could not afford to pay
more soldiers to protect them. In short, the Oristas did not trust their new elder
brother and steered Menéndez to a location that marginalized the Spaniards
while prioritizing their own economic, territorial, and defense needs. They also
had the power to enforce these boundaries on the Spaniards.[23]

The coastal Natives also sought, with only partial success, to integrate
Santa Elena into their exchange economy. For both Indians and Europeans,

social relationships were very important to trade, which was always more than a set of economic transactions. However, Natives understood trade within a system of gift giving, and as such it expressed relationships of power, not just transactional exchanges of goods and services. To accept a gift without giving something of value in return was to place yourself in the giver's debt, and to give without receiving something in return was to have power over the recipient. To neutralize the power of gifts, it was important that exchanges be mutual and reciprocal. This was the case with the Oristas' initial exchanges with Menéndez. After concluding their peace agreement, they shared a meal, with the Orista women bringing maize, acorns, fish, and oysters while the Spaniards supplied wine, honey, and biscuits. The return of the two captives from Guale created a huge obligation on the part of the Orista cacique, which he discharged by giving land to Menéndez and making him an elder brother. When the neighboring caciques came to the settlement to greet Menéndez as elder brother, they gave deer skins and pearls in exchange for Spanish hatchets.[24] Significantly, because these exchanges were made between the caciques and adelantado, the leaders who represented their respective communities, they were corporate and collective, not individual, exchanges. They were aimed at protecting the autonomy of the towns. By exchanging gifts of roughly equal value, Spaniards and coastal Indians treated each other as equals and maintained a balance of power between their peoples.[25]

This system broke down, however, after Menéndez left Santa Elena on other imperial business. As Rogel wrote, the soldiers began to treat the Indians "as if they have been conquered in war." Standing on their rights as elder brothers to "command them at their will," they abandoned the principle of reciprocity and required Natives to pay tribute by supplying and carrying maize to Santa Elena. When the people of one town, Ahoya, resisted these demands and killed a Spanish corporal, soldiers burned their town and imprisoned their cacique. The cacique of Orista then volunteered to store and transport the maize, not as a form of tribute but as a gift that the Spaniards were obligated to return. This sent a signal to neighboring towns that Santa Elena was now in Orista's debt. The cacique was asserting and declaring his power, not subjecting his people to Spanish rule. This was evident two years later, when the commander at Santa Elena, which had run out of food yet again, demanded that Orista host and feed forty soldiers from the garrison. The Oristas resisted, Rogel noted, and forced the Spaniards to honor the rules of the Indian exchange economy by offering "gifts and toys."[26]

Finally, both Spaniards and Natives completely miscalculated when it came to incorporating Spanish missionaries and Christianity into the coastal Indians' world. Jesuit and Franciscan missionaries sought to impose a mission system in which Indigenous people would be "reduced," that is, gathered into permanent settlements where they would be instructed, converted, and policed. In other parts of Florida later in the sixteenth century, such as Guale, missionaries got buy-in from Native micos by giving them gifts, which the micos, in turn, distributed to lower level caciques, thus pulling their towns into the micos' and the Spaniards' orbit. In exchange for these gifts, Indian leaders permitted the missionaries to live among them, accepting, at least on the surface, acculturation and Christianity, and Christian Indians supplied labor or corn to support the missions. These Native *cristianos*, or converts, also contributed to a labor draft to support Spanish military forces that provided security to the mission towns.[27]

Initially the Oristas seemed eager to convert to Christianity, but, as the Jesuits and Franciscans would later learn, it was for all the wrong reasons. The cacique told Menéndez that he and his people wanted to become true Christians because "those of Guale wanted to be, for those people were not to be better than they." For his part, the cacique of Guale insisted that Menéndez "leave him people to live in his land" and teach them how to be Christians "since he had done so for Orista." The coastal people understood little about Christianity as religion and practice, but they recognized its diplomatic value at once. After all, Menéndez had defined Christianization as the rejection of the "false Christianity" of his bitter enemies, the French Protestants, and he made it a condition of Orista's alliance with Santa Elena and its peace with Guale. The Indians were willing, even eager, to trade in Christianity as a form of diplomatic currency that maintained a balance of power between rival tribes. In addition, they would soon realize that missionaries were eager to protect Indians from abusive soldiers, and they liked having the friars around to mediate conflict with secular Spanish authorities.[28]

However, the coastal people had no use for Christian practice and ethics and showed little interest in the actual religion peddled by the Jesuit and Franciscan missionaries who followed Menéndez. They laughed at Rogel's teachings. Although he offered them tools and seed corn, they refused his pleas to give up their mobile lifestyle, grow more maize, and settle in one village year-round to be properly reduced and converted. As noted earlier, they had no intention of forsaking Toya, and they rejected Rogel completely when he spoke ill of the Demon. Moreover, because their autonomous towns were decentralized, there was no Native hierarchy through which the Spaniards could channel gifts and consolidate power. In short, Orista and its neighbors paid lip service to Christianity when it suited their diplomatic and trade goals or helped to check the aspirations of their enemies, but they absolutely rejected it as a substitute for their traditional religion or a tool for Spanish subjugation through the mission system. The Natives were unable to bend the missionaries to their will and keep them on their own terms—as friends and mediators—and they were unwilling to tolerate the missionaries when they challenged Indigenous practices and beliefs. This represented a failure on the part of the coastal towns, for the friars played an important role as go-betweens for coastal Natives and Spanish authorities. When the missionaries left Santa Elena in 1574, they took with them any hope of containing the violence that simmered beneath the surface of Spanish–Indian relations.[29]

THE ESCAMAÇU WAR

In the end, Indians' efforts to marginalize Santa Elena failed; and, unable to incorporate the Spaniards into their world on their own terms, coastal people turned to violence to check Spanish aggression. Like their social, economic, and religious responses to the newcomers, Native warfare was grounded in the world they had created, a world of small, separate, interconnected settlements. No match for well-armed and armored Spanish soldiers, they adopted the military strategies of the weak: deception, secrecy, and inter-Indian diplomacy. In doing so, they triggered one of the most destructive yet least known wars in the history of the colonial southeast, exceptional both in its ferocity and in the scale of Indigenous peoples' alliances and coordination.

Isolated episodes of anti-Spanish violence between 1566 and 1575 stemmed from chronic food shortages at Santa Elena. Farmers complained of poor soil on Port Royal island, and they were plagued by drought in the 1560s and flooding in the 1570s. Spanish officials mismanaged the food supply. Rations were inadequate, and Menéndez refused to let settlers have a share of the colony's cattle until the animals had multiplied for ten years. In the meantime, some colonists starved to death as their cattle ate what little corn the soil produced, and their pigs and goats died in the fields or were killed by Natives. These conditions increased Spanish dependency on their Indigenous neighbors and fueled tensions over scarce resources, some of which, such as the killing of the corporal at Ahoya, ended in bloodshed.[30]

However, by 1576, other kinds of problems were exacerbating these tensions over Spanish food dependency. Menéndez had died two years earlier, and the Franciscans had left the colony soon thereafter. Plans to find or build an inland passage to Zacatecas were dashed by hostile Natives in the interior, throwing doubt on Santa Elena's identity and reason for being. Stories of soldiers abusing and bullying Natives began to pass from town to town. The colony's new governor, Fernando de Miranda, adopted a policy of oppression toward the coastal towns. He gave orders to his second-in-command, Alonso de Solis, to kill any Natives who refused to comply with Spanish directives. When a cacique in the Guale province murdered his Christian Indian rival, Solis brought the killer to Santa Elena and publicly tortured and executed him.[31] This was a far cry from the protective "elder brother" role the coastal towns had envisioned for Menén-dez. His death, coupled with the Franciscans' abandonment of Santa Elena, seemed to open a grim new chapter in Indian–Spanish relations.

Tensions came to a head on June 17, 1576, when a group of twenty-two soldiers entered Escamaçu demanding food and shelter. The soldiers carried matchlock muskets, which were fired using slow-burning fuses. Their fuses were lit, meaning their arms were at the ready. The group was led by Ensign Hernando Moyano, who had a reputation for ruthlessness. On an expedition into the interior some years earlier, Moyano had led a force that killed hundreds of Natives and enslaved many others. His presence in Escamaçu surely put the Indians on edge. The Escamaçus were in the midst of a feast—perhaps the feast of Toya, which the Orista celebrated in late spring—and they refused to share their food. Moyano defied the Indians, drew his sword, and took food from their kettle, whereupon the Escamaçus gathered their women and children and melted into the woods. According to Andres Calderon, the sole Spanish survivor of this encounter:

> After this came an old cacique who spoke with the said Ensign, asking him what he did there, whether he wished to make war on the Indians, and for what reason he made them go to the woods; and the said Ensign had an-swered him that he did not come to make war, but to lodge himself with them and ask them for food: that they themselves had chosen to go into the woods; and the said cacique had replied to him: "Then, why dost thou keep the fuses lighted, [if] thou wishest them to return? Put out the fuses!" So the said Ensign had ordered that the fuses should be extinguished; and when the cacique saw that they were out, he gave a shout, and then the said Indians came forth and slew them all.[32]

The anthropologist Charles Hudson has written that southeastern Indians in general, "as members of small-scale societies, constantly under the scrutiny of their fellows . . . fully understood the value of secrecy" and were masters of the surprise attack. Hudson noted their admiration of stealthy predators such as the cougar, although the Escamaçus also admired and feared the secrecy of poi-sonous snakes, which one medicine man reportedly sent "severall miles over riv-ers and brooks to bite a particular Indian."[33] The attack described by Calderon was clearly deceptive—note especially the old cacique's use of the familiar and

friendly "thou" as opposed to the formal and impersonal "you" when petition-
ing Moyano—and it was brilliantly executed. Even with the numbers on their
side, Indigenous fighting men rarely enjoyed an advantage over armored and
well-armed Spanish foot soldiers. Only deception could give them this advantage, and the Escamaçus made the most of it in their engagement with Moyano.

The Escamaçus' slaughter of Moyano and twenty of his men was an unprecedented act of aggression against the Spaniards, and its causes were complex.
As already noted, although the Spaniards were experiencing food shortages,
coastal Indians were not, so food scarcity was not a contributing factor from
the Indian perspective (indeed, one historian has argued that the coastal towns
waged their war because food was abundant and their warriors were strong).
Moyano's reputation for brutally conquering and enslaving Indians in the interior surely put the Escamaçus on their guard and might have prompted them
to make a preemptive strike. Lingering tensions over ongoing abuses by Spanish
soldiers and Solis's recent execution of the Guale headmen played a role, as did
Moyano's theft of the food, an act of aggression that violated Indian norms of
exchange and treated Escamaçu like a tributary of Santa Elena. The brazenness
of the theft, which was committed openly during a public ceremony, could not
have been better calculated to insult the Escamaçus or demonstrate Moyano's
contempt for them. To add injury to insult, if the ceremony was indeed the feast
of Toya, Moyano's theft of the food would have deeply offended Escamaçu's
life-sustaining god, who might only be appeased through an act of supreme
violence. Such a combination of factors, ranging from mounting frustrations
to fear, public insults, and sacrilege, is needed to explain the extraordinary violence the Escamaçus visited upon Moyano and his men.[34]

The Moyano massacre triggered a prolonged and widespread conflict between coastal Natives and Spaniards. In the weeks that followed, Escamaçu
warriors intercepted and killed three soldiers fleeing Guale. The Guales soon
joined the fight, killing five resident Spaniards and murdering a delegation of
nine treasury officials on route to Santa Elena, and a group of unidentified Natives ambushed a Spanish boy and eight soldiers outside Santa Elena's garrison
(including Solis, who headed the detachment of soldiers).[35] However, these op-
portunistic and isolated killings tell only part of the story, and they threaten to
drown out the voices in the council houses, whose more important but largely
silent diplomatic victories underpinned the violence. The Escamaçu warriors
who killed the three soldiers were taking their trophies—the twenty severed
heads of Moyano and his men—as a present to Guale, vindicating Solis's execution of their headman and binding their intertribal alliance with Spanish blood.
Guale forces joined Escamaçu, Orista, and other coastal towns in a frontal

assault on the Spanish fort, San Felipe. Five hundred fighting men laid siege to the fort and forced the governor to evacuate his troops and abandon the settlement, which the Indians then burned. The rapid mobilization of Indigenous coastal towns from Orista south to Guale revealed a diplomatic network that transcended local identities, cultural differences, and historic animosities. The small and autonomous Native towns strung along the coast, thinly populated and occupied by farming hunter–gatherers, with no centralized authority and a history marked by jealousy and competition, too scattered even to sustain the interest of missionaries, now acted as one people, connected, unified, single-minded, and collective, dwarfing the handful of Spaniards left at Santa Elena and growing more powerful than they ever imagined.

The evacuation of Fort San Felipe did not put a stop to Indian diplomacy but instead pushed it to a new level. The coastal tribes sent emissaries as far south as St. Augustine, a ten-day journey. In the summer of 1577, the new governor of Florida, Pedro Menéndez Marqués, found that "all the coast Indians are in rebellion, and allied with those of Santa Elena and Guale." Native insurgents had destroyed St. Augustine's town and forced its residents into the fort, and Marqués now feared that the fort itself was on the verge of collapse. He soon left St. Augustine to start rebuilding the fort at Santa Elena, and in his absence, Guale and Escamaçu war captains again ventured south to strengthen their alliance with the St. Augustine Natives and plan a coordinated assault on the garrison. Thus, by late 1577, the Escamaçu War had escalated into a regional conflict that united Natives all along the southeastern coast. Building on their military victory at Santa Elena, Escamaçu and Guale leaders had achieved a remarkable diplomatic feat, forming a pan-Indian alliance whose goal was to end the Spanish occupation of La Florida and drive the Spaniards into the sea. The fortuitous wreck of the French ship *El Principe* at Port Royal, which added one hundred French castaways to Indian forces, further strengthened the Indians' hand and made them more confident than ever of an imminent triumph over the Spaniards.[36]

The Indians' far-flung alliance, however, was tenuous. When Marqués reinforced the garrison at St. Augustine, the southern Indians hesitated, and the alliance crumbled. Marqués also outmaneuvered the Indians at Santa Elena. Instead of cutting wood on Port Royal Island and exposing his men to ambush, he shipped materials from St. Augustine to construct the new fort. In the meantime, the center of Indian military resistance had shifted to Coçapoy, the largest and inmost of the coastal towns, which held nearly half the French captives from *El Principe*. When his new Fort San Marcos was complete and reinforcements had arrived, Marqués waged a scorched-earth campaign against his Indigenous enemies, rooting out the French, burning twenty towns, and killing hundreds of Natives. The Oristas mustered three hundred fighting men, but without the element of surprise, they were no match for Spanish guns and armor, and Marqués routed them. He brought two hundred soldiers to Coçapoy, where he torched the town and killed its defenders, burning some forty Indians to death and making hostages of the cacique's family, whom he exchanged for the Frenchmen. Marqués visited similar carnage on the towns of Guale. By 1580, the coastal people were pacified, although sporadic attacks on Spaniards continued until 1583. Thus, after fourteen years of colonization, the Spaniards finally conquered the Indigenous communities of the lower Carolina coast, but it was a hollow victory. Unlike Pedro Menéndez de Avilés, Marqués had no broader vision for Santa Elena, nor did the garrison serve any larger strategic or economic purpose beyond protecting itself. Coastal people, having failed to either incorporate Santa Elena into their world or to destroy it and expel the Spaniards, learned instead to live with it.[37]

The precise impact of the Escamaçu War on the coastal towns is unknown. The destruction was widespread: hundreds killed, twenty or more towns burned from Guale to Orista, Natives' food stores destroyed. Hunger, sickness, and grief undoubtedly added many more deaths to the number killed in battle and taken captive. It would take generations to recover from such devastation, and as fortune would have it, that is exactly what the coastal people got. In 1587, the Spanish crown made a strategic decision to consolidate Florida's forces at St. Augustine, and the Spaniards abandoned Santa Elena forever. Quite suddenly, the curtain closed on Carolina's coastal Indians, and they were left alone, with only minimal contact with outsiders, for over seventy years.[38]

Only a handful of sources provide glimpses into the coastal peoples' world over the next seven decades. Waves of dearth and plenty continued to wash over the coastal towns, and the Natives adapted as they always had, temporarily relocating their settlements and falling back on ancient subsistence strategies. After 1600, Escamaçu, the southernmost town, repaired relations with St. Augustine and maintained regular communication, much of it centered on sporadic trade. In 1605, its cacique was reputed to be a Christian, at least nominally; and in 1630, the Franciscans claimed that the "most populous Provinces of Santa Elena and Cayagua" were pleading for missionaries to be sent among them. Civil authorities were not convinced of Indians' love for the Franciscans and showed little enthusiasm for stationing troops that far north merely to protect the missions, so they rejected the friars' petitions. Yet the Franciscans' enthusiastic descriptions of the "most populous" coastal towns suggest that, by 1630, the coastal peoples' populations had recovered from the devastations of

Spanish colonization and war. Despite regular contact with St. Augustine and Guale, their numbers remained stable, apparently untouched by the epidemics that ravaged Native communities elsewhere in Florida in the 1610s and 1650s. When the curtain rose again with the arrival of the English in the 1660s, it revealed a very different world, one far more prosperous than that of the Spanish period, a world teeming with abundance but also violent, unstable, and filled with anxiety.[39]

CHAPTER I

Maneaters

In June 1661, some five hundred Indigenous warriors and their English partners descended the Altamaha River and attacked the Guale mission of Santo
Domingo de Talaje near the Georgia coast. They came without warning, in a
fleet of two hundred canoes and rafts, pulled along in silence by the current as it
gathered force near the river's mouth. Unlike other Indians in Spanish Florida,
these carried guns, and they spoke Iroquoian, which was unintelligible to the
Guales. The invaders showed no mercy. Reports described how they overran
Talaje and its mission, "sacking the churches and convents and killing the Christian Indians." This sudden and massive attack by strange people, their faces
painted with stripes, terrified the villagers of Talaje. Many fled to the nearby
mission of Sapala, which was situated more securely on one of the barrier islands, where they prayed for deliverance.[1]

Florida's Governor Aranguiz y Cotes had heard reports of these "striped
Indians" from Apalachicola in northwest Florida, where they had done "much
damage" and "laid waste to the land" the previous year. He immediately dispatched companies of soldiers by land and sea to defend Sapala and drive
out the enemy, but the invaders were not deterred. Using boards torn from
the church at Talaje, they built a makeshift boat to take them to the island.
Fortunately for the Guales, when their attackers tried to cross the sound, the
current carried them out to sea, and all seventy men aboard drowned. Spanish
and Guale forces counterattacked the others and forced them to retreat into the
interior—but the damage had been done. The people of Talaje abandoned their
village and resettled on St. Simons Island, safely removed from the mainland.
They were among the first of many people of the southeastern borderlands to
be displaced by these invaders. They would eventually learn that even the protective waters of the coastal islands would not keep them safe.[2]

The Spaniards called these "striped" Indians *Chichimecos*, meaning "wild
people" or "barbarians." Elsewhere, they were known as Eries and Rickaheckrians. The Native people of coastal Carolina simply called them Westos, or
enemies, a name that was later adopted by the English, and it stuck. What they
called themselves is not known, but their Indigenous victims all agreed on one

thing: They were maneaters. The reports that reached Aranguiz y Cotes in 1662 claimed that the Chichimecos "ate human flesh," and nearly a decade later, the Indians around the new English settlement at Charles Town told Maurice Mathews that the Westos "eat people and are great warriors." These claims must not be taken lightly. Seventeenth-century Iroquois practiced ritual cannibalism, in which entire villages, men and women alike, tortured, killed, cooked, and ate captive enemies to absorb their spiritual power. The Westos shared this Iroquoian culture. With their guns, their great numbers, their ruthlessness, and their reputation as maneaters, the Westos struck fear into the hearts of Native people across the southeastern borderlands.[3]

Like the Yamasees' and Scots' colonization of Port Royal, the Westo migration was a turning point in the history of the colonial southeast—not because the Westos were fierce warriors and cannibals, but because they were such efficient and enthusiastic enslavers. For two decades, they terrorized Indigenous communities across the southeastern borderlands, from Escamaçu and Guale in the east to Timucua in central Florida, Tama and Cofitachequi in the piedmont, Apalachee in western Florida, and along the edges of the powerful and populous towns of the Chattahoochee River valley. They laid waste to vulnerable settlements, killing their male defenders and taking their women and children captive for sale to the English, first in Virginia and then, after 1674, in Charles Town. The Westo invasion introduced an era of great violence, instability, and displacement in the Anglo–Spanish–Indian borderlands. It fueled the collapse of Carolina's coastal peoples, the retreat of the Guale missions and settlements, and the migration and coalescence of the Yamasees. It lined the pockets of English merchants and fed the bodies of Indians to English slave traders, who were the real maneaters in the colonial southeast. In doing so, the Westos added one more piece to what historians have called a "patchwork of slaveries," the broad and complex fabric of exploitation that came to characterize the region after 1670.

By destabilizing the region and changing its landscape and trade dynamics, the Westo invasion opened the door to Scottish and Yamasee colonization of Port Royal and played an important role in the transformation of the colonial southeast. This chapter tells the Westos' story, which goes hand-in-hand with the stories of English colonization and the rise of commercial slavery. It begins by describing the Spanish colonial world and its northern borderlands in 1660. It then examines the Westo invasion, its impact on the Indigenous peoples of the region, and the exploitative and unstable world the Westos and English co-created between 1660 and 1680.[4]

SPANISH FLORIDA AND ITS BORDERLANDS
IN THE MID-17TH CENTURY

By 1660, more than seventy years after they abandoned Santa Elena, the Spaniards had imposed a new order on Florida's Indigenous people through the mission system. Despite their failure at Santa Elena, the Franciscans had not given up on Florida. In 1597, they returned to Guale, and over the next six decades, they built a string of missions along the coast from the St. Johns River north to the Savannah. They also extended their missions west to the Timucua towns of central Florida, and by the 1630s, they were planting churches and convents among the Apalachees of western Florida, hundreds of miles from St. Augustine. The Spaniards' mission system, not their military, was the main vehicle for colonizing Florida and consolidating control over its far-flung Native peoples.

This control was far from absolute. Power was shared between Indigenous leaders and Spanish religious and civil authorities, and Spaniards' ability to command Indian tribute (labor and corn) depended on a steady stream of European goods, backed by military force. To get access to Native towns, missionaries plied caciques and micos with gifts, which they gave in turn to their people in exchange for cooperation and labor. Indian peasants planted fields of corn to support local convents, churches, friars, and officials, but Indian elites, not Spanish officials, stored and controlled corn surpluses. In addition to this local tribute, or *sabana*, the government in St. Augustine compelled these "reduced" or conquered towns, or at least their young men, to contribute to a labor draft, called *repartimiento*. Some laborers worked as messengers or carriers, and others provided manual labor to maintain the fort and other public works in St. Augustine. The repartimiento was basically a labor tax, and although it was coercive and subject to abuse, it usually included some modest compensation. When Spanish labor demands outpaced gift giving, when the repartimiento became excessive, or when the friars alienated powerful Native leaders or pushed too hard in suppressing traditional practices, the Indians rebelled, frequently targeting the friars and Christian caciques who collaborated with them. All three of Florida's provinces (Guale, Timucua, and Apalachee) experienced rebellions between 1597 and 1656, and all were swiftly and brutally suppressed by Spanish military forces. Despite this periodic unrest, on the whole, the mission system offered something to both Indians and Spaniards at every social tier: labor for the government, corn for the missions, souls for the friars, prestige goods for Indigenous headmen, and Spanish soldiers to protect mission communities from their enemies. As long as it balanced the interests of missionaries,

officials, soldiers, Native leaders, and laborers, which it generally did, this system maintained stability and order across Spanish Florida.[5]

Southeastern Indian towns north of Florida, outside this mission system,
may have achieved their own kind of equilibrium in the sixteenth and seventeenth centuries. The great Mississippian chiefdoms described by Soto and
Pardo in the mid-sixteenth century—Cofitachequi in the South Carolina piedmont, Ocute in central Georgia, Joara and Guatari in the North Carolina foot-
hills, and Coosa in the Tennessee valley—contracted or collapsed between 1600
and 1660. As these chiefdoms weakened or broke up, no highly centralized powers or new chiefdoms formed in their place, and power reverted to autonomous
towns. There is not much evidence before 1660 that these towns began to draw
together into new, coalescent societies; that is, confederations or amalgamations
of culturally similar peoples, such as the later Yamasee and Creek Indians.[6] In
addition, most towns outside the mission system had little or no direct contact
with Europeans in these decades. This minimized the disruptions caused by disease and gift exchange.[7] No longer obligated to produce corn surpluses to support chiefdoms, these towns were free to explore new, more egalitarian forms of
social organization and manage their own labor and food surpluses. As a result,
like Orista and Escamaçu, which coexisted as autonomous towns in a relative
balance of power, they may have experienced a welcome time of security and
stability in the century before the Westo migration.

Of course, Native towns could never take their security for granted. War was
an integral part of Indigenous culture. It not only was driven by issues of territory or group survival but also was tied to kinship, manhood, and social status.
Intertribal violence, such as Kiawah's killing of Escamaçu's *mandador* (captain)
in 1605 or Guale's taking of the two Orista captives in 1566, was a regular feature of Native life. This violence invariably involved captive taking.

Traditionally, captivity was a highly malleable institution in Native societies.
Whether they were by-products of war or victims of small-scale raids, by defini-
tion, captives were "others." They were not part of the captors' kin group, they
were not protected by the mutual obligations that bound kin to one another,
and thus they were disposable. In Mississippian chiefdoms, many captives were
converted into slaves to enhance chiefly status or provide menial labor or sex.
These slaves were bound to the lives of their masters, and they lived and died
in their service. As the chiefdoms declined, the purpose of captivity changed.
Captives might be adopted into a kin group to replace dead loved ones, serve
as wives, or simply increase population. They might be given as prestige gifts,
which conferred power on the giver. Some were ransomed or exchanged, and
many others were traded or sold to outsiders. In addition to these direct uses,

captives served as a kind of lubricant that greased the wheels of diplomacy and
missionization. Spanish officials such as Pedro Menéndez de Aviles brokered
captive exchanges and thereby earned the gratitude and loyalty of the towns
he sought to control (in his case, Guale and Orista). Spanish missionaries on
the Mexican frontier also brokered these exchanges. By acquiring captives and
returning them to their families, they created bonds of friendship with the Native communities they hoped to Christianize. Captivity thus had a long history
among Native people, predating contact, and Indians adapted it to their changing circumstances to meet the needs of the moment.[8]

Like so much else, the extent of captive-taking in Florida's northern borderlands, outside the mission system, is unknown for the first half of the seventeenth century. Reports of raids by non-mission Indians on Florida's mission
settlements were infrequent. Until 1659, the only raiders mentioned in Spanish
documents were Chiscas (also called Uchisis or Yuchis). These people had once
inhabited what is now northeast Tennessee before they were displaced during
the Pardo expedition of 1569—in fact, by Moyano and his men, who killed as
many as fifteen hundred Chiscas and took many others captive. At some point
thereafter, the Chiscas abandoned their ancestral lands. For decades, they were
known "to wander at will" through Florida's provinces, attacking outlying mission towns in Apalachee and Timucua. Around 1640, they made peace with
St. Augustine and settled on the edges of Apalachee, but within a few years, as
Spanish gifts dried up, they relocated to the Chattahoochee Valley and resumed
their raids. In 1651, they attacked Guale, taking captive "many women and
children of Christian and friendly Indians," according to Florida's Governor
Nicolás Ponce de León, and forcing him to shore up his frontier defenses. Unlike
the later Westos, the Chiscas did not carry firearms and had no known ties to
European traders. They would have used captives in traditional ways, adopting
or trading them but not selling them to commercial slave traders or planters.
Spanish authorities dealt with the Chiscas aggressively, although they viewed
them as an annoyance, not an existential threat.[9]

This Spanish colonial world was no Eden. Although Indian headmen retained much of their power under the mission system, they and their people
were dependent on Spanish goods, which were frequently in short supply. They
were also expected to surrender to Christianity and Spanish acculturation,
although they strove to do so on their own terms, appropriating Catholic elements they could use while rejecting others. Indeed, they continually resisted
Franciscans' efforts to suppress their traditional dances and ball games. Spanish
military forces provided an unprecedented degree of security, but St. Augustine,
which was always strapped for cash, could not afford to build and staff garrisons

for more than a handful of missions. As a result, mission Indians remained vulnerable to attack from slave raiders on the frontier and French and English pirates on the coast (and, in Apalachee, to their traditional enemies, the Apalachicola peoples). Of much greater concern and impact, the continual movement of goods and people between St. Augustine and the missions spread disease and death. Epidemics ravaged the missions in the 1610s, and Guale was hit with both plague and smallpox in the 1650s, resulting in a significant drop in population over the course of the seventeenth century. Mortality was exacerbated by the labor demands of sabana and repartimiento, which were frequent sources of tension and stretched Indigenous towns' resources thin. Native communities' capacity to recover from epidemics was further hampered by their compact and sedentary settlements and the nutritional deficiencies and food shortages that resulted from colonization. St. Augustine's failure to maintain a robust stream of gifts also fueled migration out of the mission system, which further contributed to Spanish Florida's declining Native population.[10]

Yet, by 1660, the world that the Spanish missions created was orderly and predictable, and it minimized violence from both within and without. Although St. Augustine fretted continually about English and French intruders on the Atlantic and Gulf coasts, these settlements were remote and posed no credible threat to Florida. Apart from the Chiscas, St. Augustine maintained peaceful relations with Indigenous peoples beyond Florida's borders, not least of all with its old enemy, Escamaçu. These Indians also inhabited a stable world whose autonomous towns coexisted, more or less, peacefully with one another and maintained balanced populations.

THE WESTO INVASION

The Westos introduced a major element of instability into this world. Their migration was the first step in the transformation of the southeast from a quasi-feudal Spanish colonial order to a protocapitalist British system. The Indigenous towns of coastal Carolina were among the first casualties of this transformation. The Westo invasion put an end to the coastal peoples' seasonal mobility, compressed their settlements, fractured their diplomacy, displaced many of their people, depopulated their towns, and forced them to give up their autonomy. Their world collapsed.

The Westos originated in the Great Lakes region, and their migration was rooted in the penetration of this region by French and Dutch fur traders in the early seventeenth century. The Europeans traded metal goods and increasingly guns for beaver furs, which were in great demand in Europe. By the 1620s, French traders had long-established trade ties with the Huron (an Iroquoian people) and their Algonquian neighbors in Canada, and the Dutch, based in New Amsterdam (later New York), traded with an Iroquois confederation known as the Five Nations. Iroquois and Algonquian peoples from this region had long been enemies. Competition between the Five Nations and their Indian neighbors to control the fur trade intensified this conflict, which became more deadly as the Europeans, flush with profits from the trade, armed their Indigenous partners with guns.

More than trade and firearms, however, what really escalated the violence was the Iroquois practice of mourning the dead. The Iroquois believed that the spirits of the dead would not rest unless they were replaced through the adoption of enemy captives. Usually, captured male warriors were ritually tortured and executed, whereas women and children were spared and adopted by the aggrieved families. As Iroquois deaths increased as a result of the beaver wars and the spread of disease, the demand for adoptees rose and set off a vicious cycle of violence. More trade and war meant more disease and death, which led to more war to replace the dead. Violence spiraled out of control. In the 1640s and 1650s, the Five Nations relentlessly made war on the Algonquian and Iroquoian people of the Great Lakes region. The Algonquians fled beyond their reach, but the Five Nations destroyed and absorbed the Huron and other Iroquoian-speaking people who did not belong to their confederation. One of these tribes, the Erie, splintered, and one of its branches, the Rickaheckrians, migrated into Virginia. They were a casualty of the Mourning Wars, conditioned by extraordinary violence and determined to arm themselves with European guns.[11]

The Rickaheckrians brought the disorders of the Mourning Wars southward. In 1656, they settled along the fall line in Virginia, where they were given an unfriendly welcome by a combined force of Pamunkey and English militia. Although the Rickaheckrians won this battle, they did not remain long in the region. After building ties with Virginia traders, who supplied them with guns, they migrated further south into the Tama region of what is now central Georgia. Here, as in Virginia and later in Carolina, they lived along the fall line, where smoother currents and deeper channels made the rivers navigable and gave access to towns downstream all the way to the coast.[12] From this central location, they raided Apalachee towns in 1659 and the Guale missions at Talaje and Sapala in 1660. After the attack on Sapala, Spanish forces captured and interrogated four of these Chichimecos, learning of their ties to the English and their appetite for slaves.[13]

The Westo invasion shattered the peace and stability of Florida and its northern borderlands and put everything in motion. Wherever the Westos went, people fled. In 1662, they hit Huyache, a non-Christian town on the border of

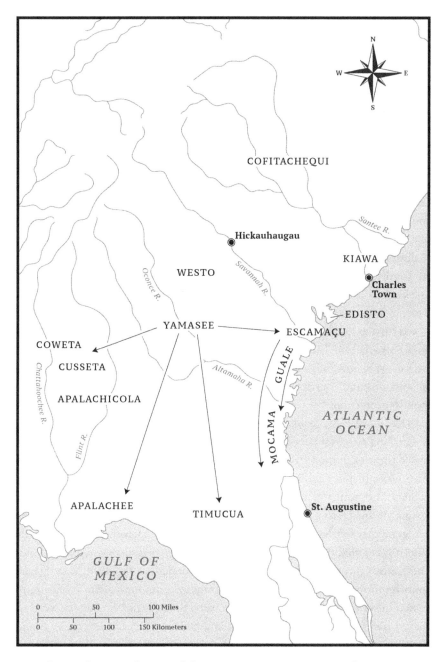

The Southeast in the Era of the Westo Invasion, ca. 1670. The arrows
denote the dispersal of the Yamasees and the retreat of Guale.
Graphic design by Amanda Espericueta.

Guale and Escamaçu, where they "put to the knife as many people as they found in it." In response, the Spaniards moved their northernmost mission southward. They also strengthened their frontier defenses by making their new northern outpost, Santa Catalina, a permanent garrison. Westo attacks against the independent, non-Christian towns of the interior are not documented, but their consequences were. Reports told of "pagan Indians" fleeing their homes for the refuge of missions on the Spanish frontier. Conditions must have been worst in the old province of Tama, which was far from the missions but close to the center of Westo power. In 1663, missionaries told of a new people, the Yamasees, who had fled from Tama into the coastal area just vacated by Huyache. The Yamasees were unknown before 1663. They were a product of the Westo invasion, which drove several disparate towns together for protection and created a new people, a "multiethnic conglomeration" and "aggregation of Indian towns of diverse origins, forced together of necessity." As such, they were the first of the southeast's coalescent societies, which later would include the Catawbas, Creeks, and Seminoles, to come together as a shield against the Indian slave trade. In any case, the Yamasees did not remain long in Huyache. As the Westos moved further northeast to the fall line of the Savannah River, directly upstream from Huyache, the Yamasees relocated southward to the coastal mission provinces of Mocama and Guale. There, they added to the shrinking population of the missions and contributed much labor to the repartimiento in exchange for Spanish protection.[14]

This movement, displacement, and compression also changed the world of Carolina's coastal people, although this was not evident to the English who visited the area in the 1660s. In that decade, English traders and explorers made three visits to the Carolina coast: an unnamed trading voyage in 1662–1663, William Hilton in 1663, and Robert Sandford in 1666. Their reports lifted the curtain on the coastal towns, which had been largely closed to outsiders since the Spaniards left Santa Elena in 1587. Unlike the Spanish colonizers of the sixteenth century, the English described a world of prosperity and abundance. The Natives thrived in crowded villages surrounded by "fields of Maiz greenly flourishing" with "many little houses straglingly amongst them." Having retreated into the interior earlier in the century, the Edistos (the English word for Orista) had now returned to the coast and built their chief town on an island. There, a "long traine of Indians" escorted Sandford to their village, a "whole rabble" gathered in the council house to greet him, and a "great troop" brought him back to his ship and slept in shelters on the shore. On St. Helena Island, Sandford saw "a great variety of choice pasturage" along with "severall fields of Maiz of very large growth" planted in the same soil that had so frustrated

Spanish farmers a century before. Hilton also found corn aplenty on St. Helena Island, where the Escamaçus grew three crops a year along with beans, peas, squash, pumpkins, and melons. Escamaçu's council house, flanked by a sentinel house and surrounded by smaller homes, was two hundred feet in diameter with walls twelve feet high and could accommodate a whole rabble of its own. These were not merely the exaggerated descriptions of colonial boosters: Archaeological surveys confirm the existence of the buildings that Hilton described, and Scottish colonizer William Dunlop later found hundreds of acres of cleared ground on St. Helena Island when he surveyed it in the 1680s.[15]

In view of the coastal Indians' historical settlement patterns and economic practices, these descriptions raise two questions that their English visitors, who were newcomers to the region, did not think to ask. First, why were these towns situated on the Sea Islands? Although Sandford sailed farther up the Port Royal River, he found no more Natives or corn fields. The Edistos had abandoned their chief inland town, which had stood on the mainland fifteen miles north of Santa Elena, and moved instead to present-day Edisto Island. The Escamaçus had moved to St. Helena Island, where the soils were inferior (as both Spanish farmers and Hilton attested) to those of the inland sites they occupied in the sixteenth century. Smaller communities, such as Stono, Wimbee, Kussah, and Combahee, also occupied coastal or sea island locations at this time. Second, why were they growing so much corn? Spanish documents from the Santa Elena era describe nothing like the intensive farming practices that Hilton and Sandford found in the 1660s, nor did the Spaniards ever associate coastal towns with such abundance. Edisto and Escamaçu were growing large surpluses of corn, and they were doing so on the "worst Lands," as Hilton called them, the sandy soils and wetlands of the Sea Islands. Had they settled into permanent villages, abandoning the mobility they had practiced "for thousands of years," and with it their varied diet and identity as seasonal hunter–gatherers?[16]

They had, at least for the short term. The prosperity and abundance on the surface of these descriptions actually points to coastal peoples' great fear of a Westo attack just under the surface. The Sea Islands placed a barrier between them and their warlike enemy, as it did for the people who fled Talaje, Huyache, and Tama. With Westos living at the fall line of the Savannah, the coastal peoples would be foolish to break into small bands to hunt and gather inland during the winter. Like Natives throughout the southeast, they too were a people on the move, although they had not yet experienced a Westo attack and were more compressed than displaced.

The coastal tribes' interactions with the English voyagers provide further evidence of their anxiety over the Westos. Tensions ran high when Hilton visited in 1663. Thirteen English castaways from a previous trading voyage had been taken by the Natives; the Stonos killed three, and of the remaining ten, the Edistos and Escamaçus each held five. The Edistos were open to negotiating with Hilton for the return of their captives, but the Escamaçus had already promised to send theirs to St. Augustine and were hostile toward Hilton. They not only refused to return their captives but also tried, unsuccessfully, to capture several of Hilton's crew after inviting them to visit their village. After several days of fruitless negotiations, Hilton sailed for Barbados, leaving behind five of the English captives but taking five Indian hostages with him. These included two high-ranking men: Shadoo, the Edisto cacique, and Wommony, the son of the cacique of Escamaçu. The coastal peoples probably associated these English explorers with the Virginians, who were friends with their Westo enemies, and they trusted neither Hilton nor even the powerless castaways. The English–Westo partnership may explain why the Stonos killed their three captives. The Escamaçus, who as the southernmost people had ties to St. Augustine, showed contempt for the English and looked instead to the Spaniards for protection. Both they and the Edistos viewed their English captives as pawns.[17]

Curiously, just three years later, these same towns were eager to strengthen their ties with the English. Wommony and Shadoo had been returned to their people, and they gave Sandford a warm welcome. No one was more surprised by this than Sandford himself. He feared the Indians, especially Escamaçu, and when he thought that his ship might sink in Port Royal Sound, he imagined a "slowe and painfull" death from people "whose piety it is to be barbarous and Gallantry to be inhumane." Instead, the Edistos greeted the English with "Ceremonyes of Welcome and friendship (by stroaking our shoulders with their palmes and sucking in theire breath the whilst)." Shadoo gave Sandford the seat of honor in his council house and even slept aboard his vessel "without the society of any of his people." This remarkable gesture of trust contrasted sharply with the Edistos' caution and suspicion in 1663.

The cacique of Escamaçu also came aboard the ship. He gave Sandford a present of skins and entertained him in his council house while Wommony guided the ship's longboat on a scouting expedition through the inland water passages. Moreover, before Sandford departed, the cacique asked him to take his sister's son with him. This was another extraordinary act of trust, for in the Natives' matrilineal system, the sister's oldest son was the cacique's's heir. Sandford agreed; for security, he left the ship's surgeon, Henry Woodward, in Escamaçu, which filled its people with "Joy and thankfullness." This exchange was sealed with public speeches and rituals, signifying a formal pact or "League" between the English and Escamaçu. In a gesture of fictive kinship, the Indian boy's sister was assigned to serve Woodward. After witnessing this agreement, a visiting Kiawah also begged to be taken with the English "that his Nacōn or tribe might be within the League." Sandford hesitated, but the Kiawah insisted and "would not bee denyed." To conciliate the Escamaçus and declare his submission, the Kiawah cut his hair "after the manner of the Port Royall Indians."[18]

Sandford knew nothing about the Westos—few English did, outside of the slave traders in the Virginia piedmont—but he detected a note of urgency in coastal peoples' overtures to the English. "All along," he wrote, "I observed a kind of Emulacōn" among the Kiawahs, Escamaçus, and Edistos "concerning us and our Friendshipp." They vied with one another for Sandford's favor and urged the English to "come amongst them." They would live together in peace, the Indians assured their visitors, and they promised that the English would never have "any occasion of dischargeing our Gunns but in merryment and for pastime." The Natives' attention to English guns is telling. Perhaps they hoped that an alliance with the English, some of whom were trade partners with the Westos, would protect them from their enemies. They no longer saw the English as threats but as potential allies. The desperate steps they took to befriend the English—entrusting the cacique's nephew to Sandford's care, thrusting themselves upon Sandford, and cutting their hair in the Escamaçu fashion—revealed their rising anxiety. Perhaps they were hearing rumors of a planned Westo assault on their towns. In 1663, the coastal peoples, with their populous towns, Spanish friends, and "fields of Maiz greenly flourishing," still had the confidence of their sixteenth-century forebears. They knew their own power, had no use for European colonizers, and could afford to kill, enslave, and scorn the English. Just three years later, they needed friends with guns. They used rituals of exchange and hair cutting to seal their league with the English, and they competed with each other to have the English "come amongst them" on generous terms.[19]

It was already too late. Within months of Sandford's visit, and before he could return with the cacique's nephew, the Westo hammer fell on the coastal towns. Escamaçu was hit especially hard. According to a report from the Sewee people to the north, the Westos "ruinated" their village on St. Helena Island, killed "severall" of its inhabitants, and "destroyed and burnt" habitations from Port Royal to Kiawah. As a result, the caciques from two coastal towns, St. Helena and Ahoya, fled with their families to Guale, where they asked for permission to resettle and come under Spanish protection, although they later changed their minds and returned to Port Royal. The Edistos may have dodged the Westo bullet, as they seemed to be unscathed when English colonists passed through Port Royal in 1670, but the Westo attack was a death blow to

Escamaçu. Their ancestral lands were soon overrun with refugees and strangers. Dislocated and defenseless, caught between anxious Spanish and English colonizers, they became an emblem of the displacement, violence, and instability of the Westo era.[20]

PAX ANGLICA

In the interior regions of Tama and the Catawba valley, the Westo invasion resulted in creative diplomacy and new social formations; namely, the coalescent societies of the Yamasee and Catawba peoples. However, in coastal Carolina, it had the opposite effect, fracturing Indian diplomacy. During the Spanish colonial era of the previous century, the town headmen frequently met together in council to negotiate troublesome situations regarding the Spaniards. They established the terms for Spanish settlement. In 1576, when the colonizers violated those terms, they engineered a regionwide pan-Indian alliance that drove the Spaniards out of Santa Elena and even threatened to destroy St. Augustine. There were still echoes of this historic diplomacy in the united front that faced down Hilton in 1663. Yet three years later, only faint traces of the old alliances remained, as Kiawah, Edisto, and Escamaçu jostled for favor with Sandford; and unlike the Yamasees, the coastal towns were wholly unable to put up a united front against the Westos. This probably speaks more to the sheer power and ruthlessness of the Westos than the limits of Indian diplomacy. After all, coalescing was not enough to keep the Yamasees safe; they also relocated far to the south in Mocama, which Carolina's coastal peoples were unwilling to do. In any case, coastal Indian diplomacy completely collapsed after 1670, when the English returned and established a permanent settlement in Kiawah. Fragmented and reeling from the Westo raids, the coastal towns surrendered their autonomy and placed themselves under the protection of the English. This opened the door for the English to impose their own terms of peace on their Indigenous neighbors. "Our Indians," as the English would call them, traded short-term security for dependency, and most—although not all—submitted to the indignity of becoming disposable "settlement Indians."

In Escamaçu, on the southern border of coastal Carolina, the breakdown of Indian diplomacy was on full display in the dizzying months after the settlement of Charles Town. The old towns had splintered following the Westo attack. Some families fled to Guale, others remained at Santa Elena, and untold others were killed and enslaved by the Westos. Strangers took their place, claiming the vacant lands for themselves and capitalizing on Escamaçu's weakness. One such group was Ospo, a Muskogean-speaking people who had lived in Guale, had ties to St. Augustine, and may have been part of the Yamasee formation. By

1670 the Ospos had settled near Santa Elena and opened backdoor diplomatic channels with both Charles Town and St. Augustine. Losing both their territory and their status as go-betweens to the Ospo was too much for the remnant of Escamaçus still living at Santa Elena. Their opposition to Ospo set off a chaotic flurry of diplomacy with the Spaniards, as both groups looked to curry favor with St. Augustine as the main purveyors of intelligence about the English.[21]

St. Augustine was not a strong outpost. It had always been acutely aware of its vulnerability, never more so than after 1670, when the English established their colony at Charles Town. Florida's governor fretted continually about an English attack, and in 1670, he dispatched Antonio de Arguelles, who commanded the garrison at Santa Catalina, to learn what he could about the strength and intentions of the English from the Indians at Santa Elena. Arguelles found two groups of Natives there: the old Escamaçus, whom he now called "Chiluques," meaning "people of a different tongue," and the Ospos, who spoke the familiar language of Guale. The Escamaçus/Chiluques told Arguelles that the English had "many men, ships, and artillery." But the cacica or headwoman of Ospo, whose name was Pamini, secretly contradicted them, telling Arguelles that the English had only two small boats in the harbor and that "no succor had come to them." They were weak, she told Arguelles, and they posed no threat to the Spaniards. Pamini had direct knowledge, for she frequently visited Charles Town with her daughter. However, she feared that the English would kill her if they knew she told the Spaniards how weak they were, so she disclosed this intelligence to Arguelles in confidence, and he believed her.[22]

One year later, nine messengers came to Guale with dire news. They were Escamaçus/Chiluques, not Ospos, but they claimed they were sent by the cacica of Ospo to warn the Spaniards of a planned English attack. According to their leader, Bluacacay, the cacica had told him "that the [English] settlement grows and that the castle is getting bigger and that many Negros have come to work and that they were now making ready ships" in preparation for war. Arguelles was skeptical, but the new commander at Santa Catalina, Don Matheo Pacheco, sent five of the messengers to St. Augustine to be deposed. Bluacacay stuck by his story: Pamini, who had been to the English settlement, had told him that two ships waited outside the bar at Charles Town, one quite large, and they were making plans to attack either Santa Catalina or St. Augustine. They even had letters of war from the king authorizing an attack. The other four deponents echoed Bluacacay's testimony, although all they knew came thirdhand through Bluacacay, not from the cacica or from direct knowledge of the English. This confirmed the governor's fears. In response, he prepared his defenses and dispatched Joseph, a Christian Indian from Guale who spoke the language of

Escamaçu, to Santa Elena to gather more intelligence. Joseph would find out if the Escamaçu messengers were putting words in Pamini's mouth or if she had lied to Arguelles the previous year.[23]

At Santa Elena, Pamini sent her brother and two others with Joseph to visit Charles Town for themselves. Joseph was there three days, and he reported that the settlement was well fortified, generously provisioned, and bustling with activity, but its five hundred inhabitants were focused on building and planting, not preparing for war. The cacica's brother, Jarnoche, confirmed this account. To cover for his sister, he told the Spaniards that the English had previously "wanted to come to this harbor [to attack St. Augustine] and that afterwards they had abandoned the plan." As a Christian, Joseph gave his testimony under oath, and it carried more weight with the Spaniards than did the news shared by pagan Indians.[24]

Just months later, however, another Chiluque messenger, Diacon, gave a very different description of Charles Town. Joseph and Pamini had lied, he said. There was only one fort, not three as the others had claimed, and it was pathetic, made up of just "four poles set on the ground and a few more lying around." The neighboring Indians were killing the colonists' livestock, and the English were getting desperate. Over one hundred people had left in two ships, presumably to find food, leaving just thirty to forty armed men and a handful of women and children in the settlement. Moreover, Jarnoche's denial of English intentions against the Spaniards was a ruse, for he had offered to guide the English in an attack against the mission and garrison at Santa Catalina. The Ospos were enemies of the Spaniards, Diacon said, and their words could not be trusted.[25]

This babel of mixed messages drove Florida's new governor, Don Manuel Cendoya, to distraction and did nothing to quell his fears of an English attack. Unsure of whom to trust or what to believe, in late 1672, Cendoya sent one his own soldiers, the multilingual Antonio Camunas, on a diplomatic mission to Charles Town. Pamini, whose trustworthiness had been undercut by Diacon and by her history of giving conflicting information, was eager to restore her credibility. Over the objections of her brother, she insisted on escorting Camunas to the English settlement, although she refused to enter the settlement with him for fear of the English. Was she afraid of the English because they knew she was working with the Spaniards? Or was she playing a double game, trying to stay in the good graces of Charles Town by keeping her relationship with the Spaniards secret from the English? The Spaniards did not know, but, as Camunas learned after spending eight days in Charles Town, Pamini had been telling the truth, and Diacon had lied. He found two hundred fifty Englishmen capable of bearing arms plus one hundred African slaves in the settlement. Camunas's report was reinforced by testimony from a runaway servant, Bernard Patrick, who said that there were eight hundred people in Charles Town and that they talked much of invading St. Augustine, although they made no plans to do so. Cendoya was not reassured. He asked the king for four hundred additional troops, along with permission to launch a preemptive strike and destroy the English settlement before it was too late.[26]

This frenzied diplomacy was fed by the shifting power dynamics and instability that the Westos and English brought to the Spanish borderlands after 1660, of which the Escamaçus were the chief casualty. As the southernmost town on the Carolina coast, Escamaçu had long enjoyed diplomatic ties to the Spaniards, and it took pride in its Spanish connections. When Hilton visited in 1663, he found a Spanish cross outside the council house and heard Indians speaking "many Spanish words" and boasting about their trade and communication with St. Augustine. As the Westo threat loomed larger, the Escamaçus courted Sandford and even appealed to English colonists in 1670 to settle at Port Royal, but this did not necessarily point to a change in loyalty. Instead, the Escamaçus hoped to position themselves between these two enemies and influence English–Spanish relations in the borderlands. They were undercut by the cacica of Ospo. Like the Escamaçus, she kept one eye on Charles Town, one on St. Augustine, and a third on the Westos, but she was a more skillful diplomat and won the confidence of the Spaniards while maintaining the trust of the English. All the Escamaçus could do was react to her initiatives, which they did clumsily, carrying mixed messages and sowing confusion, not trust, with St. Augustine. Their position deteriorated, as evidenced by their renaming in the Spanish documents. "Escamaçu" disappeared from official correspondence. As a place, it was now referred to by its Spanish name, Santa Elena; and as a people, the Escamaçus became Chiluques, recognized by their strange and unintelligible language, not their historic relationship with the Spaniards.[27]

The cutthroat competition between Escamaçu and Ospo was part of a broader failure of inter-Indian diplomacy among the coastal towns after the Westo invasion. The English were the chief beneficiaries of this diplomatic fracturing. They stepped into the gap and pulled most of the towns into their orbit with a combination of trade goods and promises of protection from the Westos. Kiawah and Edisto quickly fell in line. The Kiawahs mediated an English visit to Cofitachequi in the piedmont. Eager to trade, Cofitachequi joined the English alliance and promised to shield the coastal plain against the Westos "if ever they intend to Molest us." The Wandos, Etowahs, and Sewees came to Charles Town's defense when Spanish Indians attacked in 1670. These Indians showed "great kindness" to the English, William Owen wrote, "applauding [them] for the Hoes, Axes, beades and knives" while "inveighing against the Spaniard" with "the greatest passion that could be." Owen acknowledged that all of these people shared a common fear of the Westos, their "mortall enemie" of whom they were "more afraid than the little children are of the Bull beggars in England." Stephen Bull echoed these observations. He wrote, "Our neighbouringe Indians do promise Ayd upon all Exigencies" in exchange for "protecon from us which we have promised them" against the Westos. "Over awed by our gunns," the Indians "showed great Joy that wee are Setled amongst them" and promised "assistance against the Spaniard or any Indian Nacon that shall oppose us." By allying themselves with Charles Town, the coastal peoples accepted English protection, but at this early stage, they clearly regarded the alliance as mutual and reciprocal. Indian arrows would join English guns in the common defense of their settlements against shared enemies, the Westos and the Spaniards.[28]

Four years later, the dynamics of this English peace changed, and its true measure came to light, when, to everyone's surprise, the Carolina colony made a treaty with none other than the Westos themselves. The Westos initiated this deal for reasons of their own. Perhaps they hoped to normalize relations with Charles Town, which was threatening to go to war against them. More likely, they wished to trade directly with the English but were prevented from doing so in Virginia by the Occaneechees, who had a fortified town astride the main trading path where it crossed the James River. On the English side, the chief architect of the Westo alliance was Henry Woodward, who was arguably the single most important figure in the early history of South Carolina. As noted earlier, in 1666, Woodward, a surgeon aboard Sandford's vessel, offered to stay with the Escamaçus as security for the cacique's nephew when the boy left with the English. Woodward learned the language and customs of his hosts before he was taken into custody by the Spaniards and temporarily imprisoned in St. Augustine. After being liberated by the English pirate Robert Searle, he returned to Carolina and played a major role in English–Indian diplomacy and trade. In 1670, he negotiated the alliance with Cofitachequi and solicited Indian aid during a severe food shortage, and in 1674, he journeyed inland at the invitation of Westo traders and left a remarkable (and the only surviving) description of their town, Hickauhaugau.[29]

Located near the fall line of the Savannah River some eight days inland from the coast, Hickauhaugau was a pure expression of Westo power and militarization. The town was situated in a sharp bend in the river and was surrounded on three sides by water. Unlike most southeastern towns, but like those of Iroquoia, it was constructed to prevent enemy incursions, with a double palisade on the inland side and a single line of poles along the river. The Westos lived in Iroquois-style longhouses covered with bark and adorned with the scalps of slain enemies. They kept one hundred or more "faire canoes" on the water's edge "ready uppon all occasions." On his arrival, dozens of Westo warriors, decked out in their "anticke fighting garbe," greeted Woodward with a shout and a volley of fifty or sixty small arms. The Westos, Woodward noted, were "well provided with arms, ammunition, tradeing cloath & other trade from the northward," where they sold deer skins, furs, and slaves. The chief regaled Woodward with "long speeches intimateing their own strength (& as I judged their desire of friendship with us)." At his departure, they gave him an Indian boy and promised to visit the English in the spring with deer skins, furs, and slaves.[30]

The agreement with Woodward had clear benefits to Westos and English alike. Anti-Westo alliances were alive and well beyond the coastal towns. During Woodward's visit, a Savannah emissary visited Hickauhaugau and warned the Westos that a combined force of Chickasaws, Cussetaws, and Cherokees, each tribe powerful in its own right, was plotting to attack them. The Westos greeted this news with skepticism, but they could not deny that they were surrounded by enemies, and they could use some powerful friends in the region. As an added bonus, Charles Town was much closer to Hickauhaugau than Virginia. The Carolina trade would allow Westo traders to avoid the Occaneechee middlemen, and guns could be had in one place as well as the other. However, the English were the big winners from this trade agreement. The Westos were a valuable trade partner, and they controlled access to other towns of the interior. They would supply English merchants with plenty of deer skins, furs, and especially slaves, which were by far the most profitable commodity in Carolina. As a condition of their agreement, the English secured a guarantee from the Westos that they would not attack Charles Town's neighboring Indians along the coastal plain. This deal made the Westos into partners, not enemies, and it directed their aggression outward, away from the English and their Indigenous friends on the coast. The coastal towns would remain secure, but their security would now depend primarily on the English–Westo agreement, not on the coastal peoples' own arms. Their arrows no longer mattered. The coastal towns were excluded from the negotiations and were not party to the agreement but were represented instead by the English. No longer considered allies who joined arms against common enemies, the English–Westo partnership turned them into dependent tributaries or settlement Indians. This was the price of an English peace.[31]

Not all of the coastal towns were happy with the Pax Anglica, nor did they surrender so easily to English hegemony. In 1671, the English declared war against the Kussos (the Coçao of the Spanish era) and their "co-adjutors," some unnamed Indians from the southern part of the province. They accused these Natives of stealing corn, threatening the colonists, and joining the Spaniards to "cut off" the English plantation. The English showed no mercy; they reduced the Kussos to tributary status and forced them to pay one deerskin each month as a reminder of their subordination. Even then, some refused to submit, for three years later, a group of Kusso renegades, men of "noe certaine abode" who led the "miserable, skulking" life of those outside the Pax Anglica, set off more alarms when they "secretly murdered" two Englishmen. Yet the harsh example of the Kussos was lost on their neighbors, the Stonos. In the summer of 1674, just months before Woodward's visit to Hickauhaugau, the cacique of Stono tried to stir up the old alliances and "rise in rebellion against this [English] Settlement." That the cacique believed a coordinated uprising was even possible suggests that anti-English sentiment was widespread throughout the towns.[32]

Yet, like the Escamaçus scrambling to maintain their legitimacy with the Spaniards, these violent outbursts were acts of desperation. They were also isolated incidents, and they were put down by a ruthlessly efficient English colonial administration and its Indian friends. Since the late 1660s, years before the English set foot in Kiawah, the coastal towns had been in crisis. They would not recover. Forced by the Westo threat to give up their seasonal mobility and unable to put up a united front to deter the Westos or control English settlement, they surrendered their autonomy and placed themselves under English protection or fled to Spanish Florida as strangers moved onto their lands. Ironically, the peace and security the English restored to the coastal plain turned against the Indigenous towns. Stripping them of their autonomy, it brought the coastal Indians' world to an end.

THE WESTO WAR

Charles Town's pact with the Westos barely lasted five years. During that time, the commercial Indian slave trade took root in the colony as untold numbers of slaves changed hands among the English—untold, because the proprietors discouraged Indian slavery and expressly prohibited the exportation of Indian captives out of the colony. Legitimate trade in skins and furs alone produced a lot of profit for Carolina traders. Henry Woodward's account books show that his 1675 haul, which may have been his first exchange with the Westos, generated net profits of three hundred ninety-eight pounds sterling for himself and the Lords Proprietors. Woodward traded coarse cloth, kettles, trinkets, knives, hatchets, guns, and ammunition for bear and deer skins and beaver pelts. He also listed an unspecified number of slaves as "not sold." Slave exchanges took place off the books. As a result, few records have survived to show the extent of this trade. However, events in 1680 suggest that it was, as one historian has noted, "the most lucrative economic avenue available" to colonial elites, and they fought bitterly with one another to control it. It stood at the center of Carolina's economy and English–Indian relations. The Westos staked their lives and reputation on it. Such high stakes destabilized the Westo–English trade agreement and eventually led to war and the destruction of the Westo as a people.[33]

Not all of the English were happy with the Westo trade deal. As it turned out, the Lords Proprietors, who governed Carolina (at least on paper) from their base in London, declared that it would be better for the security of the colony to limit competition over trade with the powerful inland towns. The proprietors would, therefore, keep the Westo trade with its sizable profits in their own hands, and only their appointed and licensed agents in Carolina would be permitted to trade on their behalf. Henry Woodward was chief among their hand-picked favorites. The proprietors' self-serving monopoly stirred up the resentment of a group of far more self-serving colonial leaders whom historians have called the "Goose Creek men." Led by Maurice Mathews and James Moore, the Goose Creek faction looked to wrest control of the lucrative inland trade from Woodward, and they took steps to obstruct it and bring down both Woodward and the Westos, if necessary. In 1677, just weeks after Woodward's official appointment as the proprietors' agent, Mathews used his position on the colony's Grand Council to bring charges against the Westos. The Grand Council alleged that they had murdered two Englishmen, and, worse yet, they were "very forward and intent to inquire and find out the way manner and strength of the settlement," presumably to learn its vulnerabilities and attack it. The Grand Council restricted the Westo traders to the outskirts of the settlement until they had "given satisfaction for the blood and murder of the two English by them destroyed."[34]

Three years later, the Grand Council still had not received satisfaction. In April, they sent a delegation to meet with Westo leaders at a neutral location, not to reach an amicable settlement but to provoke a confrontation. They reminded the Westos to stay out of the colony for their own good, "least that they should fall among som of the people whose friends they had causeslie killed for whose bloud no Reparaion hath yet been made." They also warned them not to "Intermedle nor disturbe" the settlement Indians. These old and largely empty threats were intended to taunt the Westos. By repeating them, the English triggered the desired reaction when Ariano, an "Aged and a Considerable person of their nation," rose to speak. Ariano turned the tables and blamed the English for tensions between their people. Woodward had told the Westos everything,

Ariano said. They knew that the English were laying plans to "come to destroy them in their towne" and that James Moore and Jonathan Boone planned to use the pretext of a diplomatic visit to Hickauhaugau to spy out the settlement and discover its weaknesses. Woodward advised them to "knock Captain Moore and Mr. Boone on the head meaneing they should kill them." They also knew that the English planned to invite the Westos to Charles Town under friendly pretenses, only to take them captive and sell them off as slaves across the sea. Ariano's outburst gave the Goose Creek men everything they needed to move against Woodward and the Westos. Weeks later, alleging that the Westos had violated their pact by attacking the coastal Indian towns, they placed Woodward under bond and armed the Savannahs, an Algonquian-speaking people, to make all-out war on Hickauhaugau.[35]

The proprietors attributed the Westo War to the machinations of the Goose Creek men, and historians have followed their lead. Mathews, Moore, and the other "dealers in Indians" resented the proprietors' monopoly and Woodward's privileged access to the inland trade. To take control of this trade for themselves, they put words in Ariano's mouth and spun those words into stories of Woodward's perfidy and Westo treachery. In this interpretation, the war was manufactured by a self-serving clique that was pulling the Indians' and Grand Council's strings to bring about the destruction of the Westos for their own personal gain. Yet this Anglocentric, puppet-master argument for the origins of the Westo War tells only half the story. The Westos were no English puppets, nor were they simply victims of the machinations of the Goose Creek men. Viewing the Westo War from an Indian perspective completes the picture, placing the war in its broader regional context and connecting it to other important but heretofore isolated events taking place at the same time in Escamaçu and Guale. It also shows that the Goose Creek men were not far off their mark in their assessment of the Westo threat to Carolina.[36]

A good starting place for recovering this perspective is Ariano's speech. This is a rare opportunity, for Westo voices are seldom, if ever, heard in English sources. The Grand Council minutes do not capture its tone or inflections, but the substance is clear enough. Ariano believed that the English were bent on destroying the Westos. The Grand Council's emissaries were actually spies, and their seemingly friendly invitations were traps. Their words were lies, and they could not be trusted. Because the English delegation did not deny this claim, and because they came to this council with only warnings and taunts and made no overtures of peace, they, not the Westos, had broken the 1674 pact. As a result, both the English and their allies, the settlement Indians, were now enemies of the Westos, and the coastal towns were once more fair game for Westo raiders. With the plot thus exposed, the Goose Creek men were caught in their own web. They, not the Westos, had broken faith and created enmity between their people.

The Westos lost no time in capitalizing on this changed relationship. Two weeks after their meeting with the Grand Council, a force of some three hundred warriors struck Guale. Spanish officials were shocked to learn that the Westos were joined by two other peoples who had recently been "treating and trading with" the Spaniards "in good friendship:" the Uchisis and the Chiluques/Escamaçus. The raiders' first target was the Yamasee town of Colon in the southern part of the province. They then attacked the town and garrison of Santa Catalina on the northern border of Guale but were repelled by its Spanish and Indian defenders. According to the English, around this same time the Westos took captive a number of Carolina's settlement Indians and sold them directly to English settlers for powder and bullets.[37]

These bold attacks on the Spanish missions and the settlement Indians were sure to provoke reprisals from St. Augustine and Charles Town, and they have all the hallmarks of desperation. Cut off from official trade with Charles Town, the Westos needed guns, powder, and shot. The fastest route to getting them was to overtake the Spanish garrison. Failing that, the coastal Natives were easy targets for slavers, and English settlers were eager buyers with little to fear from cashing in on the local black market for Indian slaves. On the other hand, the presence of Chiluque and Uchisi warriors suggests that these attacks might have been assertions of Westo power more than desperate weapon raids. The Chiluque–Uchisi alliance signaled a realignment of Spanish- and English-allied Indians to the Westos, who also had friends among the powerful Coweta towns of the Chattahoochee. A successful strike by these combined forces against the Spanish garrison would send a message to Indigenous peoples across the borderlands that the Westos and their allies were bidding for control of the region. Furthermore, they were taking trade into their own hands by bypassing official channels and dealing directly with English households. Also, they were defying Charles Town's warnings against molesting their "Neighbour Indians," not only taking settlement Indians as slaves but doing so with the help of other settlement Indians who had previously accepted English protection. If they could arm themselves without permission from the Grand Council, and if they could orchestrate a more general realignment of Natives in their borderlands, the Westos could put the English in their place and force them to trade on the Westos' terms.

It was not to be. Newly armed with English guns, the Savannahs destroyed Hickauhaugau. They brought hundreds of Westo captives to the English, who sold them as slaves to the West Indies. Other Westos may have returned to Iroquoia, and still others blended in among the Coweta. By 1682, there were no more than fifty still living in the region.[38]

In the aftermath of the war, to feed their appetite for Indian slaves, the Goose Creek men trumped up charges against one of their own protected tribes, the Winyah, and set their Savannah allies against them. The desire for profits thus destroyed the Pax Anglica, and with the Westo maneaters eliminated, the English settlement began to cannibalize itself. As a result of these wars, the Lords Proprietors came down hard on the "dealers in Indians." In two sharply worded letters to colonial officials, they removed Mathews and Moore from the Grand Council, ordered the local assembly to establish a fair and open process for exporting enemy Indians by licensed agents, and made an eloquent plea against the inhumanity of the slave trade. "By the purchase of Indians from the Sevanas," they wrote, "you induce them through covetousness of great weapons and other European goods to make war upon their neighbours, ravish the wife from the husband, and kill the father, take the child, and burn and destroy the dwellings of the poor people who cheerfully received us into their country, and cherished us when we were weak, or at least never did us any hurt. And, after this, we have set them to do all these horrid things in order to get slaves for the Indian dealers." This spirited opposition of the proprietors, along with the Savannahs' inability to acquire slaves outside the coastal plain, led to a lull in Carolina's commercial Indian slave trade, at least for a season.[39]

Historians have rationalized Westo violence, claiming that they were victims of multiple forced migrations who used slaving as a "survival strategy," a way to "cope with contact" and "adapt to desperate times." The Westos were not the "bloodthirsty slavers" depicted in "distorted" sources but relied heavily on legitimate trade in animal hides. They used violence not just to take slaves but also to expand their hunting grounds to sustain themselves. Their betrayal and destruction by the English was a "horror story," made more poignant by the "tragic tales" of Westo refugees fleeing the murderous Savannahs.[40]

However, from the perspective of the Indigenous people of the colonial southeast, the Westo era was a reign of terror, most of all for Carolina's coastal people, whose world collapsed as a result of the invasion. The Westos came into a world of farmers and hunter–gatherers where they could have found enough land to sustain themselves with minimal violence. Instead, they launched wars of aggression against peaceful and comparatively defenseless people who never offended them, attacking and burning their towns, killing their defenders, and carrying off as many as they could as slaves to adopt, sell, or kill and eat. They brought unparalleled violence and destruction to a stable region, spreading terror, loss, sadness, and collapse in every direction. In league with the English, and driven by a desire for power and wealth, they transformed Indigenous captive-taking into a commercial enterprise whose market knew no bounds. Ironically, its appetite for slaves eventually consumed the Westos themselves.

A Refuge for the Gospel

In the early 1680s, Scotland was both an economic backwater and a site of intense religious persecution. These two overlapping contexts formed the backdrop for the Carolina colony. The colony's organizers were Presbyterian dissenters who refused to submit to the established church and who envisioned their colony, Stuarts Town, as a refuge for the gospel and its persecuted followers. At the same time, they came from the middling and upper strata of Scottish society, and they hoped to make Stuarts Town into a lucrative venture that would produce American trade goods, create a market for Scottish exports, and invigorate the national economy. The dynamic interplay between these two objectives, religious safe haven and profitable colonial port, shaped the colony from its inception in 1682 to its failure in 1689.

In other words, there were two Stuarts Towns, each one trying to solve its own problem, each problem national in scale. These two Stuarts Towns were not necessarily incompatible; in theory, they were actually complementary. The spiritual ideal gave a larger purpose to the business venture, and the commercial enterprise sustained the religious mission. However, these two objectives also competed with one another, and sometimes they came into conflict. When one took precedence over the other, it threw the entire project out of balance and threatened to destroy or delegitimize the colony. This happened in 1684, at the height of religious crisis, when the colony's leaders, desperate to preserve the church, threw caution to the wind and launched the venture, although they lacked the organizational stability to promote and finance it. It happened again in Carolina, when Stuarts Town was facing imminent financial collapse and its leaders suspended their vision of a godly community and embraced a new imperialist identity instead. This opened the door to forms of exploitation never imagined in their religious vision, including the exploitation of their fellow Presbyterian exiles. Distressed by economic insecurity, the colony cannibalized itself.

THE COVENANTERS' WORLD

The cosmos of the Scottish Presbyterians who colonized Stuarts Town was very different from that of Carolina's coastal Indians. The spiritual powers that governed their world were engaged in an epic battle for the souls of women and men. Satan, the Father of Lies, was their adversary. Satan's shock troops on earth were led by Antichrist, who commanded the Roman Catholic Church in the person of the pope. Antichrist appeared to be Christian but was actually the opposite. He deluded his followers into thinking they were following Christ along the narrow path to heaven, when in reality, they were being led by Satan down the broad road to hell. Antichrist especially hated the religious truths found in the Bible and used his formidable powers to suppress them.

Facing off against Satan and Antichrist were the forces of Christ, who based their understanding of sin, salvation, and the Christian life on the plain teachings of the Bible, not the humanmade traditions at the heart of Catholic practice. Their gospel declared that salvation was a free gift from a loving and gracious God to sinful humans, not a reward that people earned by their so-called righteous actions, as the papists taught. This gift was made through the sacrifice and merits of Christ alone. It was mediated through the spoken and written word—preaching, teaching, and Bible study—not through the rituals and incantations of priests or the monotonous refrains of set prayers. These truths about the way to salvation were clearly spelled out in the Bible, and it was the task of the true church to proclaim them in obedience to Christ's command to make disciples of all nations. By doing so, the church was the means of grace; it was God's main instrument for saving his beloved people.

For centuries, Satan had buried these truths under layers of false teachings promulgated by the Catholic church. By the grace of God, the Protestant Reformation had liberated the gospel from Antichrist and made the scriptures available to ordinary people in their own languages. In the late sixteenth century, this Reformed Protestantism triumphed in Scotland, whose national church embodied Christ's teachings and shielded the gospel against the advance of Antichrist. To Scottish Presbyterians, history was nothing less than the unfolding of God's plan to free human beings from sin and hell. The Scots had been appointed as God's agents, in their generation and in their small corner of the world, to preserve the true church and, if need be, to suffer for the gospel. Their lives were thus encased in a spiritual battle pitting church against state, good against evil, Christ against Antichrist, and heaven against hell.

Scotland's Christian fortress was breached in 1660 when Charles Stuart was restored to the thrones of England, Scotland, and Ireland. Charles was head of the Church of England, which retained the episcopal, or bishop-led, structure of the Roman Catholic Church along with some of its rituals and theology. In this episcopal system, power flowed from the top down. The monarch appointed bishops, who were responsible for ordaining and disciplining priests and protecting the flock from false teachings and practices. After his restoration, Charles declared himself head of the Church of Scotland, installed bishops to rule it, and imposed uniform worship based on the Church of England's Book of Common Prayer. For Scottish Presbyterians, who viewed the frame of church government as a protective shell surrounding the gospel of Christ, this was an existential crisis, not just an argument over arcane questions of governance and structure. The gospel was safe if placed in the hands of godly laypeople and their ministers who were called to serve the church. It would be corrupted, however, putting the souls of men and women in danger of eternal damnation, if the church were ruled by state actors who thirsted for wealth and power, not righteousness, and who felt few qualms about distorting or weakening the gospel's message of salvation. Such men were putty in the hands of Antichrist.

The Church of Scotland's bottom-up, presbyterian form of government was designed to keep the state out of religious affairs. This system would make Christ, not the king, the head of his church, and it would rid the church of all traces of Antichrist. It did this mainly by placing power in the hands of church courts made up of lay elders (called presbyters) and parish clergy. They, not secular authorities and their political appointees, would be responsible for calling ministers, disciplining members, and ensuring correct doctrine and practice. This presbyterian system was a representative and "federal" form of government. At the parish level, congregations chose their elders, called their own ministers, and disciplined their members for nonattendance or moral lapses. Elders and ministers from neighboring parishes met together in presbyteries, which screened ministerial candidates, ruled on matters of doctrine, and served as a court of appeal for church members who had been disciplined. Groups of presbyteries formed still higher courts, called synods, which, in turn, sent representatives to a national body called the General Assembly. Although the Church of Scotland was established by law as the official national church, and although it was supported by taxes, it was governed solely by these assemblies of churchmen. The state's role was to act on behalf of the church, not control it.

To Scottish Presbyterians, this system was more than just the best defense against Antichrist. Rather, it was mandated by scripture, commanded by God, and it was therefore sacred. Moreover, in 1638, they had made a national covenant, witnessed by God and sealed with a solemn oath, to defend this presbyterian system of church government and keep it free from state interference. Decades later, they insisted that they were still bound by their oath and that the covenant was both national and perpetual (i.e., binding on all Scots for all time). In 1662, 1681, and 1684, state authorities issued new oaths, or religious tests, to force these Covenanters to renounce their covenant oath. These tests became flashpoints of violent conflict as Covenanters steadfastly resisted the crown's corrupt takeover of their church.

Despite this common world view, not all Covenanters were alike. Although they adhered to the Covenant and shared a commitment to presbyterianism and the headship of Christ in their national church, their attitudes toward the state and their approaches to resisting it varied. Some were moderates who quietly worked behind the scenes or within the system to effect change. This group included ministers who had accepted an "indulgence" from the state: They were not required to renounce the covenant, and the indulgence gave them permission to remain in the ministry as long as they stayed within the bounds of their parishes and did not meet with other ministers. Over time these indulged ministers formed shadow presbyteries, creating an "alternative church" that helped Presbyterians resist episcopal takeover. Many of these moderates would have agreed with the Hamilton Declaration, a Covenanter document that acknowledged the authority of Charles II yet also stood by the Covenant, humbly pleading with the Crown to restore presbyterianism to the Church of Scotland. Other Covenanters were less cautious in their defiance of the law. They met openly in mass conventicles, harbored fugitives, and refused to attend parish services or take the king's oath when asked. Many of these resisters were arrested, fined, and imprisoned, sometimes repeatedly. Still others were uncompromising radicals. They despised indulged ministers and called the Hamilton Declaration a betrayal of the Covenant. Many of this group agreed with the more extreme Sanquhar Declaration that renounced the king as an enemy of Christ, excommunicated him, openly rejected his authority over both church and state, and advocated violent resistance to episcopal rule.[1]

Violence was endemic to the Covenanters' world, for the war with Antichrist was a battle of flesh and blood, not just words and ideas. Since 1660, the conflict between Scottish Episcopalians and Presbyterians had set off intermittent flashes of violence. It escalated in 1679 when Presbyterian radicals assassinated the Archbishop of St. Andrews and took up arms against royal forces, who routed them at Bothwell Bridge outside of Glasgow. Royal suppression of dissenters intensified after the Bothwell uprising, as did Presbyterian resistance. The stakes were high: on the one hand, the authority of the king over religious matters within his realm; on the other hand, the preservation of the gospel and defense of the Kingdom of God. In such a contest, there was little room for a middle ground. When conditions further deteriorated in 1683, with the discovery of plots to assassinate the king and rebel against his kingdom, the center collapsed completely. As the state's judicial machinery relentlessly ground down the resistance movement, Covenanters languished in prison, paid crippling fines, and faced dispossession, torture, dismemberment, execution, or banishment to the English plantations. By July 1684, when the Stuarts Town colonists set sail for Port Royal aboard the *Carolina Merchant*, the world they left behind was being torn apart by religious violence. These bleak prospects distressed John Erskine, youngest brother to the colony's leader, Lord Cardross, as he watched the *Merchant* sail out of Gourock. "The number, presumption, and interest of papists was now fast growing in Scotland," Erskine wrote. "The corruptions and antichristian latitude of bishops and their dependents," along with their "tyranny and usurpation," all showed that they were intent on "extirpating Presbyterians out of Scotland."[2]

THE CAROLINA COMPANY

The Scots who conceived and organized the Carolina colony in 1682 were Covenanters, but they were guided by commercial as well as religious motives. Like religious violence, their economic problems were tied to the restoration of Charles II. After 1660, the king and England's parliament launched a major effort to strengthen trade and consolidate the English empire. This took legal form in the Navigation Acts, a bundle of laws aimed at excluding foreign competitors, including Scotland, from trading with England's colonies. Under these laws, only English-owned ships could trade in English colonial ports. The most profitable colonial staple products, such as sugar and tobacco, had to be shipped to England or one of its colonies before being sent to foreign countries, and European goods had to pass through an English port to be taxed before going to the colonies. The Navigation Acts were designed to channel the wealth produced by England's colonies to the "mother country" and to prevent foreign nations from cashing in on English colonization.

England and Scotland were subject to the same king, but until 1707, Scotland had its own parliament. As a result, under the Navigation Acts, it was treated as a foreign country and was prohibited from direct trade with the English colonies. Spain also excluded Scotland from its American markets. To make matters worse, Scotland's trade with its most important commercial partner, the Dutch Republic, was disrupted by the Anglo–Dutch Wars of the 1660s and 1670s. Thus, while England's wealth grew exponentially as a result of the Navigation Acts and the seizure of Holland's North American colonies, Scotland's economy, although by no means stagnant, lagged far behind its neighbor to the south.[3]

It was no accident that, by 1680, as religious conflict between Presbyterians and Charles II was reaching a boiling point, Scottish merchants and political leaders began pressuring the Privy Council for a colonial port to give them a wedge into the American market. The Privy Council was the administrative arm of the crown in Scotland, and it wielded great power. Scotland's anemic exports, as West Indian planter William Colquhoun told the Privy Council in 1681, had depressed the economy and produced a "habituall disease of the body of trade" that could only be cured by an American colony. Such a colony would not only restore health to the nation's ailing economy but would also remove many of the "idle and disenting persons" who grew like a cancer on its body politic.[4] In addition to increasing trade, a colony would enable Scottish authorities to export dissent and poverty by ridding the country of religious troublemakers along with the growing rabble of "vagabonds, whores and thieves," as one petitioner put it, who burdened Edinburgh and Glasgow with their poverty. Religious conflict and empire went hand-in-hand; both the persecution of Presbyterians and Scottish poverty were, to a great extent, the products of an expanding English state. It was no surprise that advocates of colonization linked them.[5] The Privy Council did not need convincing on any of these points. Backed by James Stuart, Duke of York, the king's brother and presumed heir to the throne, it secured the blessing of Charles II to establish American colonies that would be exempt from English trade restrictions. The king was "graciously desireous to countenance and promote so laudable an undertaking," probably in part, as the Duke of York later said, because the Presbyterians "would carry with them their disaffected people." In any case, with the passage of the *Act for Encourageing Trade and Manufactures* in 1681, Scots created a legal foundation for legitimate trade (as opposed to smuggling, which they already practiced) within the English empire. The Scots could now establish their own colonies in English colonial territories, and they could trade freely and directly with these colonies.[6]

After weighing the opportunities and risks of sites from New York to Surinam, merchants and investors settled on two locations: East New Jersey and Port Royal, South Carolina. Port Royal was an especially attractive prospect for colonization. It had a fine natural harbor that, with improvements, would make an excellent port. Five rivers emptied into the sound, providing plenty of riverfront access to planters seeking to move their crops to market. Its subtropical climate and long growing season suited it perfectly to plantation agriculture. It was also within the West Indian plantation complex and offered convenient access to British settlements in the Bahamas, Jamaica, Barbados, and Virginia. This made it an ideal location for drawing in the many Scottish servants and families scattered across the Caribbean. Besides these natural and geographical advantages, Carolina was governed mainly by Anthony Ashley-Cooper, Earl of Shaftesbury, the leader of England's Whig opposition to the Crown and a great friend of Scottish Presbyterians. With Shaftesbury in their corner, the

Scots hoped to carve out an autonomous settlement that operated more-or-less independently of the English provincial government in Charles Town, which lay about sixty miles to the north of Port Royal.[7]

Port Royal did have one major drawback: its location in the debatable territory of the Anglo–Spanish borderlands. No one knew if it was on the English or Spanish side of the line, because there was no line. After fifteen years of war over control of Jamaica and other West Indian colonies, the 1670 Treaty of Madrid between Spain and Britain tried to settle this dispute by giving the British king "full right of sovereignty" to the American territories he already possessed. Unfortunately, the treaty failed to specify precisely what those territories were. Port Royal was about midway between Charles Town, which clearly belonged to the English, and Florida's Guale missions, which were indisputably in Spanish territory. Spain had some claim to it by virtue of its sixteenth-century colonization of Santa Elena, although it had not occupied the site in almost a century. The English who came to Carolina in 1670 thought it might be theirs and originally planned to settle there, but they chose instead to move further north, in part because of its nearness to Spanish Florida. Colonizing Port Royal thus risked provoking a Spanish attack. Yet the Scots were undeterred, declaring a preference for locating south of Charles Town "that wee may be as near the Spaniards as possibly wee can be, [so] that we may have a present trade with them." As later events would show, this was a lie, but a necessary one, because the Scots, like the French and Spaniards a century earlier, could not resist the many natural advantages Port Royal offered for a colony.[8]

To turn this dream of Scottish empire into reality, investors pooled their money and, in 1682, organized the Carolina Company. This was a private joint-stock company that sold shares to investors ("undertakers," the company called them) to raise funds for provisioning, outfitting, and staffing the colony. Investors would profit from selling Scottish goods abroad and by shipping and selling whatever goods the colony produced—timber, silk, indigo, and perhaps tobacco or sugar—or acquired through trade with Native people. Unlike similar English companies that colonized Massachusetts and Virginia, the Carolina Company was a strictly commercial enterprise. It did not have a charter from the Crown and had no power to govern the colony. Although it planned to recruit servants to expand production and thereby generate more trade goods, the company made no provisions, at least initially, for owning servants itself or directly profiting from unfree labor. It was basically an investment scheme that provided the organizational infrastructure to amass capital and funnel it into colonization and foreign trade. By the summer of 1682, the company had enlisted dozens of shareholders and authorized its treasurer to collect £10 from each to fund an exploratory voyage to Carolina. The voyagers would scout the area for a suitable settlement, take soundings of the depths of channels along the islands, and make a detailed report of the soil, climate, vegetation, commodities, and proximity to the Spaniards. In addition, the company negotiated generous terms of settlement with Shaftesbury and the other Carolina proprietors, designed to give the Scots autonomy from Charles Town and to guard "against the oppression of the people by their Administrators." Clearly, the leaders of the Carolina Company were more concerned about English than Spanish interference in their colony, at least from the vantage point of 1682.[9]

The early records of the Carolina Company—cargo and subscription lists, bonds with merchants and investors, plans for recruiting laborers, invoices, articles of agreement, committee meeting minutes—reflect its managers' preoccupation with the business side of colonization.[10] Yet the financial concerns on the surface of these documents masked a deep anxiety about national religious life. A closer look at the company's leadership, shareholders, terms of agreement with Shaftesbury, and the report from its exploratory voyage brings these anxieties to the surface and reveals the religious dimension of the company's colonial scheme.

The Carolina Company was dominated by Covenanters. Its principal leaders, Sir John Cochrane of Ochiltree and Sir George Campbell of Cessnock, both came from Covenanting families and were leaders in the Presbyterian resistance movement. Cochrane had been arrested in 1678 for attending conventicles, and Campbell allegedly had supplied the Bothwell rebels with arms when they occupied Glasgow in 1679. Both would later be implicated in plotting to revolt against the Stuarts to free the Church of Scotland from episcopal control.[11] In addition, most of the company's subscribers made up a dense network of family, friends, and business associates, many of whom shared a common commitment to Presbyterianism. A cursory analysis of the subscription list shows that a significant proportion of the shareholders—at least one-third, possibly many more—were Covenanters who were prosecuted for nonconformity or who had known associations with those who did. These included men such as John Hutcheson, who was summoned by the courts on suspicion of taking part in the Covenanters' 1666 Pentland Rising (Hutcheson did not help his case when he refused to say "God save the King" before the judges). Several undertakers, including Hallcraig, Alexander Cunningham of Craigends, and James Dunlop of Househill, were imprisoned or made to post bonds for refusing to take the oath. Another prominent investor, the Earl of Loudon, was charged with harboring rebels and was later implicated alongside Cochrane and Campbell in plotting against the Crown.[12]

In addition to its stakeholders at home, the Company's dual concerns over finances and faith were reflected in the decision to put William Dunlop in charge of company affairs on the ground in Carolina. Dunlop was a man of many gifts and impeccable Covenanter credentials. Born in 1654, he came of age during the prolonged state of war between Presbyterians and the state after the Restoration. In the 1650s, his father Alexander, minister at Paisley, had joined the Protesters, an extreme and uncompromising Covenanter faction that insisted on absolute independence of the church from state meddling. After the Restoration, Charles II required ministers who had been appointed by presbyteries to conform and accept reappointment by bishops. Alexander refused to submit and resigned his charge. He was hauled before the Privy Council, which banished him from the realm for refusing to take the king's religious oath (the council later relented because of his health and confined him to the town of Culross instead). William was eight years old when his family moved to Culross in 1662. He grew up in a time when hundreds of nonconforming ministers were put out of their parishes and lay resisters were meeting secretly in their homes or in the fields in defiance of the law. His mother, Elizabeth, was among them and was later arrested and banished from Edinburgh for attending one of these illegal conventicles.

As the eldest son of activist parents who suffered for their principles, William inherited strong religious convictions and habits of spirited resistance to state intrusions on Scotland's autonomous church. He married his cousin, Sarah Carstares, a devout Presbyterian whose brother William plotted assiduously to overthrow Charles II. After receiving his master's degree in theology in 1675, Dunlop joined the resistance by taking a position as chaplain in the household of the Earl of Dundonald, a staunch Covenanter and father to Cochrane of Ochiltree, future leader of the Carolina Company. Dunlop was licensed to preach, but not by the bishop, who pressured Dundonald to dismiss him. He did, but Dunlop complied only on paper. By one account, he took part in drafting the moderate Hamilton Declaration, which he smuggled out of Edinburgh to the rebel camp at Bothwell. Five years after the Bothwell uprising, with Dunlop safely in Carolina, physicians who had attended Dundonald reportedly testified that they heard Dunlop pray for the rebellion, which would have been treasonous.[13] Because he was neither an ordained minister nor a public official, he was not required to take the king's oath and thus avoided the fines and imprisonment faced by many of his associates. He was also a pragmatist who saw little value in publicly rejecting the authority of the king and learned how to work with people who did not share his religious principles. "He preached well," John Erskine wrote when he heard Dunlop at a clandestine service on the

eve of his departure to Carolina, "and was otherways accomplished." These ac-
complishments included strong communication and managerial skills, energetic
leadership, a university degree (a rarity in Carolina), and passion for his work,
all of which would serve him and the Stuarts Town colony well.[14]

The terms of agreement between company officials and the Lords Proprietors also show how close to the surface the company's religious anxieties were
in 1682. That summer, Cochrane and Campbell met with Shaftesbury to negotiate the terms of their proposed settlement. The defeat at Bothwell Bridge, the
hardening of episcopal control, and the prospects of a Scottish port in North
America convinced these men that the time was ripe for a Presbyterian colony,
and they stepped forward to lead the initiative. They promised Shaftesbury a
thousand settlers, but in exchange, they wanted changes in the Fundamental
Constitutions, which laid out the frame of government for Carolina. Self-
determination for Stuarts Town was foremost on their minds. Cochrane and
Campbell demanded clear title to the land from coastal Indians. They wanted
a location geographically separated from Charles Town and protections against
irregular elections for the colonial assembly. They also asked for the power to
appoint justices and magistrates and administer justice within their own jurisdiction. The Scots mistrusted the English colonial government at Charles Town,
and they wanted—and were granted—as much autonomy as Shaftesbury could
give them.[15]

Cochrane and Campbell also insisted on provisions to ensure the independence of the church. The Fundamental Constitutions already made generous al-
lowances for religious liberty, and in this area, it was one of the most progressive
governments in the world. To be clear, the document did not enshrine *individual*
freedom of conscience; atheism was illegal, and all adults were required to be
members of a religious body. However, it did guarantee protection for *corporate*
practice, granting full toleration to dissenters, Jews, and even Roman Catholics.
At the same time, however, the colonial charter gave the Church of England,
which it deemed "the only true and Orthodox" profession, the sole privilege of
state support. In other words, the Fundamental Constitutions granted toleration but also made the Anglican church the only established, or state-supported,
religious institution. The Scots objected to this language, and in January 1682,
the truth claims of the national church were removed, although it alone still received state funding as the "religion of the Government of England." After further negotiations, in August 1682, Shaftesbury made even greater concessions.
The proprietors gutted the establishment provisions by exempting all persons
"not conformable" to the Church of England from paying for its upkeep and
allowing other Protestant churches to tax their own members. Not satisfied with

promises of toleration, which meant nothing to Scottish Presbyterians under the heel of a Scottish Episcopal establishment, Cochrane and Campbell won provisions for multiple establishments. This placed Presbyterians and other dissenters on equal footing with the Church of England.[16]

Like the terms of agreement, the Carolina Company's 1682–1683 exploratory expedition to Port Royal also had strong religious undertones. The company commissioned the *James of Erwin*, a ship belonging to Glasgow merchant Walter Gibson, to trade goods in Charles Town and explore the coast to its south. The company's instructions to the crew reflected its business interests: take soundings of the channels; look for navigable rivers; make note of the soil, timber, and climate; and report on Port Royal's proximity to Spanish settlements and prospects for trade. The expedition's leader, John Crawford of Crawfordland, was a company shareholder and Covenanter. He sent back a glowing report of "a most healthy country," with rich soils, fine rivers and harbors, and abundant natural resources, reflecting the economic objectives of the investors. However, he also made some curious choices that spoke to the spiritual and social concerns of his fellow Covenanters. Although it was nine hundred miles from Carolina, Crawford devoted about one-third of his short report to describing Bermuda, which was not only a "most Fertile" and healthy place but also an exceptionally sober and pious one. It boasted nine churches, five ministers with good houses and generous incomes, and, best of all, "no Sectaries" (a handful of Quakers excepted). Crawford did not have to remind his readers that Bermuda was dominated by independent English churches that dissented from the Anglican establishment. Without saying so outright, Crawford presented his readers with a working model for a Presbyterian community in Carolina.

In a similar vein, Crawford's description of Port Royal's Indigenous people reflected the social and cultural assumptions of his Presbyterian friends. The Natives lived in simplicity and plenty, he wrote. "By their faces, Colour of Hayr, worshiping the new Moon, and some other Ceremonies resembling it" they were thought to be "Captive Isralites" who "might be easily gained to Christianity, and good order, if pains were taken on them, with good example." These were encouraging signs. The Scots were eager to establish close political and economic ties with Port Royal's Indians, who, Crawford assured them, "have great kindness for the English, but not for the Spaniards." William Dunlop had missionary ambitions and went to Carolina in part to "bring thes pur creturs to Crist," as his sister Margaret later reminded him. It would be no surprise if company officials dreamed of an intimate interracial community of Scots and Christianized Indians, living harmoniously in well-ordered towns under the cope of Reformed Protestant practice.[17]

Indeed, Crawford's reference to "Captive Isralites" suggests that some colonizers might have dreamed of something much more historic. In the mid-seventeenth century, theorists on both sides of the Atlantic argued that Native Americans were descended from the lost tribes of Israel, who had been taken into captivity by the Assyrian empire in the eighth century B.C.E. The prophets had declared that the physical return of Christ would be preceded by the conversion of the Jews. In the minds of some Covenanters, by converting Port Royal's Indigenous people, the Carolina colony could play an important role in God's plan to redeem humanity, bind Satan, and bring about the thousand-year reign of the saints on earth. This kind of prophetic framework for the colony would become more pronounced as persecution of Covenanters intensified in 1683.[18]

In sum, the colonial enterprise envisioned by the Carolina Company was one part business venture and one part religious escape plan. As the English state expanded during the Restoration period, forcing religious conformity on Scots while excluding them from international trade, it created both religious crisis and economic sluggishness in Scotland. Advocates of Scottish empire saw colonization as a solution to both of these ills. So too, both commerce and religion were integral to the business of the Carolina Company. The company's "laudable undertaking" was part of a larger plan to breathe life into Scotland's ailing economy, but religious anxiety, with all its historical and eternal implications, lurked just beneath the surface of its worldly business. The company's investors made up a tangled knot of disgruntled, multigenerational, intermarried Presbyterian dissidents. Its colony would be led by a seasoned Covenanter, William Dunlop, who was equal parts pragmatist and preacher. Its terms of agreement with Carolina's Lords Proprietors reflected Scots' religious fears and their determination to have absolute control over their own civil and religious affairs, and the report from the *James of Erwin*'s voyage expressed their longing for a peaceful, stable Presbyterian community that might even speed along the return of Christ. Until then, its "most Fertile" location would put money in its investors' pockets.

A SAFE HAVEN

Even as the Carolina Company laid plans to outfit the *James* for its voyage to Port Royal, many company officials were turning their attention from colonizing to conspiring against the Stuarts. In England, Shaftesbury had tried and failed in 1681 to pass a bill in parliament blocking the succession of James Stuart, a Catholic, to the throne. He was imprisoned and tried for treason, and although a sympathetic jury acquitted him in February 1682, the tide was turning against him. In July, new elections gave royalists control of London, setting the stage for a crackdown on Whigs. In desperation, Shaftesbury and other leading Whigs turned to plotting to overthrow the Stuarts, and they sought to bring disaffected Scots with them. William Carstares, brother-in-law to William Dunlop, went to Holland to discuss plans for a Scottish revolt with the exiled Earl of Argyll. The Cochrane–Campbell visit with Shaftesbury in August likely included discussions of a coordinated rebellion, but if so, no concrete plans came out of these talks. Fearful and frustrated, in November, Shaftesbury fled to Amsterdam, where he died in January 1683.[19] However, the plotting proceeded apace. In April and May, several Scots, including John Crawford, John Cochrane, and George and Hugh Campbell, all prominent within the Carolina Company, traveled to London on the pretext of company business. Instead, they met secretly with a mysterious group called the Council of Six, which had taken the lead in plotting against the government after Shaftesbury's departure. Together, they laid plans for a coordinated Scottish–English insurrection.[20]

Things took a turn for the worse in July 1683, when news broke of a plot to assassinate the Stuarts as they passed by Rye House mansion after attending the horse races. Because the races were cancelled, the plot was aborted. However, its exposure brought to light a widespread conspiracy involving English Whigs and republicans (people who were opposed to the very principle of monarchical government), Scottish Covenanters, and high-ranking nobles. These included the Earl of Argyll and even the king's illegitimate son, the Duke of Monmouth. In August, warrants for treason were issued for more than a dozen Scots, including Cochrane, the Campbells, and Crawford, plus the Earl of Loudon and Alexander Munro, who were also undertakers in the Carolina Company. Cochrane and another investor, Sir Patrick Hume of Polwarth, fled to Rotterdam, as did William Carstares. The others were arrested and imprisoned in Edinburgh, and forfeiture proceedings were undertaken against their estates. With its leaders exiled or imprisoned and its business venture tainted by charges of treason, by the fall of 1683, the Carolina Company was in tatters.[21]

After these plots were exposed, the Scottish government came down hard on Presbyterians, leading to a new phase of persecution that early Covenanter historians would call the "killing time." The Privy Council created new special courts to prosecute Presbyterian dissidents and collect fines from landowners who violated the ban on conventicles. It also empowered the army to break up conventicles and carry out summary executions in the field if needed, basically militarizing law enforcement. The Bothwell rebellion remained a sore point. New "reset and converse" laws made it a crime to aid, harbor, or talk with rebels, many of whom had been living at large since 1679. These laws were applied retroactively, so anyone who had fed, housed, or communicated with a known rebel over the previous four years and failed to report him was subject to arrest. John M'Qharrie and James Smith were sentenced to death for being present at Bothwell, although they denied taking up arms. The executioner cut off their right hands before hanging them, whereupon M'Qharrie held out his bloody stub and defied the hangman, "forbidding people to be afraid of suffering, and calling it the blood of the Covenant." George Martin, John Kerr, and James Muir had not been at Bothwell but were put to death for refusing to call it a rebellion or affirm that Charles II was lawful king of Scotland. Husbands were deemed legally responsible for their wives' attendance at conventicles or nonattendance at parish services; they could avoid the heavy fines only by turning their wives over for imprisonment. Ministers were removed from their pulpits for failing to read the king's proclamation against the Rye House plot; those too poor to post the exorbitant bond, such as Anthony Shaw, were imprisoned. Church attendance was closely surveilled, new oaths were invented to reinforce it, and neighbors were paid five pounds to inform on nonattenders. Those who resisted were placed under bond, imprisoned, or transported to the plantations. A hypervigilant state was breeding widespread fear and suspicion across the Scottish lowlands, giving rise to John Erskine's fear that the government was, indeed, intent on "extirpating the Presbyterians."[22]

Thus, by early 1684, circumstances had changed profoundly since the Carolina Company's founding two years earlier. Campbell's arrest, Cochrane's flight, and Shaftesbury's death threw the company into disarray and disrupted its ability to raise capital and organize settlement. Fears of Presbyterian extirpation were real—the authorities made no secret of it—and they only intensified as the state's campaign to root out resistance to episcopacy hardened in the killing time. The Covenanters' plotting had failed, the state was winning, and Presbyterians were running out of options. In this dire context, the colonial scheme took on a greater sense of urgency. Stuarts Town was born out of this apocalyptic moment, as reflected in its changing leadership, their prophetic views, and their plans to establish an ideal Christian community in Port Royal.

As the Carolina Company collapsed, William Dunlop, who was still fully committed to the colony, scrambled together funding from his friend and fellow Covenanter, James Montgomery of Skelmorlie, along with Glasgow merchant Walter Gibson. In addition, a new and more formidable leader emerged to take control of the colonization project: Henry Erskine, Lord Cardross. Unlike Dunlop, who kept a low profile within the Presbyterian resistance movement, Cardross had paid a high price, and a public one, for his Covenanting principles. In the 1670s and 1680s, he and his estate became a microcosm of the sufferings of Scottish Presbyterians. In 1675, royal troops had come to arrest his chaplain, the outlawed minister and "denunced rebel" John King, for violating his bond and holding conventicles at Cardross's home. A party of four hundred servants and tenants, many armed with "swords, forkes, pickes, half pickes, and such lyk weapons," rescued King and pursued the soldiers back to Stirling (one of them, Alexander Ure, a "taall reid haired man, who had a corn forke with ane aiken shaft," would come with Cardross to Carolina). King was among the radical ministers whose followers later harbored the assassins of the archbishop, and he was eventually executed for his role in the Bothwell uprising. Cardross was sentenced to four years in prison and fined five thousand pounds sterling for harboring King, allowing conventicles in his house and grounds, and having his children baptized by expelled ministers. He was released from prison in 1679, but his troubles did not end there. By 1684, royal troops had been quartered in his home twice, he had been dispossessed of some of his properties, and the privy council had rejected his appeals. Unable to pay his debts, in the weeks before his departure to Carolina he constantly kept on the move and frequently slept in the fields to avoid his creditors.[23]

On the basis of his close ties to King, Cardross would have been familiar with the prophetic "remnant theology" preached by the most radical Presbyterian ministers. Covenanters derived their idea of a saving remnant from the Bible. It was bound up with the promises that God had made with his original covenant people, the Israelites, whose cities were destroyed and lands forsaken as they were carried into captivity by their enemies. Old Testament prophets such as Isaiah assured them that God would keep his covenant, return a purified remnant of his people to the promised land, and restore their glory. Like the ancient Israelites, Scottish Presbyterians considered themselves to be a covenant people of God, and it was no surprise that the most radical Covenanters embraced remnant theology in the late 1670s. They were fighting a losing battle against a relentless state, and they took comfort in believing that a merciful God would set aside a remnant to be spared the terrible judgments visited on Scotland. The promise of such a remnant reminded them that their suffering was not in vain. Remnant theology, as one historian has noted, was "especially dear" to outed preachers such as John Welsh, David Cameron, and John King, whose hearers shared "an unshakeable conviction of divine mission."[24]

Lord Cardross and his wife were doubtless among these true believers. They harbored King when he persisted in holding conventicles at their home after his release from prison. They allowed their tenants to attend conventicles and refused to discipline their servants when they formed a mob to free King during his 1675 arrest. King's own faith in a godly remnant, made explicit in his final words written before his execution in 1679, surely resonated with Cardross.

Addressing "the truly Godly" men and women who mourned the sufferings of the church, King exhorted them to "be of good Courage," for "surely the Lord has a handful that are precious to him, to whom he will be Gracious; to these is a dark night at present," a time of "sad disasters" and "snares," so "Cleave fast to your Reformed Religion, do not Shift the Cross of Christ." As Presbyterian persecution intensified in the mid-1680s, this precious remnant would set its sights on Stuarts Town, where the church and the gospel it proclaimed, although suppressed at home, could flourish.[25]

Traces of this prophetic and covenantal thinking can also be found among more moderate Presbyterian dissidents of the mid-1680s, including the pragmatic William Dunlop. Although his worldly ambition eventually propelled him to the top tier of power in Carolina and Glasgow, Dunlop had a strong sense of divine mission rooted in the historic crisis that gripped Scotland. Letters from his wife, Sarah Carstares, who planned to join her husband in Stuarts Town, show that they both viewed colonization as a calling from God, one that went beyond William's dream of converting Native people to Christianity. Sarah prayed that God would use William "for servise to Him in thy generation," and when William was diverted by plantation business, she reminded him of the "great and main work which God hath called you more especially to follow." He echoed this language in his correspondence from Carolina. "Both a visible providence and Mercifull cast me here and hath preserved me here under aboundance of disappointments and difficulties," he wrote, and he was determined to remain until he was "cast out in a corner uselesse to myself and others," for "no man is born for himself nor called to serve himselfe alone." Dunlop would remain in Carolina long after Cardross and Covenanters at home abandoned it. Only when he was convinced that Presbyterian persecution had ended and the gospel was safe would he agree to return home "so as to be serviceable to my generation" in Scotland.[26]

At the heart of Dunlop's and Cardross's plans for the colony was a vision of Reformed Protestant community hatched in the early days of the Carolina Company. As they wrapped up negotiations with the Lords Proprietors in August 1682, Campbell and Cochrane had promised to "proceed vigorously to carry on our plantation and bring with us . . . a considerable number of Gentlemen and ministers and . . . a strength of people well provided of all things necessary." They ultimately expected ten thousand settlers, mostly Presbyterian refugees from Scotland and Ireland augmented by English from Charles Town, sugar planters from Antigua, and exiled French Protestants. Stuarts Town would be a settlement of families. The first wave of colonists promised to settle their families there as soon as the proprietors agreed to some "reasonable and necessary" requests. Dunlop and Cardross both expected their wives and children to immigrate when the town was fortified and the houses were ready. Although families diverted resources from the urgent business of clearing, building, fortifying, and planting the settlement, they were so integral to the communal vision of Stuarts Town that they would be subsidized by the colony as long as they agreed to remain for three years. In other words, entire families would be bound to the colony through a kind of familial indenture. This was a potentially risky and expensive experiment, to be sure, but "it is to be hoped," Dunlop wrote optimistically, "that God will blesse this designe."[27]

Dunlop's plan for subsidizing families was part of his "Project for a Settlement," his social blueprint for Stuarts Town drafted before or during the voyage to Carolina in the summer of 1684. Although official leadership belonged to Lord Cardross, Dunlop acted as manager of the colony, and his "Project" reflected its religious and communal priorities and social structure. Once the first makeshift dwellings were completed, Dunlop proposed that "the first building shall bee the church . . . plac'd near the center of the place first marking the ground for the houses." Cardross's house would be built next, although Dunlop hoped that Cardross would "take note of the weakness of the colony" and keep his dwelling modest so as not to overburden the laborers. This would be followed by the ministers' dwellings, "which will bee nearer to the Church in the constant use of those that shall Exercise the charge." The common people's houses would all be built to the same specifications and "conforme to the streetes and the plan of the fortification," each with "a small court or yard with a little garden." The forest would be fully cleared for plowing in the Scottish way of cultivation, and "Publick Easing places"—presumably parks or toilets—were to be set aside along the water for the benefit of servants and slaves. Dunlop's plan also made provisions for the general welfare. In addition to subsidizing families, all people in need "shall Ingenuously declare what they are able to Contribute for their subsistance to the End that those which shall bee in a condition to succour others bee not charged beyond their power: and those that with difficulty can give may not bee discouraged." Families were expected to be neighborly and "help one another to the best of their power by their Industry and Worke." Dunlop's plan thus projected an egalitarian community built by a labor collective, attuned to the needs of families and indigent people and literally centered around the church and its ministers, like an Israeli kibbutz or Christian socialist commune.[28]

The Carolina colony had never been merely a business venture, and as the state cracked down after the failed Whig plots of 1683, it was no longer merely a safe haven for religious refugees. Holland served that purpose. Instead, fueled

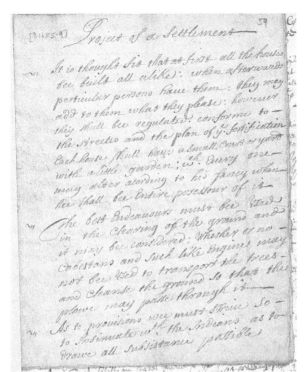

William Dunlop, Project of a Settlement (1684). Dunlop Papers, MS 9255, National Library of Scotland. Image courtesy of the National Library of Scotland.

by fears of Presbyterian extirpation and grounded in the belief that God would set aside a remnant to preserve the true church amid the terrible judgments befalling Scotland, Stuarts Town was reimagined as a flanking maneuver against antichristian bishops—"the pretended officers of the church," as John Erskine called them—along with the "interest of papists" which was "fast growing in Scotland."[29] Its purpose was collective, corporate, social, and historical. The colonizers would build a godly and well-ordered community in Carolina, where thousands of Reformed Protestants from the British Isles and British Atlantic world joined with praying Indians in orthodox Christian practice, where families flourished; fears and strivings ceased; and the gospel, shielded by an autonomous local government and a Presbyterian religious establishment, would be safe at last.

EXILE AND EXPLOITATION

Not all Covenanters aboard the *Carolina Merchant* went of their own free will. Cardross brought seven or eight servants, at least one of whom, Alexander Ure, went voluntarily. Dunlop brought twenty-two. Another thirty-five passengers came as prisoners who had been banished to Carolina for adhering to their religious principles. These exiled prisoners were all men, and most were tradesmen: glovers, weavers, maltmen, coopers, tinkers, and masons. Some were charged with rebellion or harboring rebels, but most remained in prison because they refused to take the oath, acknowledge the king's supremacy over the church, disown the Covenant, and call the Bothwell uprising a rebellion. The test oath, not the original charge, was the real sticking point. The story of these prisoners throws additional light on the way commercial development was intertwined with state oppression of religious dissenters. It also further illustrates the tension between the two Stuarts Towns: one a religious refuge, the other a money-making venture. The conflict between these two objectives entangled the colonizers in moral compromises undercutting their claim that Stuarts Town was a safe haven for the gospel and its persecuted followers.[30]

The forced exportation of Scottish dissenters boomed in the 1670s and 1680s. It was spurred by the demand for labor on British plantations and helped along by a loophole in the Navigation Acts that allowed Scottish ships to trade in English colonies if they carried servants, prisoners, or other "undesirables" for sale.[31] Walter Gibson, the owner of the *Carolina Merchant*, was one of the main profiteers. As early as 1681, Gibson was advertising for beggars, gypsies, and vagabonds to transport to the colonies. As the prisons filled in 1684, he made the rounds and recruited political prisoners who would otherwise face execution for refusing the oath. In addition to the thirty-five he brought on the *Merchant*, he transferred a number of consigned convicts to Robert Malloch, a merchant from Leith. In exchange for signing a hefty bond guaranteeing delivery of the prisoners, Gibson and Malloch received a fee of ten pounds sterling per head from the state in addition to whatever profits they earned from selling them.[32]

By 1684, the convict trade had become quite a racket. First, state authorities granted commissions and created special courts to apprehend and try rebels. Then they passed "reset and converse" laws that made people guilty by association, which led to more arrests. Even if they were innocent of the original charges, by being arrested, they were subject to the oath, to which many could not in good conscience swear. As the jails filled with dissenters, the Privy Council permitted the courts to sentence these prisoners—"such of the rebels as are found penitent . . . though they have not taken the test"—to banishment. Finally, the state paid merchants to ship these convicts out of the country and authorized them to sell the prisoners to American planters, whose demand for labor was fueling an international slave trade that included Africans, European servants, and Native Americans. "Great multitudes were at this time sent away to the plantations, by virtue of this power," wrote the historian and Covenanter

Robert Wodrow. Of an estimated three thousand Scots forcibly sent to the colonies in seventeenth and eighteenth centuries, some eight hundred, or more than one in four, were sent in the years 1665–1685. The majority of these were transported during the killing time of 1683–1685, making it the peak period for the Presbyterian convict trade.[33]

Strictly speaking, these prisoners were sentenced to exile, not servitude. On the ground in the colonies, this was a distinction without a difference, although the status of these convict laborers varied considerably. Some historians have argued that they received the same generous terms as free servants: three years of service and, after completing their terms, a grant of fifty acres of land plus seed corn and tools. In sugar colonies such as Jamaica, Scottish convict laborers were often used as overseers who supervised enslaved African field hands.[34] However, in Carolina, they were treated like slaves. This treatment started aboard ship. As prisoners banished in lieu of execution were no longer attached to nation or society, their lives were basically forfeited. This opened the door for ship captains to treat them as slaves aboard their vessels. In 1679, over two hundred fifty banished Bothwell rebels were locked in the hold of their ship and drowned when it sank in the cold waters off the northern coast of Scotland. The prisoners aboard Malloch's ship, wrote John Mathieson, suffered "great straits whyle on shipp board and on shoar also, by him and his who caried us captive to that land." James Gibson, Walter's brother and captain of the *Carolina Merchant*, seized prisoners' money and belongings, put them on very short water and food rations (one, John Alexander, reportedly died of thirst), and threatened them with his sword when they tried to worship below decks.[35]

Merchants such as Gibson and Malloch were entitled to recover the costs of transporting convicts to Carolina, which gave them some claim to prisoners' labor and bodies. Prisoners could resist this claim—servitude was voluntary, at least on paper—but they did so at their peril. Aboard ship, they were at the mercy of the captain. John Mathieson testified that Malloch's prisoners were "miserably beaten" and that he personally "received a great blow on my back very sore . . . so that for many dayes I could not lift my head higher nor my breast." The reason for this cruel treatment was because "wee would not consent to our own selling or slavery." By a "remarkable providence," Mathieson was freed from "these bloody butchers from Carolina," and he eventually made it back to Scotland. Two of Gibson's prisoners on the *Carolina Merchant*, John Smith and John Paton, were not so lucky. Captured after trying to escape from servitude in Charles Town, they were "most cruelly used, and beat several times in a day, and bound to a perpetuall service." In their cases, lifelong servitude was a consequence of their running away, not the initial condition of their service, although the outcome was the same. Another prisoner aboard the *Merchant*, John Dick, had paid for part of his passage and bound himself to work off the rest, but Gibson kept his money and sold him anyway.[36] The line between voluntary servitude and slavery was blurred for convicts, who were forced to volunteer, defrauded of their freedom, or treated so abusively that they ran away and thereby gave their owners legal cause to enslave them for life. Others died in the labor camps before they were able to complete their terms of service. Despite the letter of the law, for many, if not most, of these prisoners, banishment came to include lifelong slavery.[37]

Besides being a vessel for transporting the gospel to a safe haven far from Scotland's killing fields, the *Carolina Merchant* was also a slave ship. Curiously, William Dunlop was an undertaker in both these enterprises. He cosigned Walter Gibson's bonds for many, if not all, of the thirty-five prisoners, providing another layer of surety for their delivery to Carolina. Dunlop's precise agreement with Gibson is unknown, but he would not have risked getting stuck with the debt unless he or his colony stood to gain from the transport, sale, or labor of the convicts. In addition, some of the prisoners claimed that Dunlop cheated and exploited them. Although their friends in Scotland had donated a "considerable summe" of cloth and money for their use, Dunlop, who was entrusted with the donation, kept it himself instead of "doaling it among them," and they "got nothing of it." It also appears that Dunlop was partly responsible for defrauding and enslaving John Dick. Probably expecting to be sold when he arrived in Carolina, Dick took steps to ensure against it. He gave thirty shillings toward his passage and even engaged a friend "to serve in his room for the rest part of the fraught" if Gibson refused to accept Dick's bond. Instead, Gibson kept the thirty shillings and sold Dick to Dunlop, who took him "up the country" to his death. Dunlop bought seventeen servants after arriving in Carolina; presumably, most, if not all, of them were imprisoned aboard the *Merchant*.[38]

These accounts suggest that, at the very least, Dunlop and/or the Stuarts Town colony expected to benefit from the imprisonment of fellow Covenanters, and at worst, they exploited these prisoners, multiplied their misfortunes, and carried them into slavery. This seems out of step with the antiauthoritarian impulse at the heart of the Covenanting movement. Although this movement specifically focused on the separation of the church from state control, it was built on more general principles: mistrust of centralized power; a commitment to limited government; and, most of all, a foundational belief that freedom was essential to true Christian practice. Some of these principles reflected the emerging democratic values of the modern era, but they were rooted in the Covenanters' more fundamental belief that they could not honor God without religious and civil liberty.[39] This conviction conditioned Presbyterians to equate slavery with tyranny and liberty with the will of God. As a second-generation Covenanter, Dunlop learned to associate freedom with true religion at an early age. He inherited strong habits of resistance to state intrusions on individual liberty, and he put these values into practice as a minister and movement organizer. The Stuarts Town colony was itself the communal expression of this commitment to religious and political freedom. Covenanters' religious and political principles, their history and conditioning, their ongoing experience of oppression, and their vision for a godly society, all were out of keeping with the exploitation and involuntary bondage of fellow Christians. Some were quite explicit about this. In his widely read 1687 book *A Hind Let Loose*, Alexander Shields, Dunlop's lifelong associate and a fellow student at Edinburgh (both earned their master's degrees there in 1675), charged the "Popish, Prelatical, & Malignant faction" in Scotland with emptying the prisons and selling dissenters "as slaves to Carolina." This cruel persecution of Christians was, Shields claimed, "a greater Barbarity" than could "be found, in the Reigns of Caligula or Nero." Shields clearly equated exile with enslavement, and he tied both to the menace of Roman Catholicism and the work of Antichrist.[40]

The differences between the moderate and radical Presbyterians aboard the *Carolina Merchant* may account for some of these inconsistencies. Several of the prisoners made themselves obnoxious. They refused to join in worship with Dunlop and the other passengers because of Dunlop's moderate principles. Some were undoubtedly convinced that he had taken the indulgence and betrayed his covenant oath. Yet others, as John McClintock, one of the holdouts, wrote, were "much to be joyning with the liberal ministers and putting most favourable constructions on their discourse." The stubbornness of these radicals brought out the wrath of Gibson and undoubtedly gave him justification for restricting their rations. Their rejection of Dunlop may have encouraged him to hold back their cloth and money and enslave John Dick. On the other hand, their animosity toward Dunlop as a compromised minister, and their determination to keep unity among the radicals and dissuade their fellow prisoners from "joyning" Dunlop, might have led them to exaggerate these charges against him or even make them up out of whole cloth.[41]

And yet, then as now, even people with strong principles were able to hold to and act on contradictions, especially when the stakes were high and the context had changed. As preacher and pragmatist, Dunlop embodied the tensions between the business and religious sides of the colony. He had staked his livelihood on the success of Stuarts Town. He was leaving behind the black-and-white world of Scotland's killing time and going to a place where freedom of worship was taken for granted, but labor was scarce. In Carolina, servants and slaves were like gold. They made people forget themselves. Like the foul odors and miasmic vapors that floated up from its swamps, exploitation was in the very air of the Lowcountry. Slavery was Carolina's original sin, its inescapable context. It touched everything, and it enriched and corrupted everything it touched. Stuarts Town, as a refuge for the gospel and a beacon of liberty, might have challenged this systemic evil, but its treatment of the exiled Covenanters suggested instead that it had already fallen victim to it.

CHAPTER 3

1684

UNSETTLING PORT ROYAL

In 1684, Port Royal was transformed from a sleepy, sparsely populated region of scattered Indigenous towns to a bustling and messy multicultural frontier. In February of that year, the coastal Indians ceded their lands to the Lords Proprietors, although they continued to live in their towns and remained "very kind and serviceable" to the English. In November, they were joined by religious refugees from Scotland, who planted their settlement along the banks of the Port Royal river not far from the Wimbee village. By then, a mixed medley of some three hundred Natives, made up of pagan Yamasee and Christian Guale peoples, had already migrated from the Spanish coastal mission towns and were living on the adjacent island of Hilton Head. Within weeks of the Scots' arrival, a second and much larger group of Yamasees streamed in from the in-terior and settled uneasily among the Escamaçu remnant and the newly arrived Indians and Scots. After more than two decades of living in diaspora, these Yamasees were, at best, loosely confederated and undoubtedly lived in separate settlements reflecting their distinct lineages, polities, and geographic origins. All of this movement naturally caught the attention of English traders and the occasional pirate, who gravitated toward the action. Port Royal soon became a magnet for Indian fugitives from Florida's mission towns, hoping to get lost in its crowds. It was also an increasingly dangerous passing-through point for run-away servants and slaves and other "rascal fellows" fleeing their English masters for freedom in St. Augustine.[1]

The collapse of the Escamaçu towns and destruction of the Westos had brought an end to the coastal Indians' old world, leaving a mostly vacant space and power vacuum in its place. With this sudden influx of diverse peoples into the area, a new world was emerging, although its shape was not yet clear. Colonial officials in Charles Town and St. Augustine watched anxiously, but they had many troubles of their own, and the new settlers at Port Royal were powerful enough to keep the English out of their business. As this mishmash of displaced people poured into the area in 1684, mixing and jostling and search-ing for friends, stability, and steady footing, Port Royal stood at a crossroads, its

Port Royal in 1684. Graphic design by Amanda Espericueta.

future anything but certain. This chapter highlights that uncertainty by giving a snapshot of Port Royal in 1684. It recovers the perspectives of the coastal towns, the English, the Scots, the Yamasees, the Spaniards, and the assorted ne'er-do-wells who found a temporary home in the area, at a moment when all eyes in the southeastern borderlands turned to Port Royal.

THE INDIGENOUS COASTAL TOWNS

In early 1684, the caciques and cacicas of nine Indian towns south of Charles Town ceded their lands to the Lords Proprietors. What the Natives thought they were giving up in this transaction is not clear. The province's conveyance book provides the only record of these treaties, and it is written in the stock, no-nonsense language of English land transactions. For the sum of "Tenn pounds of the lawful money of England, and other valuable Considerations to her in hand," the cacica of Edisto, like her neighboring headmen and headwomen, ceded (gave, sold, granted, conveyed) her people's lands to the proprietors. In addition to signing separate treaties, Native leaders made a joint or collective cession of their territories, removing any doubts about the validity of the agreement. At least on paper, these lands stretched from the Appalachian Mountains in the west to the Atlantic Ocean in the east, southward to the Savannah River, and northward to the Stono River, just below Charles Town. From the English perspective, the southern coastal towns had conveyed absolute ownership of their lands to the proprietors, who wished to satisfy the Scots' demand for clear title as a condition of their settlement. There is nothing to document the Indian forms of diplomacy that typically accompanied cession treaties—no ceremony, ritual, metaphor, or story. As a result, we must reconstruct the Native perspective of these transactions piecemeal from the broader context and other English sources.[2]

On their surface, these sources spin of tale of intimacy and mutual good will. The coastal people's warm relations with the English is a major theme in descriptions of Carolina from the early 1680s. Samuel Wilson, Maurice Mathews, Thomas Ashe, John Crawford, Robert Ferguson, and Thomas Newe all noted the "perfect friendship" and "continuall peace" between English colonists and their Indian neighbors, their "good Correspondence and Amity," and the Indians' "great kindness" and love toward the English. In reality, these fawning descriptions came at a low point in English–Indian relations, and they paper over the failure of Charles Town to act justly toward its Indian neighbors and earn their trust.

The proprietors' many interventions on behalf of the coastal towns point to these problems. In 1680, after Natives repeatedly complained of English violence, theft, and encroachment, the proprietors created a special commission to manage Indian affairs. This group would investigate complaints, mediate disagreements, regulate trade, and enforce the government's orders against exporting Indian slaves. The "just deallings" of this much-vaunted commission, according to Mathews, Ashe, and Wilson, were proof of Carolina's fair treatment of its Native neighbors and created a firm foundation for happy English–Indian relations. Yet just two years later, the proprietors disbanded the commission, because it contributed more to "the oppression than protection of the Indians." At the same time, they issued an outright ban on purchasing Indian captives or directly enslaving Indigenous people (except those taken in direct war with the English). They also provided a twelve-thousand-acre reserve for Native communities displaced by the land cessions, prohibited English colonists from settling within two miles of an Indian town, and ordered those settled nearby to help their Indian neighbors build fences to protect their crops from English cattle and pigs. These measures were not expressions of English good will but were intended to curb English greed and violence and compel Charles Town to protect the coastal people from its own bad actors.[3]

In the era of the Westo and Winyah wars, fear and anger, not love and trust, were the primary emotions underlying the Indians' relationship with the English. Without a hint of irony, Samuel Wilson awkwardly recognized this in his 1682 *Account of the Province of Carolina*. After extolling the "Court of Judicature" (special commission) as an example of the colony's "Christian and Moral Consideration" toward its Indigenous neighbors, Wilson declared that the Indians would never dare "break with the English, or do any Injury to any particular person, for fear of having it reveng'd upon their whole Nation." Wilson was right. The coastal towns had witnessed firsthand the effects of English ruthlessness and treachery on the Westos (which they celebrated) and the Winyahs (which must have horrified them). By 1684, after twenty-five years of Westo aggression and English colonization, they were "thin of people," Wilson noted, and some, such as the Winyahs, were "quite extirpated." According to one count, the towns of Edisto, Stono, and St. Helena (the English name for Escamaçu/Chiluque) could barely muster more than fifty fighting men combined. Assuming that these towns were typical, the total population of the nine southern towns that ceded their lands in 1684 stood at around six hundred. They surely remembered the failures of the Kusso revolt and the Stono alliance in the 1670s. Resistance and intertribal diplomacy would only end in their destruction. Outnumbered, outgunned, and dependent on English trade goods, their only sane option was to collaborate as pretended friends with the colonizers.[4]

Cession of Lands by the Caciques,
Captains, and Chieftaines of the
Several Countrys of Kusso, Stono,
Edistoh, Ashepoo, Cubahee,
Kussah, St. Helena and Wimbee
Indians (1684). Register of the
Province Book A (1682–1693),
138. The titles and marks of
the Indian signers appear at the
bottom. Image courtesy of the
South Carolina Department of
Archives and History.

As an expression of this pretended friendship, the coastal towns ceded their lands in accordance with the proprietors' wishes. But did the caciques and cacicas understand this transfer as the English did—as a surrender of all present and future claims, in which the towns gave up their rights to their ancestral lands and became tenants who occupied English lands at the pleasure of the proprietors? It is inconceivable that the coastal peoples would give up their sacred places and the source of their livelihood, encompassing some two million acres of land, for one hundred pounds sterling and "other valuable Considerations."[5] With the possible exceptions of Wimbee and St. Helena, which were adjacent to the Scots' settlement, they were not expected to relocate their towns. If they chose to stay, they were guaranteed twelve thousand acres surrounding their existing towns, which was more than enough for their homes and fields.[6] They probably believed they were keeping their towns and their hunting and gathering grounds and that, by signing the treaties, they gave the Scots permission to settle on their lands. Surely the surveyor general, Maurice Mathews, assured them that little would change as a result of these sales, despite the transfer of real property. They would resume the seasonal mobility that had been disrupted by the Westo invasion. They would hunt in the forests of the interior coastal plain, which still produced enough deer for a profitable trade with the English, to the benefit of both partners.[7] The proprietors promised to protect their towns against encroachment and their fields against English livestock. On the other hand, the coastal peoples had little bargaining power and were in no position to reject Mathews's terms. They understood that none of these promises were guarantees and that, by signing this treaty, their prospects of ever regaining real sovereignty were remote indeed.

Thus, what appears to be a straightforward land cession, telling a story of settler colonists erasing Native people from the landscape, is complicated by the Indian perspective. The coastal towns were painfully aware of their powerlessness and subordination to Charles Town, but they had good reason to think that life would go on much as it had, as long as they remained on good terms with the English and Scots. This was in February 1684. Less than a year later, all of this became moot as a result of the Yamasee migration. The Yamasees completely overshadowed the coastal towns. They came in such great numbers that neither the Scots nor the English were able to stop them, even if they had wanted to. Their great migration effectively nullified the cession agreements and exposed the thinness of British territorial claims to Port Royal. Treaties or no treaties, the Yamasees made Port Royal their own and would remain there for the next three decades.

CHARLES TOWN

Before the ink was dry on the cession treaties, Maurice Mathews was in hot water with the Proprietors of Carolina. Mathews and his fellow Goose Creek man, James Moore, were chief among the "dealers in Indians" whom the proprietors blamed for the Westo and Winyah wars. The proprietors were especially incensed by the assault on the Winyahs, which they viewed as nothing more than a slaving expedition dressed up as a public safety measure. That "poor innocent women and children were barbarously murdered and taken for slaves," the lords proprietors lamented, all for private gain, was an affront to humanity. "We cannot answer it to God, the King, our inhabitants, nor our own consciences, that such things should continue." Angered that Mathews and Moore had "contemptuously disobeyed our orders respecting the sending away of Indians," the proprietors put them out of the Grand Council and sidelined the Goose Creek faction. They also became much more assertive in regaining control of their unruly colony. It was an uphill fight. Months later, the proprietors again ordered the governor to remove Mathews as surveyor general, after he had reaped a handsome fee for negotiating the land cessions.[8]

This kind of flagrant disregard for proprietary rule was par for the course in 1684. Colonial officials enslaved Indians under English protection and then ignored orders to remove the enslavers from office. They refused to ratify changes to the Fundamental Constitutions that would give the Scots local autonomy and protect them "against the oppression of the people by their Administrators." They violated the constitutions' existing provisions by selecting their own council members instead of waiting on appointments from the proprietors. They granted commissions under the great seal of Carolina, even though the seal was kept by the proprietors in London. They allowed the government to immediately seize the property of people who died without a will, leaving creditors, widows, and heirs with nothing. To stop candidates from "runn[ing] from one place to another to awe or hinder the people in the freedom of their Elections"—in other words, to prevent electoral abuses and potential fraud—the proprietors ordered the provincial parliament to hold elections on the same day in different counties. Carolina officials ignored this order. They also schemed to restructure the land granting system to avoid paying taxes, and they passed a jaw-dropping piece of legislation that suspended local prosecution for foreign debts. This was an especially egregious act. The proprietors were dumbfounded that colonial officials would "publish to the world that if any man can get into the possession another mans Estate or goods let him come to Carolina & he shall by the Laws be protected in the unjust detention of them." The proprietors disallowed the law and responded forcefully to these other shenanigans. Besides barring Moore and Mathews from holding public office, they dissolved the provincial parliament and called for new elections. They also suspended parliament's power to approve the Fundamental Constitutions and rebuked those who tried to make Carolina a safe haven for debtors.[9]

These outrages and power struggles made it nearly impossible for Charles Town to influence events in Port Royal as they unfolded in late 1684 and early 1685. By the time the *Carolina Merchant* left Scotland in the summer of 1684, South Carolina was a political mess, governed by self-serving officials who were embroiled in conflict with the proprietors and who used their offices to enrich themselves instead of working for the good of the colony. "We regret to find that we have entrusted the government of the country to men who have no greater regard for it than this," the proprietors wrote, and they looked to the Scots to provide a counterbalance to the unruly English. As a result, Charles Town viewed the Scottish colony as a threat, not a useful buffer between the English and Spanish Florida. The Scots would have a separate and largely autonomous county. They would enjoy the favor of the proprietors and equal representation in provincial government. To the astonishment of the English, as they watched

Yamasee migrants pour into Port Royal, the Scots would be close neighbors with the powerful Yamasees. Together, they could monopolize Carolina's most lucrative enterprise, trade with Native people in the interior. Although they could interfere with the Scottish colony, the English were powerless to control it or use it to their advantage, just as they were powerless to stop the Yamasees from settling on the lands they had just purchased from the coastal towns. As the Scots and Yamasees sorted things out to the south, Charles Town officials and traders watched anxiously, looking for opportunities to either undermine or co-opt the Scots and insert themselves into trade and diplomacy with the Yamasees.[10]

YAMASEE

In 1683–1684, two separate streams of Yamasees migrated to Port Royal. The first came from the coastal Spanish mission provinces of Guale and Mocama, and the second from the Apalachicola towns of the Chattahoochee valley deep in the interior (not to be confused with Apalachee, the missionized coastal province of the Florida panhandle). Like the peoples of coastal Carolina, the Yamasees were fiercely independent and town centered, and they made every effort to protect their autonomy by distancing themselves from colonizing powers. However, the similarities ended there, for the Yamasees were a people in motion, peculiarly suited to the shifting regional dynamics of the late Mississippian and early colonial eras. They were mobile and adaptive, with long-standing trade and diplomatic ties to far-flung peoples from across the region. Unlike the insular towns of Escamaçu that viewed the new settlement of Ospo as an existential threat, the Yamasees had porous social borders and were skilled at incorporating outsiders into their polities. They brought their independence, adaptability, and vast connections with them to Port Royal, where they were like a conduit for all the intricate, intersecting dynamics of the other three great regional powers, St. Augustine, Charles Town, and Coweta/Cusseta. Through the Yamasees, Port Royal became a focal point that concentrated the tensions of the region. They also brought instability of their own, for the Yamasees were not yet a people, and after two decades of living in diaspora, their relationships with each other were fraught and uneasy. How would they reconstitute their towns and share power? Whose rituals and political influence would prevail? How would they relate to outsiders such as the Spanish, English, Scottish, and Apalachicola towns? How would they maintain peace with other peoples while giving their young men opportunities to earn martial honors in war? As the Yamasees worked out answers to these questions in the months after their migration to Port Royal, they created the social and political framework within which Europeans acted.

It was a messy process. Beset by internal divisions and leaders with conflicting agendas, they chose both red and white paths, paths of war and peace, violence and diplomacy, simultaneously.[11]

As recent scholars have shown, the Yamasees' independent streak, adaptability, and regional connections predated their dispersal in the mid-seventeenth century. They originated in the old Mississippian chiefdoms of Tama, Ocute, and Ichisi in the Oconee River valley of central Georgia. As these chiefdoms broke apart in the sixteenth century, their once-subordinate towns formed kinship-based communities centered around council houses. Here, as in the coastal Carolina towns, power was shared by the heads of lineages, who governed by consensus. The Oconee valley peoples welcomed immigrants from other abandoned chiefdoms and incorporated them into their communities. They also acquired a strong dislike for authority and a mindset marked by an "ethos of liberty," as one historian has called it. To protect their economic, cultural, and political autonomy, they lived in dispersed settlements and chose to hunt and gather rather than become dependent on maize and powerful maize-centered societies. In later years, they resisted Spanish efforts to reduce them to fixed settlements and convert them to Christianity. As Spanish trade goods moved beyond the mission provinces in the 1640s, the Oconee valley peoples expanded their associations through trade relationships with Guale, Timucua, Apalachee, and Apalachicola. Unlike the system of gift exchange in the mission towns, direct trade was open to non-elites—to anyone who had something to trade— thus giving ordinary Indians access to prestige goods and the power they conveyed. This further decentralized power by diluting the influence of hereditary micos in the Oconee valley towns.[12]

The Westo invaders landed in the heart of this country—first in central Georgia, and later on the Georgia side of the Savannah River—and the Oconee valley peoples felt the impact early and forcefully. As a result, they fled from their homelands in 1662 and dispersed across the region. An unknown number, perhaps a majority, moved further inland to Apalachicola, settling near the towns of Coweta and Cusseta, which were powerful enough to deter the Westo slavers (indeed, these towns would later absorb the small remnant of Westos who survived the English–Savannah onslaught). Between three hundred and four hundred refugees went south, first to the borderlands of Escamaçu, then to the coastal mission provinces of Georgia. As many as two hundred removed to Apalachee, and a smaller group settled among the Timucuans in central Florida. Although the Yamasees' dispersal was driven by their urgent need for protection from the Westos, the pattern of their dispersal reflects their preexisting connections, through trade and a long history of peaceful relations, with the far-flung peoples of Spanish Florida and the Chattahoochee Valley. It may also reflect preexisting divisions among the Yamasee towns.[13]

By far, the best documented group of Yamasee migrants were those who re-located to coastal Florida and Georgia. Until 1683, these Yamasees had few rea-sons to complain about their accommodations. They were required to provide corn as *sabana* to the local headmen for the privilege of living on their lands, but as *infieles* (non-Christians), they were not required to support the missions or provide labor to St. Augustine, although they voluntarily contributed labor through the *repartimiento*. This kept them in the good graces of the governor, who, in turn, took their side against overreaching landlords who tried to extract additional tribute. With reasonable labor requirements, friends in St. Augustine, little pressure to convert, protection from Westo raiders, and access to Spanish trade goods, the Yamasees were content to live under the Spanish umbrella. Over the course of two decades, they established a dozen settlements along the coast. In 1683, however, French privateers raided the coast and put the lie to Spanish promises of security. The mico Altamaha, who may also have been dis-gruntled over recent changes in the labor draft, seized the moment. If the Span-iards were unable to guarantee their security, why bother growing corn for their landlords and sending labor to St. Augustine? He organized a Yamasee exodus out of Florida and into the Anglo–Spanish borderlands just beyond the Savan-nah River, where they could live their own lives free from Spanish influence. By late 1684, Altamaha and some three hundred fellow migrants, most of them probably from southern Guale, had reassembled on Hilton Head Island, just across the sound from St. Helena, on lands freshly ceded to the English by the Witcheaugh, St. Helena, and Wimbee towns. At the same time, a second group of migrants, led by the mico Niquisalla from northern Guale, moved inland to Apalachicola. By the end of 1683, no Yamasees remained in Guale.[14]

Altamaha's exodus combined with two other factors to make Port Royal a magnet for Yamasees from across the region: the destruction of the Westos and the proximity of English traders. The Westos had "ruined" the coastal towns, deprived them of their power, and left their lands vulnerable to seizure by outsiders. Not only were these vacant lands available, but the elimination of the Westos also made them safe to occupy. It also created new opportunities for enterprising Native groups to mediate English trade with the interior. Charles Town officials had designated the Savannah Indians as their new trade partners, but the Savannahs disappointed them. As Carolina officials told the proprietors, the Savannahs "did not afford the profitable trade to the Indian dealers in beaver,

etc., that was expected." They were also poor slavers. Lacking the power to enslave inland and mission Indians as the Westos had done, and strictly forbidden
from capturing settlement Indians after the Winyah debacle, they served only as
middlemen, buying captives in the interior and selling them to English traders
on the coast. The relative weakness of the Savannahs, the demise of the Westos,
the proximity to Charles Town, the collapse of the coastal towns, and the relo-
cation of Altamaha, all made Port Royal an attractive and secure prospect for
the rootless Yamasees.[15]

These pull factors must have been foremost in the minds of Yamasee migrants from the Chattahoochee Valley, who began streaming into Port Royal in
early 1685. In February, Caleb Westbrooke, an English trader who lived among
the Yamasees and now aligned himself with the Scots, reported that "a thousand and more" Yamasees had come to the Carolina coast from Coweta and
Cusseta, "& dayly more expected." These probably included the two hundred
who had lived in Apalachee. They were led by ten micos, the most ambitious of
whom was Niquisalla, a skillful diplomat who had close ties to both St. Augustine (from his stay in Guale) and the inland towns (where he had moved in 1683).
In addition, Westbrooke reported that an untold number of "Spanish Indians
that are Christians [from] Sapella Soho & Sapicbay" had arrived at Altamaha's
settlement. These were Guales who, like their Yamasee neighbors on the Georgia coast, had grown weary of Spanish authority or were displaced by the pirate
raids of 1683, and they were welcomed by the Yamasees and Scots in Port Royal.

Westbrooke, Altamaha, and Lord Cardross (the head of the Scots' colony)
all looked on anxiously as this assortment of Native peoples gathered in force
around them. Westbrooke feared "a design of the Spaniards" to infiltrate the
Scottish–English borderlands, although he took a narrowly personal view of the
problem. "If evil is designed," he wrote, reflecting on his vulnerability as a guest
in the Yamasee settlement, "I am the first man that must feel it." Altamaha had
organized the initial migration from the coast, but he had not expected so many
people from the interior. He insisted that Hilton Head would soon fill up, and
he worried that the Yamasees would not have enough room to plant. He "did little think of this quantity" of newcomers, Westbrooke noted. Perhaps Altamaha
too felt overwhelmed, not only by the logistical challenges but also by the threat
this massive wave of settlers posed to his own standing among the Yamasees and
his leverage with the Scots. Cardross gave his consent for the Yamasees to "setle
heire within our bounds . . . during their good behaviour," but he also admitted
that "they are so considerable and warlike that we could not doe utherwayes."
The Scots, he told the proprietors, "could not weell oppose them." By March

1685, between thirteen hundred and two thousand Yamasees and Christian Guales were living in Port Royal. To put this in perspective, only sixty Scots lived in Stuarts Town, some six hundred Natives lived in the southern coastal towns, and the total population of Charles Town was around two thousand, three-fourths of whom were slaves and indentured servants. The newcomers roughly equaled the combined White and Native population of Carolina from Charles Town to the Savannah River, making them the most formidable people in the region.[16]

However, they were far from unified. Christian and pagan, Guale and Yamasee, Natives and newcomers, migrants and runaways, Yamasees who had sojourned in Guale, Apalachee, and Apalachicola—the fault lines ran in multiple directions, among notoriously "ungovernable" people who had a strong independent streak and town-based identities, an entire generation of whom had no memory of old Tama or the Westo dispersal. Archaeological evidence suggests that coastal Yamasee women might have used different ceramic designs from those of women from the interior, pointing to subtle, underlying differences in the two groups' identities that probably developed in diaspora. Also, Altamaha himself did not recognize all Yamasees as his people. Although his own warriors told William Dunlop that Spanish forces had "killed & taken away 22 Yamassie women" from Yamacraw Bluff in a 1686 attack, Altamaha insisted that the Spaniards "had never killed any of his people."[17]

What did Altamaha mean when he declared that the Yamasee women were "not his people"? That the Yamasees came together after living in diaspora for twenty years shows that they were still "of the same fire," that they were friends, not enemies, and that they recognized their peoplehood at some fundamental level. To be sure, within this common fire, the Yamasee towns were separate and autonomous political units. They were connected internally by lineages, or blood kinship, and externally to one another by more distant ties of kin and clan; but these social and political divisions could easily be contained in a common Yamasee identity. Instead, Altamaha's disowning of the women taken at Yamacraw may point to a different dividing line, one rooted in Yamasees' dualistic world view and embodied in Altamaha's relationship with the other leading headman, the mico Niquisalla.

In general, southeastern Indians had a dualistic view of the cosmos, and this was expressed in their politics by a division between civil and military power. Civil authority over internal town matters as well as external diplomacy in peacetime was the province of the white chief. The color white stood for peace, and the white chief was typically an elder recognized for his or her wisdom, restraint, and tact. White chiefs had little coercive power, but those who were skilled at mediating conflict between town factions and harmonizing competing interests were revered by their people. Authority over military matters was the province of the red chief, who was typically young and who earned his status by feats of war. The color red symbolized war, youth, and violent action. Altamaha's age is not known, but Niquisalla had an adult son and an adult nephew who were micos of two towns in Guale, and he was said to be fifty years old in 1685. On the basis of subsequent events—namely, Altamaha's leadership of the raid on Santa Catalina de Afuica—Altamaha was a red chief, whereas the elderly Niquisalla, who later mediated between Charles Town and Coweta/ Cusseta, was a white chief. In stable communities, red and white chiefs played necessary and complementary roles. The red chief was subordinate to the white chief and could not make war without the consent of the council. This system allowed Native peoples to direct the inherent violence of young men outward, away from the community, while maintaining harmony within the town. However, in deeply divided, unstable, or coalescing societies, where the lines of authority were contested, there was no ready mechanism for achieving consensus, and young men hungered for war, red and white chiefs could become rivals who worked at cross purposes in the interest of their own "people."[18]

Such people—diverse, divided, of varied origins, living in a violent and unstable world and brought together by opportunity—were prone to mistrust and vulnerable to rumor and manipulation. This created openings for people such as Wina, a St. Helena (Escamaçu) Indian, to sow discord between the Port Royal settlers. Wina had a long history as a go-between and a track record for stirring up trouble. He had taken part in Escamaçu's 1670 effort to poison relations between St. Augustine and the cacica of Ospo. In 1684, he served as interpreter for Mathews during the land cession treaties, giving him ties to high-placed English officials. In March 1685, Cardross informed the governor of the "sinistrous dealings" of Wina and another "noted Indian," Antonio, who looked to "stir up the Indians in our parts one against another & likewise against ourselves." He also accused Wina of harboring a "Spanish Indian, whom wee have ground to apprehend to bee a Spye sent from St. Augustine." That Cardross lodged his complaint with Charles Town officials and told them that the Scots "expect your justice" indicates that Wina was protected by the English. Whether he was working for the Spaniards, the English, or his own people whose lands were overrun with strangers, Wina clearly found opportunities to exploit the incohesion among the divided people of Port Royal. As the next chapter will show, Wina and Antonio were not the only Natives to do so. The divisions among the

Yamasees also played out in the diplomacy of Altamaha and Niquisalla and had major repercussions for the Scots, English, and Spaniards, not to mention the colonial southeast more generally, in 1685.[19]

STUARTS TOWN

While Yamasee migrants were flooding Port Royal, the Scots were struggling. Sickness, death, bad luck, and English interference made it nearly impossible to attract and keep settlers. As their grand ideas about creating a refuge for the gospel met the harsh material realities of colonization, the Scots shifted their focus from otherworldly to this-worldly business: turning forests into fields; laying out town lots; fortifying their settlement; and, most of all, establishing trade ties with their Indigenous neighbors. Indeed, the prospect of partnering with the Yamasees and controlling the Indian trade quickly captured their imagination. Soon a dream of Scottish empire, of enlarged territories, bountiful trade, and Spanish silver, eclipsed the religious vision and drove the settlement.

The leading Scottish colonizers made no mention of religion in their early correspondence with family, associates, and officials back home. With no religious conflict, no Presbyterian ministers, and no oppressive Anglican establishment in Carolina, the Scots who came voluntarily aboard the *Carolina Merchant* seemed to stop thinking of themselves as persecuted dissenters. This was not true for the Presbyterian radicals imprisoned in the hold. They remembered who they were; the voyage reinforced their identity as an oppressed minority and strengthened their resolve. They added stories of theft, hunger, beatings, enslavement, and other cruelties to their narrative of sufferings and shared these stories with sympathizers in Scotland. In some ways, radicals such as John Dick, John Paton, and John Smith were the first casualties of the sea change in Stuarts Town's identity. As Dunlop and Cardross turned toward the business of making a plantation, they came to value the prisoners more as convict laborers than fellow exiles. They stripped them of their liberty and took them "up the country" to die like John Dick or allowed them to be "most cruelly used" and "bound to perpetual service" like Paton and Smith.[20]

Meanwhile the Scots' numbers dwindled. Although none of the *Merchant*'s one hundred forty-eight passengers died at sea, the colonists found Charles Town to be so "extrordinerie sicklie," Cardross told the proprietors, that a "great many" of their people died soon after arriving. Privately, Cardross blamed James Gibson more than the sickly air around Charles Town for these deaths. In a letter to his wife, he wrote that twenty-seven had died, thanks largely to their "ill usage at sea," where they were given only "rotten herrings and corrupt water." This description mirrors the complaints of the prisoners and indicates that they made up a disproportionately high number of the dead. Still, sickness did its part. It was the time of year for malarial fevers, and 1684 was the worst year to date for malaria in Carolina. Both Dunlop and Cardross sickened, one with a fever, the other with ague (intermittent fever). Malaria probably finished off the prisoners, who were already weakened by malnutrition and digestive disorders. Several other colonists, discouraged by illness, high mortality, and fears of the Spaniards (after learning of a recent Spanish attack on the Bahamas), sold their servants and abandoned the venture. The English encouraged them to do so. They showed "litle kyndnes" to the newcomers, Cardross wrote, and even some of Charles Town's "grate men" stooped to persuading the *Merchant*'s passengers to desert the Scots. They also discouraged would-be colonizers from another ship that came through Charles Town, some of whom left Carolina altogether while others settled among the English. Other troubles added to the Scots' misfortunes. A ship from Belfast, possibly the *James of Ayr*, was lost at sea, along with the lives of "Divers families" who had planned to join the Scots at Stuarts Town. By March 1685, only a handful of households, with a total population of fifty-one, had settled in Port Royal. Two-thirds of the colonists aboard the *Carolina Merchant* had died or settled elsewhere, and none of the hundred or more Scots aboard the two other vessels had joined the colony.[21]

Despite these discouragements, this core group of Scots was committed to colonization, and they pressed ahead with their plans. "We have determined that this place shall be a toun," Cardross wrote, and he called it Stuarts Town in honor of his wife, Catherine Stuart. They chose a site on Wimbee Island (present-day Port Royal Island), probably in what is now downtown Beaufort.[22] As a port town, it was situated along the water, where the channel was deep enough to accommodate ships of three hundred tons. For defense purposes, it sat atop a high bluff, where the Scots would soon place three "great guns" to deter Spanish invaders. This elevated location was also "free of swamps and marishes" and had a plentiful supply of fresh water and "wholesome air," so that the colonists quickly recovered from their fevers and agues. In keeping with Dunlop's "Project of a Settlement," the town occupied about one square mile of land and was laid out in two hundred twenty lots, each with its own garden. In addition, lot owners received two acres of farmland on the edge of town. By March 1685, settlers had purchased forty-one lots, and more were expected. Several English families planned to move into the settlement, as did a planter from Antigua who, excited about the potential for growing sugar and indigo, intended to bring five or six families to plant there in August. Cardross thus managed to put a good face on Stuarts Town, despite the early setbacks: Although it was hardly thriving, its troubles were only momentary, its prospects were bright, and its people were in good health and focused on the important work before them. "We have already built severalls as fair houses as in all Charlestoun," he boasted, unable to resist comparing Stuarts Town favorably against the English, "and more are in building."[23]

However, Cardross was not content with selling town lots and talking up the virtues of Port Royal's climate and soil to indigo planters. The Yamasee migration had fired his imagination, and he set his sights on annexing Spanish territory to the British king and monopolizing the Indian trade. By early 1685, the Scots had explored the Georgia coast as far south as St. Catherine's Island and learned that the Spaniards had abandoned their frontier "on the report of our setling here." Cardross's historical knowledge was a bit shaky, as the actual cause of the retreat of the coastal missions was the Westo/Chiluque/Uchisi raid of 1680. Be that as it may, he proposed that the Scots take possession of all territory from the Savannah to St. Catherine's in the name of the king and on behalf of the proprietors. Without waiting for the proprietors' consent, he later claimed that this territory belonged to the Scots, or rather that he "had liberty to take up another County" there and make it his own if he wished. Here, too, Cardross was mistaken, as seizing that territory would have violated the 1670 Treaty of Madrid. The Scots were also laying plans to open trade with Coweta and Cusseta in the Chattahoochee Valley, which promised to be "considerable and advantageous." This was all made possible by their "firme peace and commerce" with the Yamasees, who were "verie effectionit" to the Scots but remained "Inveterat enemies to the Spainyard."[24]

Cardross's ambitions did not end there. "We thought fit lykewayes to acquaint you," he told the proprietors, "that ther may be pasage opened from this place to New Mexico, which with all the mines thereabout the indians of that countrie have takin from the Spaniard, and that they are desyrous of trade and comerice with his Majesty's subjects here." Coweta and Cusseta lived on this passage, he added, making a trade agreement with them all the more crucial to the success of this plan. Cardross was referring to the Pueblo revolt of 1680, in which New Mexico's Pueblo Indians killed hundreds of Spaniards and forced Spain to abandon its territories north of the Rio Grande for more than a decade. In this case, Cardross's history was better than his geography. There were no precious metals in New Mexico, nor was there an inland passage connecting it to the Atlantic coast.

Cardross was not the first person to make this mistake. More than a century earlier, Pedro Menéndez de Avíles had dreamed of finding a road between his colony at Santa Elena and Spain's silver mines in Zacatecas, Mexico. He commissioned two expeditions from Captain Juan Pardo to search for this passage.

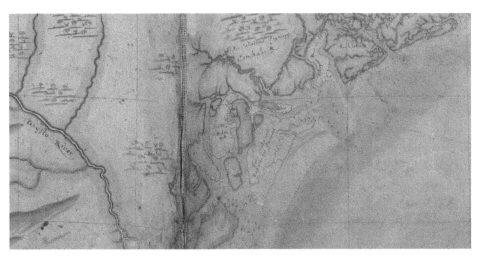

Joel Gascoyne and Maurice Mathews, *A Plat of the Province of Carolina in North America*, ca. 1685. British Library, Add MS 5414/24 Common. This detailed image shows the territory surrounding Port Royal from the Westo (Savannah) River to Cayewagh (Kiawah) Island. It is the only contemporary map that gives the approximate location of the "Scotts Settlement." Image courtesy of the British Library Imaging Services.

Sixteenth-century Spaniards also believed that there was an inland water route that connected the Chesapeake Bay to the Pacific Ocean and that the continent was much narrower than it actually is. These Spanish misconceptions about North American geography persisted into the late seventeenth century. Henry Woodward believed that the chiefdom of Cofitachequi, located about one hundred miles from the Carolina coast, bordered on Spanish territories and "probably there were mines there." Nearly two centuries after European contact, although Spanish explorers had mapped the Gulf Coast and explored hundreds of miles inland, Europeans understood little about the geography or people of the continental interior. This ignorance fueled Cardross's vision of mineral wealth flowing from New Mexico into Stuarts Town across a mythical inland passage.[25]

The English tried to put up obstacles to these dreams. Besides dissuading Scottish settlers from joining the Stuarts Town colony, they were slow to share intelligence of the "Spaniards actings motions and intentions" with the Scots, who occupied Charles Town's southern frontier. Envious of the Scots' diplomatic successes with their Yamasee neighbors, some English sought to stir up trouble and "render us contemptible," Cardross wrote, "in the eyes of the Indians about us." As already noted, his letter to the governor indicated that he held the English responsible for the "sinistrous dealings" of Wina and Antonio. Cardross hit back against this English interference with some well-placed digs against Charles Town in his correspondence with the proprietors. Although the English were "meinding their own privat Intrist" over that of the colony, the Scots would stand by their commitments and attend to the "trew Intrist" of the proprietors and Carolina. The Scots resolved to pay their quitrents (taxes to the proprietors) promptly, unlike "uthers in Carolina" who looked for ways to postpone or evade paying taxes. With the backing of the proprietors, the Scots' colony would "flourish at ane other rait than Charlestoun," and they would make it a "noble plantation."[26]

Despite their small numbers, the Scots had big dreams for Stuarts Town, envisioning it as the seat of a Scottish empire. Like a mouse fighting a lion, they moved aggressively to capitalize on Spanish Florida's weaknesses, expand their territories, and seize control of the lucrative fur and deerskin trade from the English. Although Cardross hit back against English interference, he realized that the "Jealousies" between Stuarts Town and Charles Town made the Scots vulnerable. He offered an olive branch to the governor, asking that they lay aside their differences, especially "att this tyme when wee have grounds to apprehend the invasion of a Forraigner."[27] Yet the "considerable and advantageous" earnings from the Indian trade, which had recently brought about the Westo War, the destruction of the Winyahs, and internal political turmoil at Charles Town practically guaranteed that jealousies would continue and divisions deepen.

ST. AUGUSTINE

More than a decade after the English planted their settlement in Kiawah, the colonial government in St. Augustine was still fretting about an English invasion. "This summer I have been waiting for the English enemy at every moment," Governor Juan Márquez Cabrera wrote the king in 1681. He knew that the English had armed the Chichimecos and directly benefited from the Westo/Chiluque/Uchisi raids on Sapala and Santa Catalina de Guale the previous year. Now he feared, with good reason, that they also gave covert support to pirates. Cabrera had heard rumors that English pirates were combining forces at Key West and planning a massive attack on St. Augustine. He begged the king to make a preemptive strike and "remove the lurking place and settlement of Englishmen" at Charles Town. The Crown refused, warning Cabrera that any attack on English settlements north of the Savannah River would violate the Treaty of Madrid. An attack would only be justified if the English extended their territories into Guale, or if British authorities failed to prosecute Carolina colonists who harbored pirates. Unable to stop Charles Town from using Indians and pirates as proxies to harass Spanish settlements, Cabrera did the next best thing: He beefed up his defenses by creating militias of mulattoes and free Blacks. He also continued to gather all the intelligence he could on Carolina, from the size and defenses of Charles Town to its intentions toward Spanish Florida and its relationship with corsairs trying to unload Spanish plunder.[28]

Cabrera's fears became reality in 1683, when the French pirate Michel de Grammont raided the Florida coast with a combined force of French and English corsairs. They were repelled at St. Augustine, but Grammont's subsequent run up the Guale coast so terrorized the Yamasees that they fled the province for Carolina. The withdrawal of more than three hundred Yamasees depleted the population of Guale and Mocama. In response, Florida officials moved quickly to further consolidate their thinly scattered missions, moving everyone south of the St. Marys River and completely abandoning the coast of present-day Georgia. To make matters worse, as the missions were in the process of moving, a fleet of eleven English ships led by the pirate Thomas Jingle plundered and burned the remaining Guale and Mocama towns. Their plunder included eleven unfortunate Flemish and English colonists who, though bound for Charles Town, had washed up in Guale and fallen into the hands of Spanish and Guale soldiers. The pirates relieved the Spaniards of these captives and sold them as slaves in Charles Town.[29]

As its Atlantic coastal provinces collapsed in the early 1680s, St. Augustine faced a second, although not so immediate, threat to its west: the prospect of a French settlement near the mouth of the Mississippi River. As with the continental interior, the Spaniards knew surprisingly little about the central Gulf Coast and nothing about the Mississippi, although Cabeza de Vaca had explored much of this region one hundred fifty years earlier. They mistakenly believed that the mouth of the Mississippi was a great bay, which they called Espíritu Santo. In 1678, a disaffected Spanish colonial official, the Count of Peñalosa, told officials in France of two rich and densely populated inland Indigenous kingdoms, Quivira and Aixaos, which were accessible from Espíritu Santo Bay. He proposed that the French colonize the Gulf Coast, exploit these wealthy kingdoms, and use their central location to disrupt Spanish operations in west Florida and New Mexico. The Spanish crown took Peñalosa's scheming seriously, and it ordered a report on the feasibility of colonizing Espíritu Santo for itself and establishing religious and diplomatic ties with the mysterious kingdoms of Quivira and Aixaos. A French assault on a Spanish fort in Apalachee in 1682, followed by war between France and Spain in 1683, fueled Spain's concerns about French designs on its American territories. In 1684, Peñalosa's scheme gained more traction when a former Florida official, Martin de Echagaray, made a concrete proposal to explore and map Espíritu Santo to preempt French colonization. As if taking his cue from Lord Cardross, Echagaray claimed that two rivers emptied into the mythical bay, one of which led to New Mexico. Like all unknown territories in the interior, the region was reputed to be rich in natural resources and mineral wealth, and its central location between west Florida and Tampico promised to secure control of the entire Gulf of Mexico for Spain.[30]

Thus, between 1680 and 1684, St. Augustine was besieged by threats on multiple fronts. The Chichimeco assault on Guale, two terrifying pirate raids, and the exodus of the Yamasees to Carolina had forced the Spaniards to abandon much of their coastal Atlantic territories. The inland missions had also reached a tipping point. Continual contact and Spanish labor requirements provided fertile soil for epidemic diseases, and the mission population fell accordingly, from twenty-six thousand in 1655 to just thirteen thousand 20 years later.[31] Governor Cabrera watched Charles Town grow as his own settlements stagnated or declined, and he worried continually about a direct English attack on St. Augustine. At the same time, Spanish colonial officials mulled over a French threat on Florida's western frontier. As the next chapter will show, in 1685, these threats converged. In quick succession, St. Augustine learned of an actual French colony at Espíritu Santo Bay and the Scottish settlement at Santa Elena. They also got word of the Scots' partnership with the Yamasees, their plans to colonize the abandoned Georgia coast, and their ambitions to control the Indian trade from Apalachicola to New Mexico. In this context, St. Augustine would come to view the tiny Scottish colony and its Yamasee allies as an existential threat to Florida.

SLAVES, RUNAWAYS, AND RASCAL FELLOWS

By the end of 1684, Port Royal was filling up with refugees, fugitives, and opportunists. As a colonized space, it was the product of extraordinary violence, from Westo slave raids on the coastal towns and the Westo War in the Carolina interior to pirate attacks on the Florida coast and state crackdowns on religious dissenters in Scotland. This history of violence, along with the absence of any dominant political power or social or cultural center, made Port Royal extremely unstable. It was a world of shifting circumstances, opportunities, threats, and complex rivalries, where individuals and groups moved in and out of pockets of power, and everyone was either jockeying for advantage or scrambling to survive (or at least to avoid enslavement). It was an especially dangerous place for unattached people and for free and unfree laborers at or near the bottom of the social order. Port Royal became a refuge for some of these people and a dangerous passing-through place for others. The lived experiences of captive and runaway

servants, slaves, and other "rascal fellows" associated with Port Royal lays bare
the instability, violence, and exploitation that characterized their world.[32]

In 1685, South Carolina's non-Indian population included approximately
five hundred free Whites, five hundred African slaves, and one thousand European indentured servants. Proportionally, about three-fourths of this population
was unfree, and two-thirds of these unfree laborers were White servants.[33] Indentured servitude was the dominant form of labor in the colony in general, and
nowhere more than in Stuarts Town, where there were few, if any, African slaves.
On paper, indentured servitude was a contractual, voluntary, and orderly system, and servants were free agents. In exchange for room, board, and passage,
they sold their labor for a fixed period of time. Their owners' power was limited
by their contracts, which provided at least some legal protection for servants. At
the end of their terms, servants were usually entitled to some form of freedom
dues, such as tools, seed, livestock, and/or land. This was a powerful incentive
to poor people with no economic prospects. Their condition was unfree, to be
sure, but it was temporary and voluntary, and only their labor, not their bodies, belonged to their masters. Indentured servants could compare themselves
favorably with Africans subject to chattel slavery, a permanent and involuntary
condition in which the enslaver enjoyed nearly unlimited power over the bodies
of the enslaved.

On the ground, however, the line between servitude and slavery was blurred.
The radical Covenanters John Paton and John Smith learned as much when they
tried to escape from bondage and were captured and sentenced to perpetual
servitude. Their companion, John Dick, also found that his agreement with
James Gibson to work off the balance of his passage was worthless, and he was
sold instead. He was among the seventeen servants William Dunlop purchased,
all of whom survived the Atlantic crossing as prisoners but died as servants in
Carolina. For Kate Oats, an English servant on Paul Grimball's Edisto Island
plantation, servitude was anything but voluntary. At age seven, Oats said, she
was "deceived"—that is, kidnapped, like a great many servants "spirited" into
involuntary servitude in the seventeenth century—and taken to New Providence, Bahamas, where she was sold into bondage. Ten years later, after Spanish
privateers sacked New Providence, her owner brought her to Charles Town,
where he sold her to Grimball. Oats remained on his plantation for two years,
when another group of Spanish raiders plundered Edisto Island and took her to
St. Augustine. For Oats, Paton, Dick, and Smith, there was little practical difference between servitude and slavery. Cheated or coerced into bondage, beaten
into submission, enslaved for life, or carried off as plunder like other goods and

chattels, their indentures offered little protection against kidnappers, abusive masters, and unsympathetic colonial authorities.[34]

Freedom also was not guaranteed for so-called free laborers such as the Flemish sailor Juan Clar, who slipped in and out of bondage, sometimes voluntarily, sometimes not. In his mid-twenties, Clar went to London and joined the crew of an English vessel bound for Jamaica, where his master sold the ship. Hoping to make his way back to Flanders by way of New York, he was one of the eleven unfortunate passengers whose ship was ransacked by the corsair Grammont on their way to Charles Town in 1684. Running low on provisions, they went ashore at Guale, where Natives took them captive and turned them over to the Spaniards; but before they could be taken to St. Augustine, they were liberated by English pirates and brought to Charles Town. There, Clar's pirate "liberator," Chacopal, sold him for the tidy sum of forty pounds to recover his costs. Fortunately, Clar was purchased by a Frenchman from New York who owed an old debt to Clar, and he left Charles Town on the first available ship, a free man once again. From there, he took ship to Jamaica but was put ashore in the Bahamas, where he was forced to worked eight months to pay for his food and passage. When the Spaniards raided the Bahamas in 1686, Clar offered his services to the Spanish pirate hunter Alejandro Thomás de León and joined his expedition to plunder the Carolina coast. Clar's experience shows how thin the line was between bondage and freedom and how easily one could cross over from victim to perpetrator and from plundered to plunderer. The fortunes of common laborers could change in a flash, and without well-placed friends—in Clar's case, his French debtor from New York—even resourceful and savvy travelers such as Juan Clar could end up like John Dick and Kate Oats, mired in bondage.[35]

Of all the places he traveled throughout the Atlantic world, none rattled Clar as much as Carolina, and he could not leave it soon enough. After his French friend rescued him from bondage, he "had no communication with, nor wished to have any, the said town of San Jorge [Charles Town]." Clar was not alone. The runaway servants Elmo Mermique and Glodo Satrata were equally determined to put Carolina behind them. In their early twenties, the two men had left their home in Savoy and made their way through France, Flanders, and Holland to London, where they worked for over two years before indenturing themselves to an English ship captain, the inaptly named Joseph Thoroughgood. In Carolina, they received such "harsh treatment" from Thoroughgood that they ran away, hoping to escape to St. Augustine, where they would be among fellow Roman Catholics. Mermique and Satrata were intercepted by William Dunlop at Stuarts Town and returned to Thoroughgood, who successfully petitioned the court to add one to two years to their terms of service (as further testimony of Thoroughgood's thoroughly bad character, Dunlop complained to the governor that Thoroughgood "hath neither been civill nor gratefull to me for all the care and paines I tooke of his Runaways"). Undeterred, the two Savoyards made a second attempt, but this time they happily evaded the Scots and were found instead by Indians from Guale, who took them to their Spanish allies in St. Augustine. Like the imprisoned Covenanter John Mathieson, who was "miserably beaten" and crippled for refusing to sell himself into slavery, Mermique and Satrata were surely relieved for "getting free from these bloody butchers from Carolina."[36]

In St. Augustine, these runaways probably met the former African slave Mingo and his wife, who were also fugitives from Carolina. Little is known about their backstory. They could have been among the two hundred slaves plundered from Veracruz and Campeche by English pirates and sold in Charles Town in 1685. In any case, by 1687, Mingo and his family were enslaved to Samuel Dubourdieu, a Huguenot (French Protestant) living in Charles Town. At some point, Mingo allegedly murdered an Englishman, and in August 1687, he and his wife fled the province with their two-year-old daughter. Eluding the Yamasees about Port Royal, they made it to St. Augustine, where they converted to Catholicism to safeguard their place in Spanish colonial society. There, they joined other Carolina fugitives: the Africans Conano, Jesse, Jaque, Gran Domingo, Cambo, Dique, and Robi, among others; along with European runaways such as Mermique, Satrata, Bernard Patrick (an Irish servant who had fled to St. Augustine in 1672), and Charles Robson, who, like Patrick, served as an interpreter for Spanish officials. Together, these runaways made up a kind of urban maroon community of Black and White fugitive Catholics, serving the city and living under the protection of the Spanish Crown. They remembered Carolina as a place of enslavement and death, whereas Florida represented freedom and security. Unlike the Yamasees and Scots, who came to Port Royal in search of liberty, autonomy, and opportunity, these fugitives knew it as a nest of slave catchers no better than the death trap of Charles Town.[37]

On the other hand, fugitives from outside of Carolina found Port Royal to be a perfect hiding place. Nicolás, a twenty-one-year-old Christian Yamasee from the province of Guale, quietly left the mission settlement of Sapala with other Yamasees because he feared punishment and needed "to disappear for some time." Likewise, Matheo, a Christian Indian from Santa Catalina, was driven out of Florida by fear and shame. After his village relocated to the island of Santa Maria, Matheo had words with the wife of his mico. She hit him with a stick, which led to a violent altercation between Matheo and his attacker's husband. When the village elders threatened to have Matheo arrested and sent to St. Augustine for forced labor, he fled to Carolina with the Yamasees. Port Royal's marginal location, growing Indian population, and constant movement attracted Indigenous fugitives looking a place to lay low for a while. However, sketchy European characters also made use of it, such as the "rascal fellows" William Dunlop discovered living as transients on the islands adjacent to Stuarts Town. They included Thomas Evans, Thomas Gregson ("a providence shoemaker"), and Thomas Collins ("a kind of carpenter"). The three Thomases, along with several others whose names Dunlop did not know, were building a boat to "run away out of the province," which they would surely do unless the governor commissioned magistrates to enforce the law in Port Royal. The absence of a strong civil authority lured White rascals, just as the prospect of getting lost in Port Royal's fluid and ill-defined Native settlements drew fugitive Indians.[38]

These examples could be multiplied. Indian captives were exported to the Bahamas or sold to Carolina planters (Dunlop owned an Indian slave girl). Spaniards were kidnapped by English pirates and sold as servants in Charles Town. Thomas Torre, a Spanish raider who escaped to the English and offered to lead them against St. Augustine, sold into slavery one of the Indian companions who had escaped with him.[39] Carolina in the mid-1680s was awash in exploitation. It was one massive labor grab whose guiding principle was to enslave anyone and everyone—children, Indians, Africans, Spaniards, free laborers, runaways—using any means necessary, legal or illegal. In this world, liberators could also be captors, and most people either lived in bondage or walked the knife's edge between freedom and slavery.

Port Royal stood at the center of this world. In 1684–1685, it became a magnet for all kinds of people: some looking for safety, opportunity, or autonomy and others simply trying to escape exploitation or punishment. Its future would not be determined only by its context—its history of violence, its social and political instability, or many slaveries—but also by the conflicting and intersecting agendas of its diverse people and the choices they made as they sought to secure their own place in the colonial borderlands.

CHAPTER 4

Consuming Fire

By late 1684, the proprietors had put a stop to Carolina's Indian slave trade. The Winyah War was the last straw. That "pore Innocent women & Children" who fell under English protection were "Barberously murdered taken & sent to be Sold as slaves" was an affront to God and king. The proprietors deplored the recklessness and greed of the "dealers in Indians" at Goose Creek, who used their public offices to enrich themselves. Their self-serving actions had damaged the colony's reputation and security and would discourage immigration. The proprietors sidelined Maurice Mathews and James Moore and stripped the Grand Council of any role in regulating Indian slavery. They also placed strict conditions on the export of Indigenous slaves: Only Natives captured in a war with the English could be enslaved and sold abroad, and only after the provincial parliament (not the Grand Council) investigated the circumstances of their capture and approved their sale. Captives bought from Native middlemen such as the Savannahs could not be shipped out of the colony. Without well-placed allies in key government posts, and with no export market for captives, the Savannahs could not get the arms and backing they needed to manage the captive trade in the interior. As a result, the flow of Indian slaves to Charles Town stopped.[1]

The prospects for a peaceful and stable Carolina colony further improved with the colonization of Port Royal by the Scots and Yamasees. The Scots wanted to befriend and convert Indians, not enslave them. As persecuted Covenanters, they were sensitive to tyranny in all its forms, and as Reformed Protestants, they clung to the belief that freedom was essential to true Christian practice. They were also eager to win approval from the proprietors. They promised to toe the line, and the proprietors counted on them to counterbalance the troublesome English at Charles Town. The Yamasees likewise valued liberty and went to great lengths to avoid dependent relationships and maintain their autonomy. Like the Scots, their hands were clean of the slave trade; they had been victims, never perpetrators, of Indian slavery. Thus in 1684, with the Westos destroyed, the Savannahs and Goose Creek slavers neutralized, the Covenanters planting a settlement of families at Port Royal, and the proprietors placing strict limits on the captive trade, both Natives and Europeans could anticipate an end to the violence and instability brought to Carolina by the Westos and the commercial Indian slave trade.[2]

Instead, the Scots and Yamasees reignited the trade and initiated a new period of explosive violence. This was partly because their hatred of slavery did not extend to the enslavement of others. Both the Yamasees and Scots understood freedom in tribal terms, not as a universal principle. As the historian Christina Snyder has pointed out, in Native societies, the opposite of slavery was kinship, not freedom. Yamasees were under no obligation to recognize the personhood of non-kin. On the contrary, they were obligated to kill, capture, or enslave non-kin if necessary to protect or advance the interests of their own people. Although slaving was dangerous business that almost guaranteed some kind of reprisal, successful raids were assertions of power and a source of pride. The same was true for the Covenanters. Although fiercely protective of their religious autonomy, in the end, they wanted power more than liberty, and they were bound by their covenant relationship with God to force their religious ideas on the people of Scotland through the national church. They thought much about spiritual slavery but little about bodily slavery. Like English Whigs, they saw no contradiction between resisting tyranny at home and investing in African enslavement abroad. As planters and overseers, they were cogs in the wheel of plantation bondage in the expanding British empire. Lacking any firm universal antislavery principles, and willing to exploit the labor even of fellow Covenanters, the Scots had few, if any, qualms about enslaving or exporting Indian captives if doing so strengthened the position of Stuarts Town.[3]

Yet, whatever their views of liberty and bondage, neither the Scots nor the Yamasees came to Port Royal with the intention of capitalizing on Indigenous slavery. Indeed, their decision to launch a raid against Santa Catalina de Afuica had little to do with social ethics, ideology, the demands of Carolina's Lords Proprietors, regional labor markets, greed, or global economic systems and had much to do with opportunities, personal rivalries, and local insecurities. The rapid transformation of Port Royal had sent waves of anxiety across the southeast, most of all in Port Royal itself. Sensing an opportunity to establish Yamasee as a major regional power while burnishing his own credentials as war chief, Altamaha seized the moment, struck a trade deal with Cardross, and sealed it with the blood and bodies of Spanish mission Indians. The Yamasees, not the Scots or English, were pulling the strings and creating the conditions for colonial trade. Their raid rekindled the dying embers of the Indian slave trade. For the next three decades, it would rage across the Carolina and Florida borderlands like a consuming fire. Stuarts Town and the Yamasees themselves would be among its casualties.

THE RAID ON SANTA CATALINA DE AFUICA

Contemporaries disagreed about who to blame for the raid on Santa Catalina de Afuica. Henry Woodward's sources assured him that his rival, the English trader Caleb Westbrooke, was behind it. Westbrooke certainly worried that the Yamasee migration to Port Royal might be part of a Spanish plot, and he might have persuaded Cardross to sponsor the raid to force the Yamasees to demonstrate their professed hatred for the Spaniards. As go-between and interpreter, Westbrooke was involved in negotiations and planning, and he joined the Scots at Yamacraw when the raiders delivered their booty. Antonio and seven other St. Helena Indians, all Woodward allies and friends of the English, blamed Westbrooke for this "unadvised project." Maurice Mathews disagreed. Mathews focused on the religious objects seized by the raiders: prayer books in Spanish and Latin, clerical vestments, a silver communion plate. Hoping to turn officials in London against the Scots, he told the proprietors and the Spanish ambassador that Cardross hatched the plot out of his hatred of Roman Catholicism. A group of Apalachee caciques who had an axe to grind with Florida's Governor Márquez Cabrera told the Spanish Crown that Altamaha initiated the raid to get revenge on the governor for mistreating him when he lived in Guale. This was part of a pattern of mistreatment from the governor that now extended to the Apalachees. And Caruse, a Yamasee headman who spoke for several of his people, reported that Altamaha and Westbrooke appealed to them "to make war on the Timecho Indians who are Christians and had a Spanish Fryar and Chappell among them." They added, however, that these two emissaries were representing the Scots and that Altamaha and Westbrooke told them that the English knew about and approved the raid. The Yamasee raiders, they declared, were only doing the bidding of the British.[4]

These self-serving claims must all be taken with a grain of salt. Westbrooke was an advisor, not a decision-maker. Thanks to the Yamasee migration, he and the Scots were suddenly in position to take control of the Indian trade and cut out Woodward and the English. By discrediting Westbrooke, Woodward hoped to weaken or eliminate his competition. By telling Woodward what he wanted to hear, Antonio and the other St. Helena Indians strengthened their hand with the English. The same was true for Mathews, who was deeply implicated in Carolina's Indian slave trade and took advantage of a rare opportunity to shift negative attention to someone else. His argument would have met with skepticism from the proprietors. No matter how much Cardross hated papists, he had more sense than to risk the disfavor of the proprietors, not to mention Spanish retaliation against his barely defensible new settlement, for the short-term gains of a slave raid—although he might do so if Altamaha took the initiative and assumed most of the risk. The Apalachee headmen used the raid to build their case against Márquez Cabrera, and Caruse deflected blame by claiming that he and his people were only foot soldiers who believed that they had British backing. Amid the growing tensions surrounding the colonization of Port Royal, the raid on Afuica became yet another talking point (albeit a very important one) between rivals. Assigning blame for Afuica allowed its interpreters to strengthen their own position, discredit their enemies, or preserve their neutrality in an uncertain world.

On the basis of the local context, with its swirl of rivalries, opportunities, and fears, the most likely scenario is that Altamaha initiated the raid, although not, as the Apalachee headmen claimed, because of his bitterness toward Florida's governor. Altamaha did not share Cardross's hesitations. He was eager to join forces with the Scots. Shortly after their arrival, he sent forty men to help Cardross build a warning system of beacons along the coast to their south. Most important, Altamaha had established himself as a "Chieftain" or grand mico, according to the Yamasee headmen, and in proposing the raid, he was asserting his role as war chief. After twenty years of living under Spanish control with few opportunities to take scalps, win martial honors, and prove their manhood, the generation of young men who left Guale with Altamaha were eager to pursue the red path. Curiously, however, Westbrooke noted that "most of the Yamasees that came first"—with Altamaha from Guale—"are left behind with their wives and children." This means that Altamaha recruited heavily from the Yamasees who came later and migrated from Apalachee and Apalachicola. Sixty warriors joined the raid, and there could not have been more than sixty warriors total among the three hundred Yamasees who initially came with Altamaha. If most of these men stayed back, then a majority of the raiders were from the interior. Altamaha was using the red path to unite young Yamasee men from the towns scattered by diaspora, and he was drawing them together under his leadership. The promise of violence and war was thus integral to the process of Yamasee coalescence and unity.

Altamaha was only partially successful. When questioned by the English, Caruse and his people disavowed him, claiming that he and Westbrooke had lied to them about Charles Town's approval of the raid. The white mico (chief) Niquisalla went much further. To thwart Altamaha, he personally warned the Spaniards of the pending attack. Unlike Caruse, Niquisalla did not directly blame Altamaha. Instead, he told the Spaniards what they wanted to hear, blaming Charles Town and the "new English" at Port Royal who had ordered the Yamasees to undertake the raid. Niquisalla came too late, as his news reached provincial authorities in Timucua just six hours after the raiders had left Afuica. Still, Niquisalla believed that Yamasee unity could be won through peaceful means and that provoking St. Augustine by attacking mission Indians was dangerous and ill-advised. His actions suggest that Altamaha was operating on his own, without consent of a general council. That Niquisalla was willing to ambush his own people shows just how deep internal divisions were among the Yamasees and how far Altamaha's rival would go to thwart his power grab and maintain peaceful relations with St. Augustine.[5]

Santa Catalina de Afuica was a sleepy backwater mission village and an easy target for slave raiders. Located on the mission frontier in north central Florida, it was a hundred miles from St. Augustine and sixty miles from the small provincial garrison at Machava. Like other Timucuan missions, it had suffered steep population losses across the seventeenth century. In 1675, just sixty people lived there. Their numbers were augmented three years later when the nearby village of Afuica relocated to the Santa Catalina mission (giving it a new and hybrid name), but it is doubtful that this consolidation pushed the population much over one hundred. Although situated near the confluence of the Santa Fe and Suwannee Rivers to its south, the town was completely exposed to invaders from the north. With no palisade and no firearms, it was poorly defended. Its people lived simply. They were farmers and ranchers, not warriors, and they depended mostly on the threat of retaliation from St. Augustine to deter invaders. Their chief complaint was that their friar, Fray Lastra, would not let them perform the traditional dances, although they had been approved by the bishop. These dances were spiritual practices, and the Timucuans' commitment to them suggests that they, like many Spanish mission Indians, converted to Christianity, at least in part, on their terms.[6]

At four in the morning on March 7, 1685, sixty Yamasee warriors approached this settlement on foot from two directions, moving along the provincial road that connected it to mission towns to the west and east. Half the attackers carried firearms and cutlasses, most of them provided by the Scots; the others were armed with bows and shields. Fortune was on their side. On the previous day, Afuica's cacique and sixteen of his men had set out from the village, leaving only a handful of warriors to defend it. The attackers fell on their victims while they slept. Caught by surprise and prevented by the Yamasees from fleeing along the roads, many Timucuans escaped into the woods, where some remained for several days. Others were not so lucky. Yamasee warriors later claimed to have killed fifty villagers, although more reliable Spanish sources gave a much lower number: eighteen, eight of whom were women. The Yamasees also took twenty-five women and three boys captive. This was more than enough to pay for the twenty-three guns they received from Cardross. For four hours, they terrorized Santa Catalina. They burned and looted the friar's house and chapel, taking a communion plate, prayer books, and robes; then they razed the rest of the town, leaving only ten houses standing. By eight o'clock, they were on the move again.[7]

Two of their female captives escaped and lived to tell their stories. Although their voices are hard to hear in the official correspondence, which is mainly concerned with the number and identity of the raiders and the arms they carried, they left faint traces of the terror of the raid and the ordeal of captivity. The attack was very disorienting. The Yamasees not only caught the town by surprise—they entered shooting and screaming from two directions. Frightened and confused, the villagers were unable to defend themselves and so fled in all directions. The attackers, energized by their triumph and anxious to put plenty of space between themselves and the Spaniards, covered fourteen leagues (about thirty-six miles) that first day. The Yamasees threatened to kill any captives who could not keep up with this grueling pace, and indeed, they murdered one woman, although they later claimed that she would not eat and "died in her place of grief." The raiders told the captives they were Mobilas and Tiquipaches, although the escaped women surmised by their language that they were Yamasees. The captors derisively told their prisoners to cheer up, for they were taking them to Tama, where there would be great dancing and celebration, then to San Jorge (Charles Town), where they would be clothed and received by the English. Remarkably, after experiencing the horror of the raid, followed by an exhausting march that must have lasted ten to twelve hours, the two women escaped by moonlight, and their absence was not noticed until the next day. They reported all they had learned to the provincial lieutenant, Marcus Delgado.[8]

On March 12, Cardross, Dunlop, Westbrooke, and John Hamilton went to Yamacraw, on the south bank of the Savannah River, one day's journey from Stuarts Town, to get the "great booty" they expected from the Yamasee raiders. They were not disappointed. The Yamasees delivered twenty-two women to Cardross but kept the boys for themselves, presumably for adoption. The Scots sent eight of their captives to Charles Town; three of these women were exported, and the other five were sold to local planters. Cardross brought the remaining fourteen to Stuarts Town and sold them as slaves to the West Indies. It is possible that Dunlop kept one slave for himself, for he left an "Indian girle" behind when he returned to Scotland in 1689. She died during an epidemic in 1693. If the Scots, devout Christians all, imagined the horrors these captives endured—torn from their children, their loved ones butchered, their village burned, their lives shattered, and now, bereft of home and overwhelmed by sorrow and exhaustion, handed over to strangers in a distant land—they did not bother to write it down.[9]

FALLOUT FROM THE RAID

From a strategic standpoint, the raid on Santa Catalina de Afuica was a triumph for the Scots and Yamasees. As a direct attack into the heart of Spanish Florida's imperial missions, the raid was a clear assertion of Scottish empire, and it changed everything on the ground in the southeastern borderlands. The thrust into Timucua demonstrated strength that far exceeded Stuarts Town's numbers. The success of the raid and the disposal of the captives showed that the Scots and Yamasees could be as ruthless and efficient as the Westos. It signaled Yamasee power, not to mention the clear advantages of a trade relationship with the British, to other Native groups in the region. The effect was immediate and far-reaching, setting off a chain of hostilities as anxiety rippled through the borderlands from St. Augustine to Charles Town to Apalachee.

Emboldened by their success, the Scots and Yamasees turned their eyes toward colonizing the abandoned settlements of old Guale along the Georgia coast. They liked what they saw. The "great Setlement" on St. Catherine's Island was ready-made for colonizers, with seven or eight miles of choice cleared ground and several houses still standing. As noted earlier, Cardross believed that the Spaniards had evacuated these islands because the Scots settled Port Royal, and he wanted to take possession of them. It was a pipe dream. By the Treaty of Madrid, all territory south of the Savannah was off limits to British settlers, and the proprietors would never have consented to Cardross's plan; nor did the Scots have enough people to plant new colonies on their own, although they might have encouraged the Yamasees to occupy these lands as their partners. St. Augustine thought so, for rumors circulated in Florida that the Scots "caused their Natives to dismantle" the remains of the town at Santa Catalina de Guale and that Yamasees were living there and on Sapala in late 1686. Indeed, that year, Spanish forces would burn the settlement at Sapala, although it is not clear if Yamasees had actually been occupying it. Still, these rumors accurately reflected the intentions of the Port Royal alliance and the spirit, if not the reality, of Scottish–Yamasee imperialism. The Santa Catalina de Afuica raid had whetted the Scots' and Yamasees' appetite for poaching Spain's colonial wealth. If they could raid Spanish towns and enslave their people, why not take their abandoned lands, reorient inland Native trade to Stuarts Town, and siphon off silver from New Mexico and points south?[10]

All of these initiatives were on Cardross's agenda in the spring of 1685. However, to capitalize on inland trade, he would first have to contend with Henry Woodward. In 1682, the proprietors had granted Woodward a commission to explore the Carolina interior and establish trade with its people. Like Cardross, Woodward set his sights on Coweta and Cusseta in the Chattahoochee Valley. Unlike Cardross, he hesitated, partly because of the obstructions of his enemies at Goose Creek, and partly because these towns were friends with St. Augustine and were located in territory claimed by Spain (although they were not missionized). After the Santa Catalina raid Woodward woke up to the threat that the Yamasee–Scottish alliance posed to his commercial aspirations. Moving aggressively to recover lost ground, he set off a conflict with Cardross that turned into a minor political crisis for the province.[11]

The trouble started when the English trader John Edenburgh, a Woodward associate, went to Port Royal to trade with the Yamasees. At Combahee, not far from Stuarts Town, he was arrested by William Dunlop and brought before Cardross. According to Edenburgh, Cardross declared that "noe Englishman should trade from St. Helena to the Westoe River for all the Indians was his and that noe Englishman should trade between the Westoe River and St. Katherine for that hee had take up one County and had liberty to take up another." The Scots detained Edenburgh and looked for ways to use him to their advantage. After five days, Cardross sent him a letter offering a generous twenty-five percent commission if Edenburgh would help the Scots close a trade deal with Coweta and Cusseta. Why Westbrooke could not mediate this trade agreement is anyone's guess. Perhaps he and Cardross were on the wrong side of the Yamasee divide. As friends of Altamaha, they were tainted by their part in the slave raid, and they were not to be trusted by Niquisalla, who was the gatekeeper for the inland trade. Whatever the reason, Edenburgh had significant value, and Charles Town wanted him back. In late March, the Grand Council ordered Westbrooke to apprehend Edenburgh and summoned both men to Charles Town "to give information respecting several transactions that have lately taken place to the Southward" (i.e., the raid on Santa Catalina de Afuica). Cardross bristled at this intrusion on his jurisdiction and refused to give up the two traders. "We doubt not as to the contract that has been made between the Lords Proprietors and us," he told the Grand Council, "which we mean to keep ourselves and expect to be kept by others." In other words, mind your own business. The Scots alone had authority to regulate trade in their county and with "their" Indians.[12]

Tensions escalated in mid-April, when Woodward and four other English traders passed through Port Royal, purportedly on an expedition to explore the Savannah River. On route, they picked up Edenburgh, all without sending notice to the Scots. Cardross responded by sending a deputation led by John Hamilton and Westbrooke to arrest the English for trespassing. Cardross must have been incredulous at Woodward's story of an exploratory expedition, considering that the English had been in Carolina for fifteen years and Woodward had been up the Savannah at least as far as the fall line. He rightly accused Woodward of encroaching on the Scots' trade zone, and he undoubtedly suspected Woodward of secretly negotiating with the Yamasees or using Edenburgh to gain access. When Woodward reminded him of his commission from the proprietors, Cardross would have none of it. According to Woodward, Cardross told him that he "valued no commission from the proprietors" relating to trade because "he had as much right [to it] as any of them." He also declared, as he had done with Edenburgh, that "noe Englishman had any power to come into his precinct for that the Scotch were an Independent Government from the English." He kept Woodward and his companions confined for five days before sending them back to Charles Town, where they were summoned before the Grand Council. Their sworn testimony was added to that of Edenburgh and the Yamasee headmen, strengthening the Council's case against Cardross and his rogue settlement.[13]

On May 5, the deputy governor of Carolina issued warrants for the arrest of Cardross, Hamilton, and Westbrooke and ordered Provost Marshal John Griffith to go to Port Royal and take them into custody. Griffith returned empty handed. Pleading illness, Cardross had not only refused to be arrested but also refused to return the warrant to the marshal. The deputy governor issued a second warrant with instructions to "bring [Cardross] down, sick or well." This time, Griffith took the bricklayer James Seaton with him. As they approached Stuarts Town, Hamilton disappeared into the woods. Griffith and Seaton tracked Westbrooke to his home among the Yamasees, but his Native friends sounded the alarm, and Westbrooke slipped away. Cardross was in bed with a fever and once again sent Griffith away, this time with his regrets to the governor and council. It had turned into a fool's errand for poor John Griffith, who had only a bricklayer to help him arrest a nobleman, a gentleman, and a crafty Indian trader. In mid-July, Cardross wrote the governor to explain himself. He promised to answer the summons when he was well enough to travel, expressed his warmest regard for the government, and assured the governor of his sincere "desire to uphold your authority." The proprietors were not so magnanimous. Angered by the rude treatment of a fellow nobleman, they apologized to

Cardross for the government's "ill behaviour," and they reproached Charles Town authorities for "so far forget[ting] themselves as not to show you that Respect that is due to your quality."[14]

After all this rigamarole, in the end, Woodward got what he wanted. Through Antonio, Wina, and the interrogation of the Yamasee headmen, he already had an idea of the Yamasees' internal divisions and where the Scots and Westbrooke stood in relation to them. Edenburgh brought more intelligence. Cardross's sickness and incapacitation weakened the Scots' resistance to English interference. Woodward used these circumstances to his advantage, and sometime in June or July 1685, he made a deal with Niquisalla to mediate trade negotiations between the English and the Chattahoochee River towns.

It is a mistake, however, to overstate Woodward's role in opening trade with the interior. He was the supplicant, and Niquisalla, who controlled access to the inland towns, operated under his own agenda. The Yamasee mico had watched from the sidelines while Altamaha befriended Cardross and unified warriors from the scattered towns for the Santa Catalina raid. He had failed to sabotage the raid, and then had seen his rival strengthened by the "great booty" it brought, the bond it secured between the Yamasees and the Scots, and the way it energized young Yamasee warriors. To isolate Altamaha, pour cold water on the red path and assert the primacy of civil authority over the military, Niquisalla opened negotiations with the English for trade with the interior. Indeed, he may have had little choice. The Apalachicola towns were eager to negotiate the return of five captives taken during the Westo War and presumably still held in Charles Town. They, and not Niquisalla, may have insisted on trading exclusively with the English. In either case, Indigenous people, not Woodward and the Carolinians, were setting the terms of trade.[15]

By September, Niquisalla and Woodward were in Coweta and Cusseta, accompanied by half a dozen English and at least forty-five Yamasees. The Indians put their newfound privileges on full display: Decked out in hats and waist-jackets, they carried machetes along with thirty pistols and twenty-seven muskets. The "squad leader" of the Santa Catalina raid was among them; perhaps he brought the Timucuan adoptees with him as trophies. The Yamasees must have made quite an impression on their Native hosts. They were living embodiments of the benefits of trading with the English, and the inland people gave them a warm reception. The Yamasees boasted about the strength of their English allies, who "had that which they had need of, both powder and balls as well as provisions." The English were making plans, so the Yamasees claimed, to attack St. Augustine by sea and Apalachee by land, where they would "set fire" to all the "little places" under Spanish protection. Not far from Coweta,

Woodward had constructed a blockhouse for storing trade goods. The Natives brought bear and bison skins, beaver and otter pelts, and hundreds of deer skins, and the English supplied stockings, fine fabrics, and firearms. Niquisalla had outmaneuvered Altamaha and Cardross and supplanted the Savannahs as middleman in the inland trade. Over the course of the next year, he and his son and nephews would take Woodward deeper into the interior. Thus, the Altamaha–Cardross raid ended with a Woodward–Niquisalla alliance that would funnel trade from the Chattahoochee and Apalachee villages to Charles Town, leaving Stuarts Town in the cold.[16]

STUARTS TOWN: SETTLING A PLANTATION

In the meantime, the Scots were disheartened by news that conditions continued to deteriorate back in Scotland. In February 1685, Charles II died and was succeeded by his brother James, who had converted to Roman Catholicism as an adult. James had two Protestant daughters from his first marriage but no sons, although his second wife, a Catholic, was young and fertile, and the prospect of a Catholic succession could not be ruled out. Earlier Protestant attempts to block James's succession had contributed to Shaftesbury's demise and set in motion the plots of 1683. Now, Presbyterians at home and abroad were alarmed. Just three months into James's reign, the Earl of Argyll, a Covenanter, returned from exile and launched a coordinated uprising with Charles's illegitimate son, the Duke of Monmouth. They were roundly defeated, and Argyll and Monmouth were captured and executed. In the wake of this rebellion, Scotland's parliament passed new and ever harsher anti-Covenanting laws. It was now treason to hold to the covenant, and people who attended field conventicles would face the death penalty. Closer to home for Carolina's Scots, Cardross's brother, John Erskine, fled to Rotterdam, and Sir John Cochrane of Ochiltree, Dunlop's old pupil and one-time leader of the Carolina Company, was arrested and imprisoned in Edinburgh. When news of these grim events reached Stuarts Town in the spring and summer of 1685, they must have added greater urgency to the business of settling a plantation for Scotland's religious refugees.[17]

As Cardross's big plans for monopolizing the Indian trade and annexing Spanish Florida came to nothing, Stuarts Town's leaders, especially William Dunlop, settled down to the hard work of planting and recruiting colonists. This was easier said than done, because Port Royal remained "extraordinarie sicklie" through much of 1685. After the first wave of deaths in Charles Town in October 1684, fever and ague lingered among the colonists as they settled Stuarts Town that winter. Of the twenty-two servants Dunlop brought on the *Carolina Merchant*, only eight were still living eighteen months later. All of the seven White servants he purchased after arriving also died. In the spring of 1685, a ship from Ireland brought eighty settlers, mostly women and children; the "greater pairt" of them were dead within six months. Another Irish ship, the *Abercorne*, put in at Port Royal in the summer of 1685 to take on timber for Barbados. Its passengers sickened from malaria, and twenty-nine died. Although the death rate dropped to zero in the fall and winter of 1685, the damage had been done. By August 1686, two years after sailing with one hundred forty-eight passengers from Gourock, only thirty men capable of bearing arms remained in the settlement, and few Scots were willing to risk immigrating to the death trap in Carolina.[18]

However, Dunlop remained optimistic, and he soldiered on. "Tho no assistance should come to us," he wrote to James Montgomery of Skelmorlie, his partner in Scotland, "I am resolved by the grace of God to maintain Port Royall so long as we have 6 men alive." Hinting at secondary causes of the high mortality rate, Dunlop declared that he "would never look upon [the country] as unhealthy." Livestock reproduced themselves with enthusiasm. In November 1684, he bought a young sow for sixteen shillings, and by March 1686, she had produced thirty shoats collectively valued at fifteen pounds sterling, an enormous gain. "So doe cattell increase extraordinarily," he claimed, as did figs, apples, oranges, olives, and mulberry trees (which he extolled, as did so many Europeans before and after him, for their promising silkworms and sweet berries). Peaches were in "great plenty," Dunlop claimed, "and as little thought of as the hawse on the thorn bushes in Scotland." Indeed, one Carolina hog ate more peaches in a year than all the people of Scotland put together. On St. Helena Island, eight miles south of Stuarts Town, Native people had cleared hundreds of acres of ground before moving out to make way for the Scots. This good ground was there for the taking, and its soil, with a little time, care, and cultivation, would surely produce English grains as well as American corn.[19]

To be sure, much work was required to clear forests, create pastures and ponds, put up fences, dig wells, build houses and barns, and make the settlement profitable. "Expect nothing but Labour, for the Country is a wildernesse," Dunlop wrote, "though the labour afterward will be more easie." He asked for as many tradesmen and freemen as Skelmorlie could send. Smiths, shoemakers, tailors, and ship carpenters would find "good Imployment" at Port Royal, and they would get town lots plus acreage on the edge of town to plant all the corn they needed while pursuing their trades. White servants were of little value. They sickened and died at alarming rates, and when healthy, they "abundantly consumed" clothing and food, so that they were both unproductive and expensive to keep. African slaves, on the other hand, were already seasoned to the tropics. Hardier, cheaper to maintain, and more profitable than White servants, they made "the best and lasting servants," indeed "the only servants for this country." Dunlop repeatedly urged Skelmorlie to get slaves from Barbados and bring them to Stuarts Town. With the Indian trade closed to the Scots, the colony's profitability depended more than ever on the labor efficiency only enslaved Africans could provide. Therefore, he reminded Skelmorlie, "let your chiefe care be to provide for Negroes."[20]

Dunlop left unanswered the question of how Stuarts Town would pay for these slaves. The same disarray at home that drove the Covenanters to start their colony also left it undercapitalized, although by no means bankrupt. In 1685, Skelmorlie cobbled together sixteen hundred pounds sterling, "a great dele of money," to purchase the *Richard & John*, an English ship of one hundred forty tons and twenty guns, which he intended for trade in the West Indies and Carolina. Heartened by this investment, which included some of his own money, Dunlop sent Skelmorlie a long list of goods for the colony. The Scots needed claret and other liquors, linen, rugs, and blue or red Galloway cloth, all of which the new arrivals could trade for cattle and corn. If he sailed first to Barbados, Skelmorlie should take on rum, sugar, and molasses, as well as slaves, and he should bring the ship directly to Stuarts Town to avoid seizure of Scottish goods in Charles Town under the Navigation Acts. Money was scarce in Carolina, so "come not without 1000 pounds sterling or two." In other words, bring goods as well as cash to buy more goods. With Carolina's most lucrative commodities, deer skins, beaver furs, and Indian slaves, flowing through Woodward's hands into Charles Town, the Scots had little of value to exchange for these goods. Dunlop made the most of a "considerable parcell" of squared cedar and pine boards he stacked on the shore for Skelmorlie's ship, but he also recognized that "all the lumber she can carry hence will hardly defray charges which a tedious voyage may bring." The Scots felt the loss of the valuable commodities they had anticipated from the Indian trade. With only wood to offer, Dunlop was forced to rely mainly on credit while reminding his partners to be patient and expect short-term losses but long-term gains, for "all new settlements are gone about with great charge at first and it takes time before profit come in."[21]

On a positive note, the end to the trade war between Cardross and Woodward led to improved relations between Stuarts Town and Charles Town. The English complied with the proprietors' orders and sent three surplus cannons to the Scots, which they mounted in their small fort. The proprietors appointed Dunlop as one of their deputies, giving him a seat on the Grand Council and in the provincial parliament. Dunlop's moderation, diplomacy, and pragmatism won him several well-placed friends in Charles Town, including Carolina's governor, Joseph Morton. Morton made him militia captain for Port Royal County, a post that reported directly to the governor, thus recognizing Stuarts Town's equal standing with its English neighbor. Dunlop was also appointed receiver and escheator for the county, which gave him charge over fines, forfeitures, shipwrecks, ambergris, and land grants. He served as register for deaths and burials, a post "of no trouble and may be of no little profite." He was also entrusted with supervising public improvement projects, such as cutting a canal between the Edisto and Wadmalaw Rivers. Dunlop's skillful mediation between Cardross and Charles Town, not to mention his administrative competency, earned the respect and trust of English authorities in Carolina. Thanks to his "wise discreet deportment," as Dunlop's friend John Stewart wrote, the Scots were "better esteem'd by one and all" in Carolina. Although he came to Port Royal to "be serviceable to my generation" in its battle with Antichrist, he discovered more usefulness and satisfaction by serving the kingdom of this world, not the next. Both Stuarts Town and Charles Town benefited.[22]

Back in Scotland, however, Sarah Carstares worried that her husband's plantation business was diverting him from the "great and main work which God hath called you more especially to follow." She urged him to remember his calling and reminded him that "bringing many soulls to glory" would be "far, very far, more true advantage and honnour [than] being the first of a plantation tho' it should be never so populous." William's replies have not survived, but the steady stream of correspondence from Sarah reveals a marriage that was equal parts partnership and intimate companionship. Besides offering spiritual advice, she chided him for failing to write more frequently and urged him to contact his associates in Scotland about the investments they placed in his hands. She worried about his credit and warned him that Skelmorlie balked at answering his bills and could not be trusted. Indeed, by June 1686, she was persuaded that his Scottish partners had "all quit thoughts of you or giving any help to you." At the same time, news of Carolina's high mortality discouraged immigration so that "no person will go" to "that place"—Sarah's preferred term for Carolina, as it was for William's mother and sister, as if they were unwilling to dignify Stuarts Town by calling it by name. From the vantage point of Scotland, even during the darkest days of the killing time, Carolina looked increasingly like a death sentence to would-be immigrants and a losing venture to investors.[23]

Sarah blunted these advices and warnings by couching them in terms of tenderness and affection. William was her "dearest heart," her "very desirable husband," her "estimable dearest jewell." Every caution, every reminder, was punctuated with these terms of endearment, and she went to great lengths to express her affection and heartfelt longings. "I could not have been so happie in no creature for a husband as thyself," she wrote, for "thow hath been and art to me for all things that is satisfying comfortable and pleasent in such a relation beyound all conception." Their separation was her greatest sorrow, and she was so grieved by her inability to join him that it was "like death to me." She and Lady Cardross had both intended to sail on Skelmorlie's vessel in March 1686, but circumstances prevented it. Sarah saw the hand of providence in these delays. She wondered if "I am being left behind for some strocke which I have a great hand in provocking God to inflict," as if God were correcting her for her idolatrous attachment to her husband. No ships sailed from Scotland that summer, and she considered taking passage from London by way of New England but was concerned about the expense. She confessed that both the voyage and "that place itself" (Carolina) were "very frightening." Her fears increased after the disaster of the *Henry and Francis*, a Scottish ship bound for New Jersey in 1685. Plagued by fever, leaks, and food shortages, it spent fifteen miserable weeks at sea and lost seventy passengers and crew. Worried about traveling in the summer heat, torn between leaving the children behind or taking them with her, and discouraged from immigrating by family and friends, Sarah was repeatedly prevented from sailing to Carolina, despite William's insistence that she join him. Distressed by these disappointments and their long separation, she found comfort in the hope of meeting again in heaven, "when we shall never again be seprat we will be happie and forget all sorrow upon the account of parting and distance here."[24]

William shared Sarah's loneliness, impatience, and distress. "If she be not come away," he wrote Skelmorlie in spring of 1685, "by all means send my wife and children." He assumed that she and Lady Cardross would be aboard Skelmorlie's ship, which sailed in early March but was inexplicably delayed in getting to Stuarts Town. Cardross, too, "waitts dayly for his Lady and is impatient for her coming." By July, Dunlop was "extremely anxious" that his "chiefe," as he called Sarah, had not yet arrived. He was also troubled by the pile of debt he was amassing on behalf of the settlement. Skelmorlie owed him ninety-eight pounds, and Dunlop was sending his own creditors to Skelmorlie to collect their debts from what he owed Dunlop. He had borrowed money from Governor Morton and billed it to Skelmorlie's account, and he had covered a sizable debt that Skelmorlie owed to John Dowhill. Dunlop also incurred expenses of sixty pounds for surveying some twenty-four thousand acres and would be forced to sell his flock of cattle to satisfy the debt if Skelmorlie's ship, half of which belonged to Dunlop, did not arrive soon. As the summer wore on, Dunlop remained in "constant expectation" of the *Richard & John*, and his letters to Skelmorlie grew sharp and urgent. Impatient for Sarah, worried that his partners at home would not send the recruits needed to bolster the settlement, and desperate for slaves and Scottish trade goods, he warned Skelmorlie that he would be "much to blame and it will much damage your interest here" if the ship disappointed his expectations. Little did Dunlop know that, even as he wrote, Sarah was still in Scotland, the *Richard & John* was anchored in Antigua, and its captain had no intention of continuing the promised voyage to Carolina.[25]

THE SPANISH RESPONSE: FIRE AND SWORD

St. Augustine responded to the British–Indian activity on its frontier with a mixture of caution and fury. The delicate imperial context called for a measured approach, one that would punish its enemies and curtail their expansion without embroiling Spain in war. At the same time, this context produced growing anxiety and frustration. The English colony at Charles Town had long worried the Spaniards, and now they were further provoked by the Scots at Port Royal and the French at Espiritu Santo on the Gulf Coast. Pirates and Westo slavers had depopulated Guale, and now British-backed Yamasee raiders were threatening to do the same in Timucua. Woodward's intrusion into the Chattahoochee Valley pushed St. Augustine to the breaking point. Florida's Governor Márquez Cabrera spent much of 1684–1686 gathering intelligence on these settlements, their aspirations, their relationships with Native peoples, their dealings with pirates, and their role in the Santa Catalina raid. Cabrera was cautious toward the British colonies, but he had no such hesitations about punishing their Indigenous partners. As he slowly built his case against his imperial rivals, Cabrera vented his fury at their Indian allies, first going after the Yamasee raiders, then torching the Chattahoochee towns who dared to make friends with Woodward. Eventually, he would turn fire and sword against his European as well as his Indigenous enemies.

The earliest Spanish–Timucuan efforts to track down the Yamasee raiders failed, for the Yamasees had timed their raid perfectly. Niquisalla's warning reached Spanish authorities six hours after the attack, and by the time a Spanish relief force under Marcus Delgado arrived in Santa Catalina de Afuica, the attackers were gone. Delgado spent two days tracking them through the woods, but he was only able to find the two female captives who had escaped. Months later, a much larger provincial force of one hundred fifty-three men combed the Georgia interior. Lost in the woods for days on end, their Native guides confounded by the unfamiliar territory, they found no trace of the Yamasees. "There is no camp of theirs on the entire mainland," the provincial governor told Márquez Cabrera in November 1685, although he had heard rumors that the raiders were living on the abandoned islands of old Guale, in Spanish territory and on the very edge of the coastal missions. If true, this would have been a major provocation, though there is no evidence that St. Augustine tried to verify the rumor.[26]

Given the scale of the Yamasee migration to Santa Elena ten months before, not to mention the earlier, smaller wave of Yamasees who moved to Carolina from Guale in 1684, the Spaniards' confusion over the whereabouts of the Yamasee raiders is perplexing. Thanks to Niquisalla, officials in Timucua knew that the raiders had teamed up with the Scots and were living north of the Savannah. Perhaps they hoped to find a Yamasee camp in Tama, on the basis of the report of the two escaped captives. Perhaps they failed to communicate Niquisalla's message clearly to St. Augustine. In any case, St. Augustine's inability to locate the Yamasees was part of a more general failure to understand the physical and human worlds just beyond the borders of La Florida. Spain had colonized the region one hundred twenty years earlier. Over the course of nine decades, it had extended missions along the Atlantic coast, the interior, and the panhandle, yet its soldiers and their Indigenous scouts got lost in the woods of central Georgia. Spanish authorities confused the mouth of the Mississippi River with the bay of Espiritu Santo. Also, their relationship with the people of the Chattahoochee Valley, who lived outside the mission system with its roads and trade advantages, was tenuous, as had been their ties to Escamaçu and the coastal Carolina towns. St. Augustine was now learning that their British enemies were not making the same mistakes. The English and Scots were aggressively pushing into their frontiers and building trade and communication networks with Native people. As for the Yamasees, not until December 1685 and early 1686 would St. Augustine find new sources of intelligence that placed the Yamasee settlements in Port Royal. Until then, the Spaniards and their Native allies were in the dark, although the Yamasees made no secret of their whereabouts, and the English, Scots, Carolina coastal peoples, and even St. Augustine's Indian connections in the Chattahoochee Valley knew exactly where they were.[27]

Nothing reflected St. Augustine's weakening grip on its borderlands like Antonio Matheos's misadventures in Apalachicola. In the summer of 1685, St. Augustine heard reports that Captain Enrique (Henry Woodward) was in the interior, building trade and political ties with Coweta, Cusseta, and the neighboring towns. Governor Márquez Cabrera dispatched Matheos to find, capture, and, if necessary, kill the English intruders. Matheos looked to Spain's Apalachicola allies for help. However, as his force of Spanish and Indigenous troops moved through the province in search of Woodward, the Indians abandoned their towns and melted into the forest. Matheos could get no intelligence on the whereabouts of the English, but he heard plenty of rumors about the warm welcome Native people gave Enrique, all while turning their backs on the Spaniards. Matheos burned with anger, and in his report to Márquez Cabrera, he poured out his grief over this betrayal like a jealous lover. Although the Natives said the English came only to trade, "it is my opinion they came for something else. The reception they gave [the English] was so great that no cacique, woman, or child was left that did not come to see it." Having earlier sworn obedience to the Spanish Crown and accepted Spanish protection against Chisca raiders, they now fled from the Spaniards and showed nothing but "contempt for the compassion we have had for them." Instead, they embraced and protected the English, spiriting Enrique from one hiding place to the next as Matheos approached. "Were I not a Christian," he told the mico of the town of Apalachicoli, the only headman who came out to greet him, "I would act in such a way that they, their wives, and children should die of hunger."[28]

Matheos's Christian restraint did not last long. Shortly after returning in frustration to the Apalachee mission province, he received new orders from Márquez Cabrera to mount a second expedition. The governor had read Matheos' report alongside that of another observer on a parallel expedition, Domingo de Leturiondo. Leturiondo's report included testimony from two Apalachicola micos. They insisted that they had not invited the English into their towns and that they fled from Matheos only because he came with many soldiers and they feared he would kill them. In Leturiondo's view, the Apalachicola towns were "neutral with us and the English," and the Spaniards would never catch the English traders "as long as the Indians of that province do not want it." If St. Augustine tried to force the issue, they would have to "obliterate all the villages" of the Chattahoochee Valley. This would send the towns into the arms of the English and make them the "declared enemies" of the Spaniards. It would also leave the Apalachee missions open to a joint English–Indian attack. Márquez Cabrera ignored Leturiondo's warning. Instead, he echoed Matheos's narrative of Indian betrayal: The Apalachicola towns had given themselves to the English and showed them the territory bordering the Apalachee missions. This was a far cry from the cool reception they gave the Spaniards years before, when they greeted them "with their arms in their hands." Clearly, they feared the Spaniards but loved the English. The governor ordered Matheos to return to Apalachicola and "capture the Englishmen for having entered into the land of the King, going beyond the limits of the capitulations, stirring up the vassals who have given obedience." If the Indigenous towns persisted in aiding the enemy, Matheos was instructed to capture their headmen and "burn the villages and provisions."[29]

In late December, Matheos set off with a force of five hundred Spanish and Apalachee fighting men. As he passed through Apalachicola, he tortured three Indians, in one case by holding a loaded rifle to his head and hanging him "by the neck a little above the ground from a pine." Torture and threats of more violence brought out representatives of eight minor towns. They claimed that they only welcomed the English because five of their people were enslaved in Charles Town, and Woodward promised to return them. They also identified Cusseta, Coweta, and two other chief towns as ring leaders of the English alliance. When the micos of these four leading towns failed to answer his summons, Matheos kept his promise and burned them to the ground "without leaving anything, not even a pickle of maize" for their sustenance. Not only did these towns lose their belongings and have to rebuild their homes, council house, and storage buildings, but they also had to endure the winter without the stores of corn they had set aside for their sustenance. After this show of force, Matheos returned to Apalachee, congratulating himself when the towns along his return route greeted him with "great affection." Although confident that this combination of destruction and mercy had subdued the unfaithful Apalachicola towns, he returned without any English prisoners and accomplished only half of his mission.[30]

As Leturiondo predicted, the failure of the Matheos expedition marked a turning point in the history of the colonial southeast. Had Márquez Cabrera heeded Leturiondo's advice and accepted the Apalachicola towns' neutrality, leaving room for Coweta and Cusseta to play both sides of the imperial rivalry, he could have prevented the leading towns from decisively shifting their alliance to Charles Town. This would have given St. Augustine time to shore up its relationship with Apalachicola, whose people were wary of an English alliance. After all, they had witnessed Charles Town's treachery toward the Westos, and they were clearly put off by Woodward's use of the five Indian captives to leverage trade and diplomacy. An even more decisive outcome would have resulted if Matheos had captured Captain Enrique and his fellow traders. This would have thwarted, or at least forestalled, English expansion into the interior, along with the trade in firearms and Indian slaves with its devastating impact on Indigenous communities.[31]

While Matheos was punishing Apalachicola, Márquez Cabrera was gathering evidence of British aggression to justify a similar strike against the Carolina settlements. In December 1685, he interrogated Nicolás, the Christian runaway from Guale, who testified about the Scottish-Yamasee alliance and the disposal of the Timucuan slaves from Santa Catalina de Afuica. The following month, he questioned the two Savoyard refugees, Elmo Mermique and Glodo Satrata.

They confirmed that the Scots had armed the Yamasee raiders and purchased their captives, and they added that the English had bought two hundred slaves captured by pirates in Veracruz. In May, he received a full report from Matheos, who had sent two Apalachee spies into Apalachicola the previous year. They gave detailed information on the Yamasee–English intrusion and reported rumors that the English planned to invade the Apalachee mission province. Márquez Cabrera also suspected that Yamasees were living in the abandoned Guale towns and that the Scots had reconnoitered the coast in hopes of expanding their settlements beyond the "limits of the capitulations" of the 1670 treaty. By midsummer 1686, such clear and compelling evidence of British "damages and hostilities by land and sea" gave Florida's governor everything he needed to justify an assault on Port Royal.[32]

In August, Márquez Cabrera commissioned Alejandro Thomás de León to "traverse and clean these coasts of enemies . . . inflicting upon them all possible hostilities, and driving them away from these coasts." León was a pirate catcher and commander in the coast guard of the Indies. From Havana, he brought two galliots—small, one-masted vessels equipped with oars and prized for their speed and maneuverability—to St. Augustine, where a third galliot captured from the French pirate Grammont joined the expedition. The Flemish refugee Juan Clar was among León's crew, having joined when the Spaniards invaded the Bahamas two years earlier. Initially brought to Carolina in chains, he must have relished the irony of returning now to plunder the colony. In St. Augustine, León outfitted the ships and recruited dozens of corsairs—Spaniards, free Blacks, mulattoes, English renegades, and at least one slave—promising them a share of the plunder along with whatever they could personally pillage from the settlements. On route to Carolina, the expedition picked up a number of Guale Indians on the Georgia coast. Among them was the Christian Matheo, who had struck his mico and fled to Carolina two years earlier but was now on his way back home. By the time they reached Port Royal, the three galliots carried an estimated one hundred fifty men hungry for plunder.[33]

At noon on August 17, the galliots landed just below Stuarts Town, probably at a bend in the Port Royal River now known as Spanish Point. They were guided by Matheo, the other Guales, and/or the English runaways who knew the settlement's precise location. Dividing their forces into two bodies, the raiders came through the woods and entered the town through the cleared fields on its inland side. According to Dunlop, only half of the Scots' thirty fighting men were in the settlement, and they were "forced by their multitude to flee before we came to handy blowes." Although the defenders were able to load the three great guns in their fortifications, they were overwhelmed before they could fire them. As Dunlop and his companions fled into the woods, Cardross escaped by boat. The corsairs turned the cannons on Cardross but missed, and he made it safely to Charles Town, although with "much difficultie." Dunlop and six others remained in the woods for three nights, helplessly watching as the attackers plundered their goods and clothes, burned their houses and fences, killed their cattle and pigs, and carried off three of their people. One of the captives was a teenaged boy, John Livingston, a free settler whose father, James, was parish minister at Ancrum in Scotland. The other two were Dunlop's unnamed servants. The raiders even destroyed the squared cedar Dunlop had laid out for Skelmorlie's ship.[34]

Léon must have been disappointed by the slim pickings in Stuarts Town. After three days, he pressed northward to Edisto Island. This was a huge risk, because Edisto was in undisputed English territory, beyond the limits of his commission, and any plunder taken there could be seized by the Crown. Here again, Léon's English and Indigenous guides would have provided key information about the location and promise of Edisto's plantations, two of which belonged to Governor Morton. His large crew surely expected more for their troubles than Stuarts Town offered, and the prospect of stealing valuable African slaves would have been irresistible. Edisto did not let them down. The corsairs spent seven days there and plundered four plantations. At Morton's, they carried away eleven slaves and two servants, including Samuel Yankey, a young Englishman who had come to Carolina with Morton and served four years of a twelve-year indenture. At Paul Grimball's plantation, the raiders seized Kate Oats, the servant who had been spirited into servitude at age seven. For five days, Léon's crew plundered Grimball with impunity. They ate his bacon, smoked his tobacco, drank his rum, and seized his sugar, peas, corn, dried apples, salt, and spices. They carried off nails, tools, books, farm implements, cookware, clothes, candlesticks, bedding, leather goods, guns, and whatever furnishings they could carry. As they had done at Stuarts Town, the raiders burned his houses and fences, killed his hogs, scattered his herd of cattle, and destroyed forty acres of corn and thirty acres of peas. Grimball's detailed claim included one hundred sixty-two items totaling eleven hundred sixty-three pounds sterling. Nothing was too trivial to escape either the looters' grasp or Grimball's inventory, including his pewter mustard pot and candle snuffer dish, each valued at under three shillings.[35]

Charles Town was slow to respond to the Spanish attack. Cardross brought word to Governor Morton on August 20, three days after the attack on Stuarts Town. It took Morton three more days to meet with the Grand Council and mobilize militia units at Charles Town, Colleton, and James Island. On August 24, reports reached Morton that the Spaniards had five hundred men along with "2 or 3 great ships without the barr." This gross exaggeration frightened Morton into shoring up his defenses at Charles Town instead of ordering an immediate counterattack. He recruited Indian allies from the coastal towns and two days later ordered Stephen Bull to rendezvous with the southern militia and fall on the Spaniards at Edisto. Bull was delayed by a "wonderfully horrid and destructive" hurricane, for he did not leave Charles Town until August 29, one day after the corsairs had left the province. Although he had missed the enemy by two days, Bull found "severall markes of his malice," including the charred remains of an English prisoner. Thanks to Morton's hesitations, misinformation, and the weather, the raiders were allowed to plunder the province for eleven days with no opposition from the English or Scots.[36]

In the end, however, fate was not on the side of the invaders. Although the English were slow to respond, and although the Edisto plantations yielded all the plunder the raiders could have hoped for, the weather was against them. The August 26 hurricane destroyed the flagship and killed Léon along with Governor Morton's brother in-law, who was imprisoned aboard the vessel. The survivors salvaged what they could and burned the damaged ship along with the prisoner's corpse. With just two vessels available for the return trip, and burdened by their booty, they abandoned six of their Guale companions for lack of space, leaving them stranded in a colony they had just helped plunder. As the Guales made their way south in a makeshift canoe, they were captured by English traders returning from the interior with a sizeable cargo of furs: one hundred twenty deer skins, two hundred beaver and otter furs, and twenty bear skins. The traders threatened to kill their captives, although it is more likely that they planned to sell them in Charles Town. That night, however, the Guales secretly cut their bonds with an oyster shell, beat the English to death, and carried the skins and furs back to St. Augustine. They were intercepted by the returning corsairs who tried to add the English trade goods to their plunder. However, Márquez Cabrera intervened and allowed the Guales to keep the booty. At the same time, he seized the goods taken illegally from the Edisto plantations, which included eleven African slaves, an iron pot, a silver candlestick, and two boats. Ironically, the surviving commanders of the expedition returned to Havana with empty pockets, and the Guales they abandoned in Carolina made a handsome profit from the stolen furs.[37]

In December, Márquez Cabrera launched a second attack, this time targeting the Yamasees, who were unscathed by the August invasion. He brought together a motley and massive force made up of a few dozen Spaniards and an unspecified number of Natives, free Blacks, and mulattoes from St. Augustine, who sailed north in one of the galliots and two piraguas—small, dugout vessels with one mast. The governor also enlisted two hundred Apalachees and one hundred Timucuans to march overland as part of a joint operation. The raiders sacked and burned the Yamasee settlement on Santa Catalina de Guale. At Santa Elena, they killed Niquisalla, his son, and his nephew. Niquisalla was probably a prime target, for he had displayed his loyalty to the Spaniards when he alerted them about Altamaha's raid and then betrayed them by escorting Woodward into the interior. At Yamacraw on the Savannah, they took twenty-three Yamasee women captive—the precise number of female captives that the Yamasees had taken from Afuica (minus the two who escaped). The combined Spanish–Indian forces destroyed the livestock, fields, and settlements of the Yamasees from Santa Elena to Sapala. In addition to the twenty-three captives, they brought back thirty-seven fugitive Christian Indians along with six tons of corn and four hundred pounds of beans.[38]

In the short term, the attacks of 1686 were a triumph for Márquez Cabrera. Chastened, the Yamasee colonizers abandoned their settlements in Guale and consolidated their towns around the Ashepoo River in South Carolina, some thirty miles inland from Santa Elena. The death of Niquisalla and his son and nephew, both of whom had worked closely with him to mediate relations between Woodward and the inland peoples, would have jeopardized the Yamasees' prospects to act as middlemen in the Carolina–Apalachicola trade. The Scots were scattered and demoralized. Stuarts Town was in ruins. Dunlop estimated that his losses (combined with Skelmorlie's and Alexander Dunlop's) were between five hundred and six hundred pounds sterling and would come to much more if he was unable to resettle, replant, and recover his surviving cattle and pigs. For Carolina as a whole, Governor Morton claimed losses of twenty thousand pounds sterling and petitioned the king to demand "a speedy and full reparation" from Spain to prevent "the utter ruine of these His Majesties languishing supplicants."[39]

In the Chattahoochee towns, however, Matheos's scorched earth campaign backfired. It alienated the most powerful of the inland peoples and, as Leturiondo had predicted, sent them running to the English. The Scottish–Yamasee colonization of Port Royal and their violent run against the Timucuans thus created a dilemma for St. Augustine. Márquez Cabrera had to meet these provocations with force, but his ruthlessness did nothing to build relationships with Native peoples beyond the missions, who were key to colonizing the southeastern borderlands. Instead, it strengthened their ties to Charles Town and its traders, who viewed all Native people as prospective slaves.

Indeed, Charles Town was the biggest winner from the fallout over the Santa Catalina de Afuica raid. The Scots, Yamasees, and Apalachicola towns took the brunt of punishment from the Spaniards. Whatever threat Stuarts Town might still have posed to the English was eliminated after August 1686. By using the five Apalachicola captives as hostages to leverage trade and exploiting the rift between Altamaha and Niquisalla, the English sealed their partnership with the Yamasees and through them with the Chattahoochee towns and other inland peoples. In addition, the Lords Proprietors were discredited by their lackluster response to the Spanish attacks. Deeply dissatisfied with the leadership at Charles Town, the proprietors blamed the dealers in Indians for the attacks, claiming that they brought disaster on themselves by exporting Indian captives and entertaining pirates. As true as this was, it almost seemed as if the proprietors were siding with the Spaniards, as they refused to support any retaliatory measures. Their response gave Carolina's unruly rulers space to claim that the proprietors were blaming the victims, and it gave them leverage against the proprietors when they sent William Dunlop to take their case directly to the king.

RESOLVED UPON VENGEANCE

These long-term gains took time to unfold, however, and in the fall of 1686, they were far from evident to Carolina's leaders. These leaders instead saw gloom and doom. They complained of a "universall discontent and dejection of the Spiritts of most of the inhabitants" of the province. They were convinced that the one–two punch of the August attack and hurricane, in which "the hand of Almighty God seems to concurr with the Malice of our Enemies," would stymie immigration and "hasten our Ruin and desolation." Over the next four years, they made multiple attempts to get revenge on their Spanish enemies, recover their plundered property, and seek reparations for their losses. Ironically, William Dunlop, who was the biggest loser from Léon's invasion, rose to prominence as a result of it. Dunlop never lost hope. Driven by defending his honor as much as recovering his fortunes, he saw the destruction of the Scots' colony as a momentary setback, and he declared that he was "by all means endeavouring on resettling Stuarts Town at Port-Royal." In the meantime, he led two expeditions into Florida, one military and one diplomatic, and was eventually chosen to present Carolina's case to King William. Undaunted and resolute, Dunlop, like the English at Charles Town, found ways to turn his losses to his advantage.[40]

After its failed counterattack on the Spanish raiders, Charles Town laid plans to launch a retaliatory strike against St. Augustine and take back its plundered goods. Dunlop used his influence to push for this strike and claimed, against all precedent, that St. Augustine itself was "within the limits of this province." On October 15, the provincial parliament passed *An Act to Levy and Impresse Men, Arms etc. for the Defence of the Government*. This statute authorized the governor to grant commissions to pursue and destroy the enemy, whether within or beyond Carolina's borders. Dunlop estimated that five hundred men, including "the great pairt of the Gentry," would join the expedition, which would be led by Colonel John Godfrey and was planned for mid-November. He assured Skelmorlie that they would "either take St. Augustine from the Spaniards (and thereby clear all this pairt of the main of them) or lose our lives in so high a quarrel." In the meantime, the governor and council requested support from the Lords Proprietors. They wanted compensation for their losses and more funding for defense, including a warship and magazine. They also asked for letters of reprisal that would authorize the governor to grant commissions for privateers to attack Spanish ships. Dunlop likewise encouraged Skelmorlie and Lord Rosse, another investor who suffered major losses in the invasion, to use their influence at court to appeal to the king for letters of reprisal and marque.[41]

Godfrey, Dunlop, and company were disappointed. Before they could sail for St. Augustine, a new governor, James Colleton, arrived in Charles Town. He was brother to the proprietor Peter Colleton, and he was no friend of the provincial government that had so long frustrated the proprietors in London. Colleton put an immediate stop to all plans to retaliate against Florida. The proprietors gave him their full support. They reminded the Carolinians that the Fundamental Constitutions only allowed them to pursue an enemy beyond their borders in "the heat of victory." This did not extend to "granting Commissions and a deliberate making an invasive war upon the King of Spain's Subjects within his owne Territories." They vetoed the *Act to Levy and Impresse Men*, and they rebuked the provincial government for its reckless and irresponsible plans. "Noe Rationall man," they told the council, "can think that the Subjects of any Prince may be permitted without his leave or Consent to make war upon any of his Allyes for the Reparation of their private injuries or any other cause whatsoever." Privately, they congratulated Colleton for putting an end to such recklessness, which would have cost Morton and Godfrey their lives. They encouraged him instead to shore up Carolina's defenses, especially on its frontiers, and to send a civil letter to Governor Márquez Cabrera demanding an explanation for the attack.[42]

Colleton soon realized that he could not answer only to the proprietors and that he had to make concessions to the Carolinians who thirsted for revenge. Accordingly, in March 1687, he commissioned Dunlop to lead a reconnaissance expedition along the southern coast. Colleton ordered Dunlop to put up a series of beacons that would warn Carolina of any future Spanish attacks, and to recruit Yamasees to help erect and man the beacons. Dunlop interpreted his commission broadly—not just to erect beacons but also to "goe to the frontiers to see if the Spaniards were still lying within the province." On the basis of his later actions, Dunlop apparently hoped to provoke a Spanish attack. In this case, his commission allowed him to "pursue this said Enemy as far as Porta-Maria and St. Johns [present-day Jacksonville], to take kill and destroy the said Enemy" and to plunder its ships. This would allow him to avenge his honor and recoup a portion of his and his investors' losses, thus restoring their respect for him as their agent.[43]

The second attack had driven the Yamasees into Ashepoo, some thirty miles inland from the mouth of the river at St. Helena Sound. Limited to one piragua and a leaky boat commandeered from Woodward's estate, it took Dunlop nine days to reach their settlement. He was accompanied by thirty well-armed men with ample provisions, which made the desired impression on the Yamasees. They too were eager for Spanish blood and plunder, although they showed no enthusiasm for erecting, much less maintaining, beacons. Caleb Westbrooke was still living among them, and Dunlop pressed him into the expedition, along with George Smith, one of the few surviving Presbyterian radicals brought to Carolina as political prisoners in 1684. Altamaha agreed to join Dunlop and brought fifty-four Yamasees with him. They were later joined by a handful of Wimbees, so that, all together, they made up a force of one hundred, most of them equipped with firearms, traveling south along the inland passages in a dozen boats and canoes.[44]

Dunlop's journal of the expedition poignantly described the desolation of the lower Carolina and Georgia coasts after a quarter century of slave raids, pirate and corsair attacks, and dislocation. Carolina's coastal islands, once the site of thriving Escamaçu, Wimbee, Edisto, and Ospo villages, were now deserted. Stuarts Town remained in ruins. Dunlop could not even find stray cattle and pigs there to feed his men. The Indigenous settlement at Hilton Head, where hundreds of Yamasees had lived after migrating into the area in 1684, was abandoned, as was the Yamasee settlement at Yamacraw on the south side of the Savannah. Here, Spanish and Indian raiders had "killed & taken away" twenty-three Yamasee women and left behind two herds of cattle they had rustled from Port Royall. On Ossabaw Island, Yamasee hunters killed thirteen deer, yet another sign of the flight of human predators from the coast. Further south, Dunlop found only "the ruins of severall houses" in the "great Setle-ment" at the southern end of Santa Catalina Island, where sixty families had lived in and around the mission just eight years earlier. And at Sapala, the "very large plantations" were desolate. Like Santa Catalina, the Spaniards abandoned Sapala when they withdrew from Guale and consolidated their coastal missions southward. To prevent colonization by Scots and Yamasees, the corsairs burned

Sapala's orange groves, peach and fig trees, and the priest's house and garden with its artichokes and onions. They left behind only "the remains & rags of old clothes" they had plundered from Stuarts Town. After one hundred twenty years of Spanish and two decades of English colonization, the southeastern coast from Edisto to the St. Marys River, once home to dozens of Indigenous towns and thousands upon thousands of people, was completely depopulated.[45]

Although charged by Governor Colleton with erecting beacons, at no point in his southward voyage did Dunlop mention them. He was focused instead on finding Spaniards. Venturing as far south as present-day Cumberland Island, just north of the St. Marys River, Dunlop found what he was looking for: a lookout manned by a Spanish sentinel and four Natives. However, when he told Altamaha of his plan to storm the post to get intelligence from the sentinel, the Yamasee headman hesitated and made excuses. When Dunlop pressed him, Altamaha declared that "he wold not goe kill Spaniards for they had never killed any of his people." Frustrated and perplexed, Dunlop began to suspect that Altamaha had joined the expedition to betray the English into Spanish hands. "I expostulate with him his breach of promise his coming with me so far when all alongst I had told him we came to fight the Spaniard if we found them coming again," Dunlop wrote. "When he see me angry he then offered to go farther, but having discovered so much of his treachery . . . I resolved not to proceed any further." Both Dunlop and Altamaha were being disingenuous. Altamaha understood that finding a Spanish lookout sixty miles north of St. Augustine was not evidence that the Spaniards were "coming again" into Carolina and that Dunlop was grasping for a pretext to provoke a confrontation. Also, Dunlop must have wondered at how Altamaha was splitting hairs about "his people," given the murder of Niquisalla and his family, the destruction of the Yamasee towns, and the female captives taken from Yamacraw. Altamaha was clearly conflicted. He would have been foolhardy to betray the English and invite retaliation from Charles Town. At the same time, he obviously had no desire to risk another Spanish invasion for the sake of satisfying Dunlop's honor. Dunlop had misjudged him. As a result, the expedition, which lasted thirty-five days and took them three hundred miles through woods and rivers, was an unqualified failure.[46]

With their hopes of retaliating against St. Augustine dashed, the Carolinians turned to diplomacy to recover their losses and salvage what remained of their reputations. In the summer of 1688, Colleton dispatched Dunlop with an interpreter and twenty men to St. Augustine to demand satisfaction from the governor. Márquez Cabrera's turbulent rule had ended with his arrest the previous year, and he was replaced by Diego de Quiroga y Losado. Although the English knew little about the new governor, they hoped to work this change in leadership to their advantage by blaming the previous administration for the troubles between Florida and Carolina. This would keep Quiroga y Losado off the defensive and give him an honorable route to making reparations, which is all they reasonably expected.

After a series of miscues in his approach to the city, Dunlop presented his case to the governor. He spun a narrative of English good will and victimization. Although the Spaniards, under the orders of Márquez Cabrera and without the king of Spain's consent, had "hostilly invaded" Carolina and inflicted "Injuries and damages" on its inhabitants, King James had commanded his subjects "Inviolatly to preserve the peace and good amity" between Charles Town and St. Augustine. Besides stopping all plans for retaliation, James made every effort to suppress piracy in American waters, and he enjoined his Carolina subjects to do likewise. He even sent a whole "squadron of Shipps of Warr of his Royall Navye" to the West Indies to "exstirpate those Ravenous Beasts," the "sea Robbers." Dunlop's reference to the naval fleet was meant to intimidate more than reassure Quiroga y Losado. Because the raid on Carolina was undertaken without a commission from the Crown, Governor Colleton was authorized to settle matters with St. Augustine himself, and the Royal Navy, so Dunlop suggested, was at his disposal. The Carolinians demanded justice—the extradition of Márquez Cabrera to stand trial for murder in Charles Town or St. Augustine—but what they really wanted was reparations: fourteen thousand Spanish dollars (about forty-two hundred pounds sterling) plus the return of the five captive Whites and eleven slaves.[47]

Dunlop made no mention of the pirates entertained in both Charles Town and Stuarts Town, the Yamasee raid on Timucua, or the English intrusions into Apalachicola, and his plea for justice and compensation largely fell on deaf ears. Quiroga y Losado either would not or could not return the eleven slaves, but as a sign of good will, he did offer one concession: He would promise to purchase eleven other slaves—like the captives, consisting of three women and eight men—who had run away from Carolina and converted to Catholicism since coming to St. Augustine. Instead of fourteen thousand Spanish dollars, he would pay just sixteen hundred, or about four hundred eighty pounds sterling, for these men and women. This was a promise to pay, not an actual payment, and Dunlop planned to divide it between himself and the four owners of the fugitives when and if he received it. Significantly, Quiroga y Losado also gave "ample and full assurance" that future runaways would be "faithfully restored" to their English owners by the Spaniards. Dunlop could now leave Carolina satisfied that he got some concessions from Florida for his losses at Stuarts Town;

not much, to be sure, as the combined expeditions must have cost considerably more than the sixteen hundred Spanish dollars he was promised. Still, the expedition had at least salvaged his honor. He had boldly presented his demands to St. Augustine and done everything within his power to recoup the losses of his Scottish business partners. He and the government at Charles Town would now appeal to the British Crown for reparations.[48]

Although it failed to give full satisfaction, the expedition kept peace and amity between St. Augustine and Charles Town. However, it did so at the expense of Carolina's enslaved people, ultimately signaling to Carolina slaves and their owners that Florida would no longer be a safe haven for runaways. This was a major departure from nearly two decades of practice, and it was an indirect consequence of the raid on Stuarts Town. The illegal seizure of eleven slaves from Morton's plantation had put the Spaniards in a bind. Quiroga y Losado was forced to make concessions to Charles Town, so he offered to pay for the runaways and return fugitives in the future. Slaves in Carolina apparently heard only the first part of this agreement—that the Spanish governor would purchase their freedom if they escaped to Spanish Florida—because new groups of fugitives reached St. Augustine in 1688, 1689, and 1690. Quiroga y Losado wrote to Spain for direction on how to handle this crisis, and in 1693, the Crown replied that fugitive slaves who converted to Catholicism should be granted freedom and that their English owners should be compensated. The governor freed the slaves, but he neglected to pay the English. In 1697, the new governor, Laureano de Torres y Ayala, still had not paid Dunlop for the eleven runaways. That same year, seven new fugitives—six Africans and one Indian—escaped to Florida expecting to live as free people. Because he had not yet paid the outstanding debt to Dunlop, Torres y Ayala sent them back. He told the Crown that he could not afford to admit fugitives if he had to pay for them, as that would "become a trade contrary to His Majesty's will." Dunlop's deal with Quiroga y Losado first opened and then closed Florida's door to fugitive slaves. Thus, the colonization of Port Royal by Scots and Yamasees not only reignited the Indian slave trade but also closed a path to freedom for Carolina's enslaved people.[49]

Epilogue

UNFINISHED BUSINESS

Developments in Carolina and Britain gradually wore down Dunlop's resolu-
tion to rebuild Stuarts Town. As late as November 1686, three months after the
first attack, both he and Cardross remained committed to colonization and were
actively recruiting Huguenots for the settlement. However, when their wives
failed to join them in the spring of 1687, it became clear that Stuarts Town
would not be a settlement of families. Cardross abandoned the project and went
back to Scotland in July. By then, Dunlop had returned empty-handed from his
first expedition. He soon stopped speaking of rebuilding the colony, although he
still hoped to use his experience in Carolina for "settling another plantation."
Skelmorlie was not interested. As Dunlop's wife, Sarah, and his mother, Bessi,
reminded him, his associates in Scotland "have all quit thoughts of you" and
could not be counted on to give help "by men nor moni." Skelmorlie not only
refused to answer his bills but also criticized Dunlop's management of the plantation and blamed him for its failure. Having endured "privations," the death
of his servants, a ruinous attack, a month-long expedition through rivers and
woods in search of Spaniards, and even "ventur[ing] my life in settling a plantation," Dunlop was deeply wounded by his friend's betrayal. "I confesse I never
expected to be abused by Skelmorlie," he wrote. His final letters to Skelmorlie
were bitter and defensive.[1]

   Back in Scotland, conditions were improving for Presbyterians. After putting down the Monmouth–Argyll rebellion, James VII and II looked to shore
up his support in Scotland by issuing an indulgence for Presbyterian dissenters. In August 1687, Dunlop's mother wrote that Covenanting ministers were
freely preaching in homes (although not in churches) and exiled dissenters
were returning to Scotland. In this same period, Dunlop received a letter from
three nonconforming ministers, assuring him that the churches would soon be
open and imploring him to return and help with the work of the gospel. Sarah
shared more encouraging news six months later. "Our liberty continueth yet,"
she wrote, "and we are every day looking for an act of indemnity." By the time
her letter reached her husband, King James's Catholic wife had given birth to a

son. Faced with the prospect of a Roman Catholic succession, the English parliament ousted James and offered the throne to William of Orange and his wife
Mary, Protestant daughter to James by his first marriage. Scotland's parliament
soon followed suit, setting the stage for the abolition of episcopacy and restoration of presbyterianism to the Church of Scotland by 1690.[2]

More than the Spanish attacks, more even than the financial setbacks or
Stuarts Town's failure to retain colonists, these changing religious conditions in
Scotland convinced Dunlop to give up the project and go home. In May 1688,
he opened his mind in a letter to his cousins. He had come to Carolina in service to God and his countrymen. Providence had brought him safely there and
"preserved me here under an aboundance of disappointments and difficulties,"
and this made him loathe to abandon the place "for no more service than what I
have yet done."

> For no man is born for himself nor called to serve himselfe alone: this made
> me always more ready to serve others then myself and to imagine thet
> wherever I went there was something called for at my hand of service to
> thet place and those people where my Lot fell out to be; But . . . you need
> not doubt but the first and even remote prospect I have of being anyway
> Imployed especially in Scotland and so as to be serviceable to my generation
> will find welcome with me . . . . I assure you that no small matter would
> have kept me at such a distance from Sarah Carstairs all this time if I
> could but see hou to help it, but ane overruling hand [of providence] must
> be stoopt to.[3]

Dunlop returned to Britain just over a year later, and Stuarts Town was lost. It
failed in part because Lord Cardross's imperial ambitions outran his resources,
and he was unable to defend his settlement against Spanish reprisals for his attack on Santa Catalina de Afuica. In addition, his association with Altamaha
combined with circumstances beyond his control to place the lucrative Indian
trade in Henry Woodward's hands. Port Royal's high mortality also played
a role. It discouraged immigration, although not as much as the unfavorable
conditions back in Scotland. Indeed, Stuarts Town failed mainly because of the
disruptions of the killing times and, ironically, the triumph of religious toleration. The persecution of Presbyterians that drove colonization also ruined the
Carolina Company and discouraged investment and immigration, whereas
the return of religious freedom for Presbyterians in the late 1680s removed the
impetus for colonization. The timing for a new colony was all wrong; in some
sense, it was doomed to fail from its inception.[4] The Covenanters' errand to
Carolina, their plan to create a refuge for the true church where the gospel could

be preached in its purity and simplicity, turned out to be a fool's errand, and it was soon forgotten.[5]

But not by William Dunlop. Although his service to God in "thet place" was no longer required, Dunlop never stopped believing in Carolina. If he had set out to amass a fortune, Port Royal was "as fair and mor fair for it then any other I ever see, or if I desyned worldly greatnesse I may have more of it here than ever I could expect elsewhere." Carolina left its mark on him; it was a defining experience for him, a pivotal moment. "The experience I have got," he told Skelmorlie, "is worth all the money I have lost" from the Spanish attack. Service to his generation was only part of what drove Dunlop. The business of making plantations got into his blood, as it doubtless did for Cardross. Instead of cooling their heels in exile in Rotterdam or sleeping in the fields to avoid creditors and oath-takers, they were negotiating with exotic aboriginal peoples, poaching from the Spaniards, clearing forests, building empire, and having the adventure of a lifetime. Dunlop did not forget Stuarts Town.

Nor was he done with colonization schemes. In the late 1690s, Dunlop was one of the largest shareholders in the Company of Scotland Trading to Africa and the Indies. He took a lead role in promoting the company's scheme to colonize the Isthmus of Darien (Panama), convert its Native people to Christianity, and make Scotland rich by monopolizing trade between the Atlantic and Pacific at the expense of Spain. Unlike Stuarts Town, Darien was a high-profile venture, meticulously planned and well funded, that captured the imagination and much of the money of Scotland. It absorbed half the nation's coinage, with subscriptions amounting to more than four times the national government's revenues. Unfortunately, like Stuarts Town, the settlement was in territory claimed by Spain, and the colonizing plan was built on a combination of faulty assumptions and wishful thinking. The site was environmentally unsustainable, the Native Tule Indians had complex ties to the Spaniards, the English secretly undermined the colony, and over a thousand colonists died of tropical diseases and shipwreck. Darien failed spectacularly and was overtaken by Spanish forces in early 1700.

The Darien venture bankrupted Scotland and forced Scots to accept an English bailout. This set the stage for the union of Scottish and English parliaments, which put an end to Scottish sovereignty in 1707. Dunlop and Stuarts Town bear a part, if only a tiny part, of the blame for this unfortunate series of events. The Darien project was Dunlop's "constant preoccupation" in the last years of his life. It was more unfinished business that would compensate for the failure of Stuarts Town, and he poured his energy and much of his money into it. He died in March 1700, just months before news of Darien's collapse reached Scotland.

Ironically, one of the few survivors of the venture, the Reverend Archibald Stobo, washed up in Carolina when the venture's flagship, the *Rising Sun*, wrecked in Charles Town harbor during a storm. Stobo made Carolina his home, and over the course of his long career, he remained a bitter opponent of Carolina's Anglican establishment while planting multiple Presbyterian churches in the lowcountry, some of which became the earliest slave-owning congregations in the colonial southeast. No one did more than Stobo to fix religious dissent on the provincial landscape or wed it more perfectly to the plantation regime.[6]

When he left Carolina, Dunlop had been commissioned by the government in Charles Town to petition the king for reparations for the Spanish attack. Instead of returning directly to Scotland he sailed to London, where he spent at least four months in late 1689 and early 1690. During this time, he drafted an extraordinary document, *Proposalls for the propagating of the Christian Religion, and converting of Slaves whether Negroes or Indians in the English plantations.* The circumstances surrounding this document are murky, but it was probably written at the request of English reformers. These would have included the scientist and philanthropist Robert Boyle, who made multiple copies of it, and possibly the Anglican missionary Morgan Godwyn, who had spent time in Virginia and Barbados and was Britain's foremost advocate for baptizing slaves. Boyle and his friends were promoting a parliamentary bill that would remove obstacles to Christianizing enslaved people. In their view, the chief obstacle was the opposition of slave owners, who claimed that the law did not allow them to enslave Christians and that baptism would require manumission. Dunlop had gone to Carolina with the dream of converting Native people to Christianity. Like the vision for a religious refuge, this dream died hard in Carolina. Perhaps the *Proposalls* represented a last attempt to redeem it, an opportunity to wrap up more unfinished business. Although Dunlop had no standing in England's parliament and no stated desire to push for such reforms in Scotland, he shared an interest in spreading the gospel throughout the empire, and he would have gladly agreed to lend his ideas to Boyle's project.[7]

Dunlop's *Proposalls* consisted of ten items intended to create the optimum conditions for slave conversions. Like similar proposals from the seventeenth century, these guaranteed that conversion would in no way alter the status of the enslaved. The first item called for "a law declaring that no slave upon his professing of the Christian Religion shall thereby be freed of that Service he oweth to his Master; but that he and his posterity shall remain in the same Condition of perpetuall service and under the same dominion to his Master as before, except in so far as by Law is provided for." This was meant to promote Christianization by assuring slaveholders, in no uncertain terms, that their

Portrait of William Dunlop (1654–1700), unknown artist. This portrait probably dates from the 1690s, when Dunlop was Principal of the University of Glasgow. © CSG CIC Glasgow Museums Collection.

Christian slaves would have no legal claim whatsoever to freedom. It fell in line perfectly with Boyle's legislative agenda. However, unlike other proposals from the era, Dunlop's then sought to undo almost everything the first provision guaranteed. It gave enslaved Christians the right to their lives and property, provided safeguards against abuse and overwork and protection for their families, and acknowledged the validity of their testimony given under oath. It not only allowed enslaved people to receive instruction but legally obligated slave owners to "take some suitable care to cause instruct, and Catechize their slaves in the principles of the Christian religion." It even promoted emancipation by suggesting that charitable contributions be used to purchase the freedom of the "most serious of Christian slaves." Thus, the proposals affirmed slavery while stripping away many of its enslaving principles. Daring to imagine enslaved people living authentic Christian lives, they adopted the perspective of the enslaved, treating them as free agents in their own conversion, not merely as recipients of baptism. Giving enslaved Christians power over their lives, property, work, and families along with a potential pathway to freedom, they envisioned a framework for Christian slavery that bordered on antislavery.

Such radical proposals had little value to moderate reformers such as Boyle, but they say a great deal about Dunlop, and they embody the frustrations, hesitancies, and shattered religious vision of his Carolina colony. Dunlop was shaped by a religious culture that was fiercely protective of its liberties and its church's autonomy. This tradition associated Roman Catholicism, which it considered anti-Christian, with tyranny and slavery. It insisted that liberty—a great deal of liberty—was necessary to live an authentic Christian life. These beliefs and associations were reinforced by the hard experience of a quarter-century of persecution under the Stuarts. At the same time, Dunlop was principal manager of a colony whose survival, along with the preservation of the religious liberties the colony was designed to protect, depended on the exploitation of a variety of enslaved people. During his stay in Carolina, he personally experienced the many ways slavery and Christianity were entangled. He went as a missionary to Native people but ended up enslaving them. He colluded with pagan Yamasees to kill and capture Christian Timucuans and then sold those captives as slaves to pirates and West Indian planters. He intercepted and re-enslaved runaways who were fleeing Protestant Carolina for freedom in Catholic Florida. He sailed to St. Augustine and demanded the return of slaves who had converted to Catholicism. He bound imprisoned Covenanters to service for Stuarts Town, and when they died, he urged Skelmorlie to buy Africans from Barbados for enslavement in Scottish Carolina. The paradoxical proslavery/antislavery Christianity envisioned in the *Proposalls* reflects Dunlop's deep ambivalence, which was shaped by his experience as a second-generation Covenanter, minister of the gospel, colonial administrator, and enslaver.

Dunlop did not join the English reformers in their campaign to convert the enslaved people of the British empire to Christianity. Instead, he accepted an appointment from King William as principal of the University of Glasgow. This was much more than he expected, and he owed it largely to the advocacy of his brother in-law, William Carstares, who was close to the king. The king was also indebted to Dunlop for his role in exposing the Montgomery Plot, named after Dunlop's old friend, James Montgomery of Skelmorlie. Embittered at being denied a major post after the settlement of 1689, Skelmorlie conspired with Jacobites to oust William and return James Stuart to the throne. One of Skelmorlie's co-conspirators confessed the plot to Dunlop, who reported it to the king, who, in turn, rewarded him with the principalship. It was a stable and lucrative post where Dunlop had full range to exercise his passion for service.[8] His fellow colonizer Lord Cardross also took care of unfinished business and prospered under William. He raised a regiment of cavalry to enforce William's settlement and served on the king's council and the Scottish Privy Council, the very body that had imprisoned him and seized parts of his estate a decade earlier. Cardross remained a staunch Presbyterian and foe of English hegemony until his death in 1693.[9] James Montgomery of Skelmorlie fled to France, where he died in 1694.

Dunlop's departure, according to his friend John Stewart, struck Carolinians with "a deep sense of loss" and great "greiff and concerne for the absence of one so usefull to the publick." However, the failure of Stuarts Town itself was hardly noticed in Charles Town. Britain and Spain were at peace with one another throughout the 1690s, putting a temporary stop to overt hostilities between Carolina and Florida. English planters got the message from the attacks of 1686, and fifteen years passed before they took up land again in the contested territory of Port Royal. Yet Spanish violence did not deter English trade with the Native peoples of the interior. When Woodward died shortly after returning from his visit to Apalachicola in 1686, there was no shortage of traders to take his place, and they continued to traffic in deer skins, guns, and Indian captives. John Stewart traded with Cusseta for two years and went deeper still into the interior, two hundred forty miles further than Woodward had gone, to open trade between Carolina and the Chickasaw towns. George Smith, the exiled Covenanter who came to Port Royal in chains, moved in with the Yamasees after the destruction of Stuarts Town and apprenticed under Caleb Westbrooke. Smith returned from Apalachicola in 1690 with twenty-eight hundred dressed skins, four hundred of which he kept as his commission. Accompanied by the micos of Cusseta and Coweta, Smith reinvented himself as a trader and diplomat, according to Stewart, and "now forsooth he dyns when here with the governor." Trading was dangerous work—Stewart was attacked by Spaniards and their Indigenous allies, and Westbrooke was murdered by a Savannah in 1693—but the profits were irresistible. The high financial and diplomatic stakes that came with the Indian trade also guaranteed that power struggles would continue between the Goose Creek men and the Lords Proprietors. Unable to ever really establish their authority, the proprietors continued to lose ground to provincial officials in the 1690s and after, until the proprietary government was finally overthrown in 1719.[10]

The Indigenous people of the Carolina coast continued to decline. The Westo invasion had forced them to welcome instead of resist English colonization. Their populations dwindled. In the north, the Kiawahs, Winyahs, Stonos, and Kussos were crowded out by English planters, enslaved by the Savannahs, and stripped of their autonomy as they came under the so-called protection of Charles Town. In the south, Escamaçu had been overrun by the Ospos and then by the Yamasees. In 1684, the Escamaçu remnant at St. Helena along with their neighbors—Wimbee, Edisto, Kussah, and Combahee—had ceded their lands to make room for the Scots. In 1695, the province officially reduced them to tributary status. "Whereof they have not been hitherto any ways useful or serviceable, or contributing to the inhabitants of this province more than they have been particularly and specially rewarded for," according to the provincial parliament, the settlement Indians (which did not include the Yamasees) would henceforth be required to bring in one skin of a beast of prey per man each year. Any hunter who failed to comply was to be "upon his bare back severely whipt in sight of the inhabittants of the saide towne."

Nor was this the final humiliation. In 1707, they were given a new name. In an effort to rein in abusive traders, the assembly passed a law regulating trade with "any Indians whatsoever (except those commonly called Cusabes, viz. Santees, Ittavans, Seawees, Stoanoes, Kiawaws, Kussos, Edistoes, St. Helenas)." Unlike other forms of convenient shorthand that the English used—"our neigh-boring Indians," "settlement Indians," or simply "our Indians" (as distinct from Spanish-allied Indians, though the implied ownership was no accident)—Cusabo at least had the advantage of sounding like something they might call themselves. They did not, but the name stuck and has persisted into the present. It was an unthinking decision, a throwaway shorthand for a powerless people who were a burden on the province and whose names were no longer worth the trouble of enumerating. As such, it signified how far they had fallen, and it rep-resented another step toward the settler colonial erasure of the coastal peoples.[11]

In the meantime, the Apalachicola towns completed their turn away from Florida and toward Carolina. In 1689, the Spaniards built a fort near Coweta to keep the English out of the province and manned it with Apalachee warriors. The towns seemed to acquiesce, but two years later, they abandoned the Chat-tahoochee valley, migrating to Ochese Creek near the Ocmulgee River in central Georgia. This put them closer to Charles Town and beyond the reach of St. Augustine. Their exodus was led by Coweta and Cusseta, and their micos' em-bassy to Charles Town with George Smith in 1690 was meant to declare it. The Ochese Creek settlement became a magnet for Native people throughout the region, including the Sabacolas, Tallapoosas, Cherokees, and some Yamasees. The English referred to the Ochese people as Creeks, and the settlement became the nucleus of a new Indian confederation that would play a major political, economic, and military role in the region through the era of the American Revolution. Other Apalachicola peoples moved further south into the Savannah drainage, positioning themselves strategically between the Yamasees and the declining Timucuan towns.[12]

The Spanish–Indian attack of November 1686 had driven the Yamasees inland to the Ashepoo River, where Dunlop found them in 1687 as he gathered recruits for his first expedition. With the death of Niquisalla and his heirs, Altamaha had few, if any, rivals among the remaining micos. This was reflected in their shifting settlement patterns. Around 1690, the Yamasees returned to Port Royal, where they eventually established ten semiautonomous towns in two clusters. The Lower Towns all derived from the old Tama chiefdom and included both Yamasees who had migrated from the coast with Altamaha as well as migrants from the interior. Their chief town was named Altamaha, indicating that Altamaha the man had brought some unity to the disparate Yamasees and that they recognized, at some level, his primacy as mico, as did the authorities in Charles Town, who worked exclusively through him after the death of Niquisalla. In 1690, Altamaha made a seven-year contract with Governor Colleton to provide three hundred paid Yamasee laborers to produce silk and cotton (it is not known what became of this arrangement, although it probably fell through when Colleton was replaced and arrested later that year). He was still alive and well in 1702, when his actions in battle demonstrated the strength of his bonds with his people. That year, the Yamasees joined Governor James Moore on an assault against St. Augustine. Although Moore's forces heavily outnumbered the Spaniards, the expedition failed. As Moore burned his ships and fled over land, Altamaha stayed behind to cover the retreat. When the English urged him to run, Altamaha mocked Moore, declaring that "though your Governour leaves you, I will not stir until I have seen all my Men before me." Altamaha was careful with the lives of his people. He refused to put them at risk when Dunlop tried to strongarm him into attacking the Spanish sentry in 1687, and now he jeopardized his own safety to guarantee theirs, thereby earning their trust and respect. As he aged, he evolved into a white chief. By the 1710s, as relations between Yamasees and English traders deteriorated, Altamaha was using every means to strengthen diplomatic ties, not only with Charles Town but directly with London itself.[13]

At Port Royal, the Yamasees achieved what the Scots could not: they built communities. Their settlements reflected their Mississippian roots and resembled those of the coastal Indigenous people they had supplanted. The towns were fairly small, containing, on average, about eighteen houses and perhaps one hundred thirty people. They lived in round houses occupied by families of seven to nine people each. These houses were dispersed throughout the settlement, leaving plenty of room for gardens, corn fields, and open spaces for processing animal hides. Families remained close to their dead; they buried them within the walls of their houses, placing the bodies in flexed or fetal positions. There is some evidence that the Yamasees, like Escamaçu, built large, round council houses and that Altamaha lived in one atop a ceremonial mound. Like their ancestors, the South Carolina Yamasees continued to grow and gather native plants and eat wild game, fish, and shellfish for their sustenance. As they had done in Florida, Carolina Yamasees resisted Christianization (with one important exception, discussed later)—although admittedly, the English made little effort to convert them. They were a rootless people with a portable religion. Perhaps their ancestral gods traveled with them, making sacred the woods and rivers as Escamaçu had done in its myths and Orista in its worship of Toya.[14]

Yet Yamasees were not stubborn traditionalists; they were adaptive, and their culture reflected the changing world they co-created and inhabited. Alongside traditional foods, they consumed poultry, pork, and beef. Most of the mortuary objects buried with their dead were trade goods, including English pipes, beads, and rum bottles. They added new functional elements to their ceramics, such as strap handles on pots, as well as new decorative motifs. In the locations of their towns, archaeologists have recovered significantly more musket balls and flints than arrow points and projectiles, pointing to Yamasees' growing dependence on firearms and their deep entrenchment in the slave trade. Despite their proximity to Charles Town, their regular contact with English traders and diplomats, and the exposure to Old World diseases that resulted from it, the Yamasees maintained and possibly even increased their population between 1685 and 1715. This was surely due, in part, to their adoption of captives and their willingness to make room for newcomers in their settlements.[15] They also used Christianity to their advantage. In 1702, the Euhaws, a branch of Yamasees who had lived for more than a century among the Spanish missions of Timucua, migrated to Port Royal and settled among the Lower Towns. In 1713, Altamaha sent a Christian Euhaw "prince" to London to strengthen diplomatic ties with England. Like the Orista cacique who negotiated with Pedro Menéndez over one hundred fifty years earlier, the Yamasees understood the diplomatic currency of Christianity, and they used it, or tried to use it, to their advantage. Although this diplomatic overture failed, it was one of many adaptive strategies through which the Yamasees sustained themselves as they clung to their autonomy. Their dependency on trade was destabilizing, but they were not a colonized people. They were a hybrid and adaptive people who resisted acculturation and conquest. They lived in a world of their own making, a world that belonged to Yamasees as much as English.[16]

From Port Royal, Ochese Creek, and the lower Savannah River, Indigenous slavers launched raids against Spanish mission towns throughout the 1690s. In 1691, they attacked the Timucuan mission of San Juan de Guacara, which never recovered. In 1694, they raided Chacata, and in 1702, they attacked Santa Fé in Timucua as well as mission towns in Apalachee. As the Yamasees had done at

Santa Catalina de Afuica, the raiders burned the towns, plundered the missions, killed resisters, and herded women and children into slavery. The English traders who bought these captives did not share the Lords Proprietors' qualms over the "pernicious Inhumane barbarous practice" of enslaving and exporting Native people. Instead, they competed for opportunities to ply their Indian suppliers with guns and European goods. This only drove them deeper into debt and fueled more raids for more slaves.[17]

Queen Anne's War, which lasted from 1702 to 1713, renewed hostilities between Britain and Spain and escalated violence and slaving in the Anglo–Spanish borderlands. This war was the pretext for James Moore's failed assault on St. Augustine in 1702. Two years later, Moore recruited fifteen hundred Creeks and Yamasees and laid waste to Apalachee Province. It was a campaign of unprecedented carnage. The raiders killed hundreds, captured a thousand, and displaced thousands more. At the town of Abuyale, they burned and mutilated sixteen prisoners, cutting out their eyes, ears, and tongues. As the English and their allies destroyed their towns, Apalachee and Timucuan refugees fled to deep south Florida to avoid death and capture. As a result of these slaving expeditions, the Christian Indian population of La Florida plummeted, from twenty-five thousand in the mid-seventeenth century to just four hundred in 1706. The Spanish mission system collapsed.[18]

As it had done with the Westos, the slave trade now began to devour the enslavers. Queen Anne's War exhausted the supply of captives from Florida, leaving the Yamasees in particular with few options for discharging their debts to English traders. Tensions over trade dependency and debt were compounded by encroachment and trade abuses. After 1700, Carolina planters began taking up land in Port Royal, and within a decade they were edging onto Yamasee lands. The provincial government was unwilling to rein in White settlers, just as they were unable to effectively regulate the Indian trade or discipline violent traders. In 1715, these tensions reached a breaking point. When a delegation of English traders threatened to kill their headmen and enslave their people, the Yamasees lashed out, murdering the traders and sparking a war that engulfed the entire region. Catawbas, Cherokees, Upper and Lower Creeks, Choctaws, and others combined forces and fought the British on two fronts. They killed traders, burned plantations, and carried off captives. In terms of breadth and ferocity, the region had seen nothing like the Yamasee War since the Escamaçu War of the 1570s. Over time, the British wore down Indian resistance and broke the pan-Indian alliance by making separate treaties with the Catawbas, Cherokees, and Creeks. The Yamasees fought on, but they were forced out of Carolina.

Renewing their friendship with their enemies in St. Augustine, they returned at last to Spanish Florida.[19]

None of this was inevitable. Not the desolation of the Spanish mission towns. Not the displacement of the Yamasees or the migration of the Apalachicola peoples. Not the destruction of Stuarts Town. Not the shattering of the Indigenous societies in the southeast. Not even a form of chattel slavery that affirmed enslaved people as children of God but denied their humanness. To be sure, capitalism and kinship created a context that was favorable to the commercialization of the captive trade. The lure of prestige goods was powerful, all the more so because English goods, unlike those of the Spaniards, did not come with Christian missionaries, an important consideration for Yamasees and Creeks who clung to their traditional gods. Yamasee culture did not obligate them to treat non-kin humanely or see them as persons, just as Christian culture did not stop English traders and planters from treating Indians as commodities. At another time, the power and security that came with English guns might have been a factor, but from the vantage point of 1684, there was no clear regional threat to Yamasee security. The destruction of the Westos put a halt to the captive trade. The Savannahs were not strong enough to meet English demand, and the proprietors were taking extraordinary steps to isolate the dealers in slaves and end the export of Indian captives. However, the dual migration of Scots and Yamasees to Port Royal created a highly unstable moment. Competition between Scots and English, on the one hand, and red and white Yamasee headmen on the other triggered the slave raid on Santa Catalina de Afuica, and the region pivoted. Woodward teamed up with Niquisalla, who brokered the English trade agreement with the Chattahoochee towns. From there, the dominos fell: the destruction of Stuarts Town, Matheos's punitive expedition against Apalachicola, the migration to Ochese Creek, and the rekindling of the commercial Indian slave trade.

Notes

INTRODUCTION: CAROLINA'S LOST COLONY FOUND

1. John H. Hann, *The History of the Timucua Indians and Missions* (Gainesville, FL: University of Florida Press, 1996), 273; Amy Turner Bushnell, "Living at Liberty: The Ungovernable Yamasees of Spanish Florida," in Denise I. Bossy, ed. *The Yamasee Indians: From Florida to South Carolina* (Lincoln: University of Nebraska Press, 2018), 36; "The Examacon of several Yamasse Indians whose spokesman Caruse one of their Cassiques declared," in Alexander S. Salley, ed. *Records in the British Public Record Office Relating to South Carolina, 1685–1690* (Atlanta, GA: Historical Commission of South Carolina, 1929), 2: 66 [hereinafter *RBPRO*]; "Dr. Henry Woodward to Deputy Governor John Godfrey," in *Calendar of State Papers, Colonial Series, America and the West Indies, Volume 12, 1685–1688*, ed. J. W. Fortescue (London: HMSO, 1898), 83 [hereinafter *CSPC*]; "Questioning of a Guale Indian Returned from English Territory to His Native Guale, December 29, 1685," Antonio Matheos Documents, Phase III, John H. Hann Collection of Colonial Records, P.K. Yonge Library. Gainesville: University of Florida, 37–39; Antonio Matheos to Márquez Cabrera, San Luis, May 21, 1686, Matheos Documents, Phase IV, 71; John Worth, *The Struggle for the Georgia Coast* (Tuscaloosa: University of Alabama Press, 2007), 140–41.

2. I use the name "Port Royal" rather loosely to refer to the rivers, islands, coastal mainland, inlets, and sounds from Edisto Island in the north to Hilton Head Island in the south. Present-day Beaufort is at the approximate center of this area, as was seventeenth-century Stuarts Town.

3. Readers who are interested in this transformation should see Eric E. Bowne, "From Westo to Comanche: The Role of Commercial Indian Slaving in the Development of Colonial North America," in *Linking the Histories of Slavery: North America and Its Borderlands,* eds. Bonnie Martin and James F. Brooks (Santa Fe, NM: School for Advanced Research, 2015), 35–62; Alejandra Dubcovsky, *Informed Power: Communication in the Early American South* (Cambridge, MA: Harvard University Press, 2016); Christina Snyder, *Slavery in Indian Country: The Changing Face of Captivity in Early America* (Cambridge, MA: Harvard University Press, 2010); Robbie Ethridge and Charles Hudson, eds., *The Transformation of the Southeastern Indians, 1540–1760* (Jackson: University Press of Mississippi, 2002); and Robbie Ethridge and Sheri M. Shuck-Hall, eds., *Mapping the Mississippian Shatter Zone: The Colonial Indian Slave Trade and Regional Instability in the American South* (Lincoln: University of Nebraska, 2009).

4. Previous scholarship on the colonization of Stuarts Town/Port Royal has been fragmentary. For the most important recent works, see Linda G. Fryer, "Documents Relating to the Formation of the Carolina Company in Scotland, 1682," *South

Carolina Historical Magazine 99, no. 2 (April 1998), 110–34; Peter N. Moore, "Scotland's Lost Colony Found: Rediscovering Stuarts Town, 1682–88," *Scottish Historical Review*, XCIX, 1, no. 249 (April 2020): 26–50; L. H. Roper, *Conceiving Carolina: Proprietors, Planters, and Plots, 1662–1719* (New York: Palgrave-Macmillan, 2004), 75–92; Amy Turner Bushnell, *Situado and Sabana: Spain's Support System for the Presidio and Mission Provinces of Florida* (New York: Anthropological Papers of the American Museum of Natural History, 1994), 166–69; Worth, *Struggle*, 45–47; and Alan Gallay, *The Indian Slave Trade: The Rise of the English Empire in the American South, 1670–1717* (New Haven, CT: Yale University Press, 2002), 71–88.

5. This book stands on the shoulders of a quarter-century of scholarship on the Indigenous history of the colonial southeast. I am particularly indebted to multiple works by John E. Worth, especially *Struggle for the Georgia Coast*; Bushnell, *Situado and Sabana*; Joseph M. Hall, *Zamumo's Gift: Indian-European Exchange in the Colonial Southeast* (Philadelphia: University of Pennsylvania Press, 2012); Steven C. Hahn, *The Invention of the Creek Nation, 1670–1763* (Lincoln: University of Nebraska Press, 2014); Gallay, *Indian Slave Trade*; multiple works by Denise I. Bossy, all of them cited in the following chapters, especially *Yamasee Indians*; and an older but eminently useful ethnography by Gene Waddell, *Indians of the South Carolina Lowcountry, 1562–1751* (Columbia: University of South Carolina Southern Studies Program, 1980).

6. "Mr. Carteret's Relation of their Planting on Ashley River '70," in *Narratives of Early Carolina, 1650–1708*, ed. Alexander S. Salley Jr. (New York: Charles Scribner's Sons, 1911), 118.

7. Robert M. Weir, *Colonial South Carolina: A History* (Columbia: University of South Carolina Press, 1997); Roper, *Conceiving Carolina*; John J. Navin, *The Grim Years: Settling South Carolina, 1670–1720* (Columbia: University of South Carolina Press, 2020). For a more mixed and balanced perspective, see Michelle LeMaster and Bradford J. Wood, eds., *Creating and Contesting Carolina: Proprietary Era Histories* (Columbia: University of South Carolina Press, 2013).

8. *RPBRO*, 293; Testimony of John Mathieson, MS 2832, National Library of Scotland, Edinburgh, Scotland [hereinafter NLS] (quotation). On the miseries of early Carolina see Navin, *The Grim Years*, 1–15, 45–94.

PROLOGUE: THE INDIGENOUS WORLD
OF THE LOWER CAROLINA COAST

1. "Dr. Henry Woodward to John Locke, 12 November 1675," in *The Correspondence of John Locke: Volume One: Introduction, Letters Nos. 1–461*, ed. E. S. DeBeer (Oxford: Oxford University Press, 1976), 305 (origin story); Hall, *Zamumo's Gift*, 2 (feathers). For a reading of the Escamaçu origin story that places it in the context of the disruptions of the Westo slaving era, see Denise I. Bossy, "Yamasee Mobility: Mississippian Roots, Seventeenth-Century Strategies," in *Contact, Colonialism and Native Communities in the Southeastern United States*, eds. Edmond A. Boudreaux III, Maureen Meyers, and Jay K. Johnson (Gainesville: University of Florida Press, 2020), 204–5.

2. On the centrality of towns and local identity to southeastern Indians in the late Mississippian, contact, and early colonial eras, see Joshua Piker, *Okfuskee: A Creek Indian Town in Colonial America* (Cambridge, MA: Harvard University Press, 2006), 7–10; Hall, *Zamumo's Gift*, 6–7; and Hahn, *Invention of the Creek Nation*, 5–8, 20.

3. The coastal peoples' words for "headman" and "headwoman" have not survived, so I follow the lead of both Spanish and English sources in using *cacique* and *cacica*, which are derived from Taino, a Caribbean language. Unfortunately, these terms do not capture the distinctions that the coastal peoples made among their leaders, which the English differentiated with words such as "queen," "chieftain," "cacique," and "captain." However, the common use of *cacique* and *cacica* by Europeans over the course of a century suggests that these terms were accepted by Native people, even if they proved inadequate to describe their political organization. See Waddell, *Indians of the South Carolina Lowcountry*, 29–33, 262. The Muskogean word *mico*, which scholars use to refer to headmen of Muskogean-speaking peoples, is not apt for the coastal peoples, who spoke a different language. See Denise I. Bossy, "Spiritual Diplomacy, the Yamasees, and the Society for the Propagation of the Gospel," *Early American Studies* 12, no. 2 (Spring 2014), 377.

4. On the history and ethnography of the coastal towns, see especially Chester B. DePratter, "Irene and Altamaha Pottery from the Charlesfort/Santa Elena Site, Parris Island, South Carolina," in *From Santa Elena to St. Augustine: Indigenous Ceramic Variability, A.D. 1400–1700*, eds. Kathleen Deagan and David Hurst Thomas (New York: Anthropological Papers of the American Museum of Natural History, 90, August 26, 2009): 19–47; Worth, *Struggle*; Karen Lynn Paar, "'To Settle Is to Conquer': Spaniards, Native Americans, and the Colonization of Santa Elena in Sixteenth Century Florida" (PhD dissertation, University of North Carolina–Chapel Hill, 1999); Gene Waddell, "Cusabo," in *Handbook of North American Indians: Volume 14: Southeast*, ed. Raymond J. Fogelson (Washington, DC: Smithsonian Institution, 2004), 254–64; Waddell, *Indians of the South Carolina Lowcountry*; and Bushnell, *Situado and Sabana*. On the culture and social organization of southeastern Natives in general, see Charles M. Hudson, *The Southeastern Indians* (Knoxville: University of Tennessee Press, 1976).

5. Paar makes a similar argument about integrating Santa Elena; see "'To Settle Is to Conquer,'" 7. For a similar Indigenous perspective on Spanish colonization in a different context, see Juliana Barr, *Peace Came in the Form of a Woman: Indians and Spaniards in the Texas Borderlands* (Chapel Hill: University of North Carolina Press, 2007), 3. On reframing the idea of rebellion, see Robin A. Beck Jr., Christopher B. Rodning, and David G. Moore, "Limiting Resistance: Juan Pardo and the Shrinking of Spanish Florida," in *Enduring Conquests: Rethinking the Archaeology of Resistance to Spanish Colonialism in the Americas*, eds. Matthew Liebmann and Melissa S. Murphy (Santa Fe, NM: School for Advanced Research Press, 2011), 19–39. For a general framework that highlights Indian power, see Pekka Hämäläinen, "Shapes of Power: Indians, Europeans, and North American Worlds from the Seventeenth to the Nineteenth Century," in *Contested Spaces of Early America*, eds. Juliana Barr and Edward Countryman (Philadelphia: University of Pennsylvania Press, 2014), 31–68.

6. Archaeologists have not found these sixteenth-century towns, so their locations must be reconstructed using contemporary maps and written records. The two foremost scholars generally agree on the relative proximity of the towns to one another, although they differ in some important details. Charles M. Hudson places all of the principal towns directly inland from Port Royal, more or less along the Salkehatchie River; Hudson, *The Juan Pardo Expeditions: Explorations of the Carolinas and Tennessee, 1566–1568* (Tuscaloosa, AL: University of Alabama Press, 2005), 33. Waddell locates Escamaçu further south and Caçao much further north along the Santee; "Cusabo," 255–58. The remaining three towns were Ahoya, Stalame, and Mayon.

7. Victor D. Thompson et al., "The Archaeology and Remote Sensing of Santa Elena's Four Millennia of Occupation," *Remote Sensing* 10, no. 2 (February 2018), 9; Brad Botwick, "Prehistoric Settlement and Land Use in the Sea Islands: Archaeological Investigations at a Multi-Component Interior Site on Port Royal Island, South Carolina," *South Carolina Antiquities* 40 (2008), 18–19; Michael Trinkley, *Further Investigations of Prehistoric and Historic Lifeways on Callawassie and Spring Islands, Beaufort County, South Carolina* (Columbia, SC: Chicora Foundation, Inc., 1991), 216–17; James L. Michie, "The Daws Island Shell Midden: Cultural Diversity on the Lower South Carolina Coast During the Late Archaic Period," *South Carolina Antiquities* 32 (2000), 32; Mark J. Brooks et al., "Modeling Subsistence Change in the Late Prehistoric Period in the Interior Lower Coastal Plain of South Carolina," *Anthropological Studies* 7 (1984), 11–13; Juan Rogel, "Rogel's Account of the Florida Mission," in John Dawson Gilmary Shea, *The Historical Magazine, and Notes and Queries Concerning the Antiquities, History and Biography of America*, V, no. 11 (November 1861), 329; J. Michael Francis and Kathleen Kole, *Murder and Martyrdom in Spanish Florida: Don Juan and the Guale Uprising of 1597* (Washington, DC: American Museum of Natural History, 2011), 119; R[obert] F[erguson], *The Present State of Carolina, with Advice to Settlers* (London, 1682), 14.

8. For succinct definitions of Mississippian societies, see Robin Beck, *Chiefdoms, Collapse, and Coalescence in the Early American South* (New York: Cambridge University Press, 2013), 27; David G. Anderson, *The Savannah River Chiefdoms: Political Change in the Late Prehistoric Southeast* (Tuscaloosa: University of Alabama Press, 1994), 108; and Hahn, *Invention of the Creek Nation*, 14–15.

9. Hudson, *Juan Pardo*, 51–83; Chester B. DePratter, "Cofitachequi: Ethnohistorical and Archaeological Evidence," *Anthropological Studies*, 9 (1989), 133–56. There were actually two precontact mound sites near the mouth of the Savannah River, although only one, at Irene, was active in the late precontact period, and it had been abandoned by 1450; see Anderson, *Savannah River Chiefdoms*, 242, 249–50; and Beck, *Chiefdoms, Collapse, and Coalescence*, 41, 48. On the decline of chiefly power and the turn toward reciprocal, trade based relationships in the Late Mississippian period, see Hall, *Zamumo's Gift*, 20–25.

10. Waddell, "Cusabo," 259–62; Jerald T. Milanich, "Prehistory of the Lower Atlantic Coast after 500 B.C.," in *Handbook of North American Indians*, 235–36; Anderson, *Savannah River Chiefdoms*, 120; Hudson, *Juan Pardo*, 79–81. The coastal Indians bore strong resemblance to the upper Savannah River people described by

Adam King and Keith Stephenson, "Foragers, Farmers, and Chiefs: The Woodland and Mississippian Periods in the Middle Savannah River Valley," in *Archaeology in South Carolina: Exploring the Hidden Heritage of the Palmetto State*, ed. Adam King (Columbia: University of South Carolina Press, 2016), 36–41; and for that matter, to the proto-Creek peoples described in Hall, *Zamumo's Gift*, and Hahn, *Invention of the Creek Nation*.

11. For an extensive linguistic analysis, see Waddell, *Indians of the South Carolina Lowcountry*, 29–33. For interpreters, see John H. Hann, "Translation of the Ecija Voyages of 1605 and 1609 and the González Derrotero of 1609," *Florida Archaeology*, 2 (1986), 8–10, 29; and Waddell, "Cusabo," 254. On the basis of evidence about interpreters from the 1560s, Charles Hudson believed that the coastal people spoke a variant of Muskogean, but he also recognized that their place names had no known etymology. Similarly, John Worth argues that the coastal Indians understood Guale but primarily spoke either a dialect of Muskogean or a different language altogether. Hudson, *Juan Pardo*, 79–81; Karen M. Booker, Charles M. Hudson, and Robert L. Rankin, "Place Name Identification and Multilingualism in the Sixteenth-Century Southeast," *Ethnohistory* 39, no. 4 (Autumn 1992), 416–18; Worth, *Struggle*, 26. It should be noted that in the early 1680s, Muskogean-speaking Guales referred to Escamaçu as "Chiluques," the Muskogean word for "people of a different tongue." See Worth, *Struggle*, 26; and Hahn, *Invention of the Creek Nation*, 22.

12. Laudonnière's description is reprinted in Waddell, *Indians of the South Carolina Lowcountry*, 132–34.

13. Rogel's account is reprinted in Waddell, *Indians of the South Carolina Lowcountry*, 328. Also see Juan Rogel to Francisco Borgiae, Havana, November 10, 1568, in *Monumenta antiquae Floridae* (1566–1572), ed. Félix Zubillaga (Rome: Monumenta Historica Soc. Iesu, 1946), 332.

14. On the Mississippian origins of the Yamasees' uprootedness, see Bossy, "Yamasee Mobility," 205–8.

15. On the Charlesfort ordeal, see Richard Hakluyt, *Hakluyt's Collection of the Early Voyages, Travels, and Discoveries of the English Nation* (London: R. H. Evans, 1810), 383–84.

16. Hudson, *Juan Pardo*, 3, 5.

17. Hudson, *Juan Pardo*, 14–18; Gonzalo Solis de Merás, *Pedro Menéndez de Avilés: Adelantado, Governor and Captain-general of Florida*, trans. Jeanette Thurber Connor (Deland: The Florida State Historical Society, 1923), 169 (quotation).

18. On the importance of women and families to peaceful relations between Spaniards and Indians, see Barr, *Peace Came in the Form of a Woman*, 12–13.

19. Gonzala Solis de Merás, *Pedro Menéndez de Avilés and the Conquest of Florida: A New Manuscript*, trans. David Arbesu-Fernandez (Gainesville: University of Florida Press, 2017), 115–22 (quotation on 122). Escamaçu and Orista had befriended the French when they settled at Port Royal in 1662, and they now felt betrayed to find Frenchmen in the raiding party from Guale. They were, therefore, eager to accept Menéndez's alliance.

20. Hudson, *Southeastern Indians*, 184–85; Snyder, *Slavery in Indian Country*, 46–48.

21. Solis de Merás, *Pedro Menéndez de Avilés, Adelantado*, 176 (first quotation), 174 (second quotation), 177 (third quotation). For kinship structures and the role of elder brother, see Hudson, *Southeastern Indians*, 185–90.

22. Solis de Merás, *Pedro Menéndez de Avilés, Adelantado*, 175–76 (quotations). On the distances between Santa Elena and the Orista towns, see Solis de Merás, *Pedro Menéndez de Avilés and the Conquest of Florida*, 121; and Zubillaga, *Monumenta*, 400.

23. What is now Parris Island has a long history of occupation by Indigenous people, dating back more than three thousand years before contact, but it had been abandoned by the mid-sixteenth century. See Thompson et al., "The Archaeology and Remote Sensing," 9. For complaints of Spanish farmers, see *Colonial Records of Spanish Florida: Letters and Reports of Governors and Secular Persons*, ed. Jeannette M. Thurber Connor (Deland: Florida Historical Society, 1925–1930), I: 83–99, 143, 149, 155 [hereinafter *CRSF*].

24. Solis de Merás, *Pedro Menéndez de Avilés, Adelantado*, 175–76.

25. On the nature and complexity of gift giving in the early southeast, see especially Hall, *Zamumo's Gift*, 6–7.

26. Waddell, *Indians of the South Carolina Lowcountry*, 392n401 (first quotation); Hudson, *Juan Pardo*, 45–46 (Ahoya); "Rogel's Account," in Waddell, 329 (second quotation). On how Indians along Pardo's route used gifts of maize as declarations of power, see Beck et al., "Limiting Resistance." As Hall has noted, gift giving placed obligations on the giver as well as the receiver, so that it was sometimes difficult to distinguish who was tributary to whom; *Zamumo's Gift*, 7, 10, 22, 64.

27. On the mission system, see Timothy Paul Grady, *Anglo-Spanish Rivalry in Colonial South-East America, 1650–1725* (London: Pickering and Chatto, 2010).

28. On southeastern Indians' selective adaptation of Christianity and their use of conversion and Christian practice as a diplomatic strategy, see Bossy, "Spiritual Diplomacy," 369.

29. Solis de Merás, *Pedro Menéndez de Avilés, Adelantado*, 174, 178 (quotations); "Rogel's Account," 328.

30. For the chronic food shortages at Santa Elena, see Solis de Merás, *Pedro Menéndez de Avilés and the Conquest of Florida*, 125; Hudson, *Juan Pardo*, 45–46; and Paar, "'To Settle Is to Conquer,'" 58–59; *CRSF*, I: 83–89, 143, 145–93.

31. Paar, "'To Settle Is to Conquer,'" 81; Waddell, *Indians of the South Carolina Lowcountry*, 171–72.

32. *CRSF*, I: 193–201 (quotation on 195–97). On Moyano's enormities, see Hudson, *Juan Pardo*, 26–28.

33. Hudson, *Juan Pardo*, 172; "Woodward to John Locke," 305.

34. On rainfall and food shortages, see Karen L. Paar, "Climate in the Historical Record of Sixteenth-Century Spanish Florida: The Case of Santa Elena Re-examined," in *Historical Climate Variability and Impacts in North America*, eds. Lesley-Ann Dupigny-Giroux and Cary J. Mock (Dordrecht, the Netherlands: Springer, 2009), 47–58. On the role of Spanish abuses and interference with Guale politics as a factor in the Escamaçu War, see Paar, "'To Settle Is to Conquer,'" 79–81.

35. Waddell, *Indians of South Carolina Lowcountry*, 177 (three soldiers), 174 (five Spaniards); *CRSF*, I: 197 (treasury officials), 201 (one boy and eight soldiers).

36. *CRSF*, I: 265 (quotation), II: 81 (coordinated assault).

37. *CRSF*, I: 263–77 and II: 79–83, 247–49, 253–55; Paar, "'To Settle Is to Conquer,'" 206–11.

38. Paar, "'To Settle Is to Conquer,'" 5.

39. Hann, "Translation of the Ecija Voyages," 7–9, 12; "The Fray Alonso de Jesús Petition of 1630," John C. Hann Collection of Colonial Records, MS O24, P.K. Yonge Library, University of Florida, Gainesville (missions, population); Hall, *Zamumo's Gift*, 69 (epidemics). There is no evidence of devastating epidemics or population loss resulting from the colonization of Santa Elena, and given the relative isolation and stability of the coastal towns from 1590 to 1660, it is reasonable to assume that their populations recovered from the ill effects of colonization and war, as did many other Indigenous communities; see Tai S. Edwards and Paul Kelton, "Germs, Genocides, and America's Indigenous Peoples," *Journal of American History*, 107, no. 1 (June 2020): 52–76.

CHAPTER 1: MANEATERS

1. Worth, *Struggle*, 15–18 (quotation on 15). Two accounts of the raid give widely varying figures (five hundred and two thousand) for the number of raiders. I have chosen the smaller figure, which is more consistent with the number of canoes and with other, later estimates of the Westo population in Eric E. Bowne's *The Westo Indians: Slave Traders of the Early Colonial South* (Tuscaloosa: University of Alabama Press, 2005), 25. Alan Gallay gives a much higher population estimate of seventeen hundred to eight thousand; *Indian Slave Trade*, 41.

2. Worth, *Struggle*, 17.

3. Bowne, *Westo Indians*, 25 (naming); "Mr. Carteret's Relation," 118, gives them the name "Mandatoes," but the etymology of this word is unknown, and it is surely a transcribing error for the word "man-eaters;" see Langdon Cheeves, ed., *The Shaftesbury Papers and other Records Relating to Carolina* (Charleston: South Carolina Historical Society, 1897, reprint 2010), 166. Worth, *Struggle*, 17 (first quotation); Maurice Mathews to Shaftesbury, August 30, 1671, *CSPC*, 7: 610 (second quotation); Daniel K. Richter, *The Ordeal of the Longhouse: The Peoples of the Iroquois League in the Era of European Colonization* (Williamsburg, VA: Omohundro Institute of Early American History and Culture, 1992), 35–36 (ritual cannibalism).

4. On the "patchwork of slaveries" see Christina Snyder, "Native American Slavery in Global Context," in *What Is a Slave Society? The Practice of Slavery in Global Perspective*, eds. Noel Lenski and Catherine N. Cameron (Cambridge: Cambridge University Press, 2018), 187; also see James Brooks, "Intersections: Slavery, Borderlands, Edges," in Lenski and Cameron, 434. On the impact of the Westos, see Eric E. Bowne, "'Carryinge awaye their Corne and Children': The Effects of Westo Slave Raids on the Indians of the Lower South," in *Mapping the Mississippian Shatter Zone*, 104–14; and Gallay, *Indian Slave Trade*, 41–42.

5. Amy Turner Bushnell, "Ruling 'the Republic of Indians' in Seventeenth-Century

Florida," in *Powhatan's Mantle: Indians in the Colonial Southeast*, eds. Gregory A. Waselkov, Peter H. Wood, and Tom Hatley (Lincoln: University of Nebraska Press, 2006), 195–214; and *Situado and Sabana*; John E. Worth, "Spanish Missions and the Persistence of Chiefly Power," in *Transformation of the Southeastern Indians, 1540–1760*, eds. Robbie Ethridge and Charles M. Hudson (Jackson: University Press of Mississippi, 2002), 53–59.

6. There is very little evidence of these societies in what Marvin T. Smith has called "the dark age of the seventeenth century," so my depiction here is based largely on conjecture; Smith, "Aboriginal Population Movements in the Postcontact Southeast," in *Transformation of the Southeastern Indians*, 14; Smith, *Coosa: The Rise and Fall of a Mississippian Chiefdom* (Gainesville: University of Florida Press, 2000), 9–121; Hall, *Zamumo's Gift*, 56; Robbie Ethridge, "Introduction," in *Mapping the Mississippian Shatter Zone*, 1–3; Robin A. Beck, "Catawba Coalescence and the Shattering of the Carolina Piedmont, 1540–1675, in ibid., 120–30; Charles M. Hudson, "Introduction," in *Transformation of the Southeastern Indians*, xx–xxi; Snyder, *Slavery in Indian Country*, 43.

7. Spanish traders did establish trade relationships with the Chattahoochee towns in the 1640s. Hall, *Zamumo's Gifts*, 65–68, describes this as traditional trade—deerskins for prestige goods—and not gift exchange. Although the inland towns remained insulated from the most disruptive elements of Spanish colonization, this trade made Spanish goods widely available to non-elites and had a significant impact on power dynamics within the towns.

8. Solís de Merás, *Pedro Menéndez de Avilés and the Conquest of Florida*, 115–22; Hann, "Translation of the Ecija Voyages," 7–8 (mandador). On traditional Indian captivity and slavery, see Snyder, *Slavery in the Indian Country*, 37, 43–45.

9. Hudson, *Juan Pardo*, 27–29 (displacement); Hall, *Zamumo's Gifts*, 68 (peace); Worth, *Struggle*, 52n15; Bushnell, *Situado and Sabana*, 126 (quotations). There is considerable disagreement over the identification of Chisca with the Yuchi of east Tennessee; see Jason Baird Jackson, "Yuchi," in *Handbook of North American Indians*, 426.

10. John Worth estimates that the Native population of Florida fell by ninety percent across the board between 1600 and 1680; see *The Timucuan Chiefdoms of Spanish Florida, Volume 2: Resistance and Destruction* (Gainesville: University of Florida Press, 1999), 10–12. Also see Paul Kelton, *Epidemics and Enslavement: Biological Catastrophes in the Native Southeast, 1492–1715* (Lincoln: University of Nebraska Press, 2007), 83–87. On outmigration, see Hall, *Zamumo's Gifts*, 68–69.

11. Alan Taylor, *American Colonies: The Settling of North America* (New York: Penguin Books, 2001), 102–7, 112–13 (Mourning Wars); Bowne, *Westo Indians*, 37–41 (Eries).

12. Little is known about the Rickaheckrians in Virginia, and there is only indirect evidence of their ties to Virginia traders or of the sale of Indian slaves in Virginia; see Maureen Meyers, "From Refugees to Slave Traders: The Transformation of the Westo Indians," in *Mapping the Mississippian Shatter Zone*, 81–103; Kristalyn Marie Shefveland, *Anglo-Native Virginia: Trade, Conversion, and Indian Slavery in the Old*

Dominion, 1646–1722 (Lincoln: University of Nebraska Press, 2016), 29–32; Bowne, *Westo Indians,* 37–41; Worth, *Struggle,* 17–18, 52n15.

13. There is some evidence of English-sponsored raids in Apalachee as early as 1656; see Dubcovsky, *Informed Power,* 94–95.

14. Worth, *Struggle,* 18 (Huyache, first two quotations), 20 (fourth quotation), 21 (Yamasee migrations); Alex Y. Sweeney and Eric C. Poplin, "The Yamasee Indians of Early South Carolina," in *Archaeology in South Carolina,* 62 (third quotation).

15. Robert Sandford, "A Relation of a Voyage on the Coast of the Province of Carolina, 1666," in *Narratives of Early Carolina,* 88, 91–92, 100; William Hilton, "A Relation of a Discovery, 1664," in ibid., 41, 44; "Joseph Woory (1666): Discovery," in Jennie Holton Fant, ed., *The Travelers' Charleston: Accounts of Charleston and Lowcountry, South Carolina, 1666–1861* (Columbia: University of South Carolina Press, 2013); Thompson et al., "The Archaeology and Remote Sensing," 12; William Dunlop to James Montgomery of Skelmorly, 1686, GD3/5/773, National Records of Scotland, Edinburgh [hereinafter NRS].

16. Sandford, "Relation of a Voyage," 102–3; Hilton, "Relation of a Discovery," 44. On the locations of these towns, see Waddell, *Indians of the South Carolina Lowcountry,* iii, 359 n. 3.

17. Hilton, "Relation of a Discovery," 39–43.

18. Sandford, "Relation of a Voyage," 95 (first two quotations), 91 (third quotation), 92 (fourth quotation), 105 (remaining quotations). On hair, hair cutting, and Indian identity, see Snyder, *Slavery in Indian Country,* 17–18, 36–37. The Indigenous practice of sending young men, especially the nephews of headmen, on such external diplomatic missions, was not uncommon among southeastern peoples; see Bossy, "Spiritual Diplomacy," 378.

19. Sandford, "Relation of a Voyage," 106.

20. "Mr. Carteret's Relation," 118 (quotations); "Mr. Mathews' Relation," *Shaftesbury Papers,* 170–71 (Edisto); Worth, *Struggle,* 22, 76 (Guale).

21. The Ospo spoke the language of Guale, needing only one interpreter when they gave depositions to the Spaniards. The Escamaçu required two translators: one "of the tongue of the province of Santa Elena" and a second to translate from Guale to Spanish. See the bundle of documents translated by St. Julien Ravenel Childs in 1936, Childs Family Papers, collection 1224, folders 5 and 6, pp. 2, 18, South Carolina Historical Society, Charleston. For more on the origins of Ospo, see Worth, *Struggle,* 24–25.

22. "Deposition of Captain Antonio de Arguelles, Aug. 1, 1671," Childs Family Papers, 8–9. On Chiluque, see Worth, *Struggle,* 26. On Pamini, see Dubcovsky, *Informed Power,* 108–111; and Hahn, *Invention of the Creek Nation,* 22.

23. Depositions of Bluacacay, Barchoamini, Ynna, Sthiaco, and Huannucase, Childs Family Papers, 4–8 (quotation on 4).

24. Childs Family Papers, 16, 18 (quotation).

25. Jose Miguel Gallardo, "The Spaniards and the English Settlement in Charles Town," *South Carolina Historical and Genealogical Magazine,* 37, no. 2 (April 1936), 51 [hereinafter *SCHGM*].

26. "Enclosures in Cendoya's Letter of Dec. 15, 1672," Childs Family Papers. Spain's confusion about the intentions of the English and how to respond to their settlement persisted into 1674; see Gallardo, "Spaniards and the English Settlement," *SCHGM*, 37, no. 3 (July 1936): 92, 97–98.

27. Hilton, "Relation of a Discovery," 39.

28. *Shaftesbury Papers*, 200–1 (Owen), 194, 274–75 (Bull).

29. Roper, *Conceiving Carolina*, 62 (Westo initiative). On Woodward and his early contributions to the colony, see "Council to the Lords Proprietors," *Shaftesbury Papers*, 190–91; and Eric E. Bowne, "Dr. Henry Woodward's Role in Early Carolina Indian Relations," in *Creating and Contesting Carolina*, 73–93.

30. "Woodward's Westo Discovery," *Shaftesbury Papers*, 457–62. Waddell, "Cusabo," 260, found no mention of palisades in the sources for the coastal towns, which was typical of dispersed settlements in the southeast; also see Kelton, *Epidemics and Enslavement*, 8–11; and John R. Swanton, *Smithsonian Institution Bureau of Ethnology Bulletin of the Indians of the Southeastern United States* (Washington, DC: Government Printing Office, 1946), 433–39, which finds few stockaded towns in the southeast during the seventeenth century.

31. "Woodward's Westo Discovery," 461.

32. *Shaftesbury Papers*, 342, 451; CSPC 7: 746 (tribute); CSPC, 11: 1284 (skulking).

33. Henry Woodward, Accounts as Indian agent of the first Earl of Shaftesbury 1674–1678, Personal Papers, South Carolina Department of Archives and History, Columbia, SC; Roper, *Conceiving Carolina*, 55 (quotation).

34. CSPC 10: 176 (monopoly); A. S. Salley Jr., ed., *Journal of the Grand Council of South Carolina* (Columbia: Historical Commission of South Carolina, 1907), 82–83 [hereinafter *JGC*]. On the Goose Creek men, see especially Roper, *Conceiving Carolina*, 55–67.

35. *JGC*, 83–84.

36. For the proprietors' perspective (and quotation) see *CSPC*, 11: 1284. The puppet-master argument is most forcefully made by Roper, *Conceiving Carolina*, 62–65.

37. Worth, *Struggle*, 31 (quotations); *JGC*, 84. A cryptic 1682 reference to the execution of several Westo headmen suggests that the Westo attack on settlement Indians may have followed an act of war by the English. In a letter to the council, *CSPC* 11: 1284, the proprietors claimed that "the heads of the Westos were taken whilst they were in treaty with the Government, and so under the public faith for their safety, and put to death in cold blood." The language here suggests that the execution might have taken place during or just after the April 12 meeting, when the Westo headmen were gathered together.

38. CSPC, 11: 1284; Bowne, *Westo Indians*, 101.

39. CSPC, 11: 1284; Stephen Warren, *The Worlds the Shawnees Made: Migration and Violence in Early America* (Chapel Hill: University of North Carolina Press, 2014), 93.

40. Shefveland, *Anglo-Native Virginia*, 31; Bowne, *Westo Indians*, 26; Gallay, *Indian Slave Trade*, 41; Matthew Jennings, "'Cutting one anothers Throats': British, Native, and African Violence in Early Carolina," in *Creating and Contesting*

Carolina, 122; Warren, *Worlds the Shawnees Made*, 85; Hahn, *Invention of the Creek Nation*, 34–35.

CHAPTER 2: A REFUGE FOR THE GOSPEL

1. My intent here is to capture the Covenanters' perspective of their world, not subject it to scholarly analysis. Toward that end, there has been a revival of scholarly interest in the Covenanters over the past decade, with a refreshing focus on the social and cultural history of the Covenanting movement. See especially the essays in the special supplement of the *Scottish Historical Review*, 99 (December 2020), which includes overviews of the literature in Neil McIntyre's "Preface: Experiencing the Covenant at Home and Abroad," 331–35; and Allan I. Macinnes's "Afterword: Radicalism Reasserted: Covenanting in the Seventeenth Century," 473–90. On the organization of the alternative church by moderates, see Elizabeth Hannan Hyman, "A Church Militant: Scotland, 1661–1690," *Sixteenth Century Journal*, XXVI, no. 1 (1995), 49. For a running account of the defiant, noncompliant group of resisters, see John Erskine, *Journal of the Hon. John Erskine of Carnock, 1683–1687* (Edinburgh, Scotland: Scottish History Society, 1893). On the uncompromising radicals, see Richard L. Greaves, *Secrets of the Kingdom: British Radicals from the Popish Plot to the Revolution of 1688–89* (Stanford, CA: Stanford University Press, 1992); and Emily Moberg Robinson, "Sacred Memory: The Covenanter Use of History in Scotland and America," *Journal of Transatlantic Studies*, 11, no. 2 (Summer 2013): 135–57.

2. Robert Wodrow, *History of the Sufferings of the Church of Scotland, from the Restoration to the Revolution*, vol. IV (Glasgow, Scotland: Blackie and Son, 1832), 1–6; Erskine, *Journal*, 72, 62 (quotations).

3. David Dobson. *Scottish Trade with Colonial Charleston, 1683–1783* (Glasgow, Scotland: Humming Earth, 2009), 3. T. M. Devine has argued that Scotland's economy, while sluggish in comparison with England's in the seventeenth century, was far from stagnant; see "The Modern Economy: Scotland and the Act of Union," in *The Transformation of Scotland: The Economy since 1700*, eds. T. M. Devine, C. H. Lee, and G. C. Peden (Edinburgh, Scotland: Edinburgh University Press, 2005), 19–20.

4. *Register of the Privy Council of Scotland*, third series, Volume 7, 1681–1682, ed. P. Hume Brown (Edinburgh, 1915), 600, 664–72 (quotation on 671–72) [hereinafter *RPCS*].

5. *RPCS*, 8: 526 (quotation); Alexander Murdoch, *Scotland and America, c. 1600–c. 1800* (New York: Palgrave Macmillan, 2010), 18.

6. *RPCS*, 7: 600 (quotation from king); Gilbert Burnet, *Bishop Burnet's History of His Own Time, Volume I* (London: Thomas Ward, 1724), 526; Murdoch, *Scotland and America*, 17–18; George Pratt Insh, *Scottish Colonial Schemes, 1620–1686* (Glasgow, Scotland: Maclehose, Jackson & Co., 1922), 197 (quotation from duke), 135 (Act for Trade).

7. Insh, *Colonial Schemes*, 189–90 (Shaftesbury); Kurt Gingrich, "'To Erect a Collonie of Scottish Subjects in Aney Pairt of America': The Quest for a Scottish Colony in North America in the 1680s," *Journal of Early American History* 2 (2012), 75–78 (autonomy).

8. Frances Gardiner Davenport, ed., *European Treaties Bearing on the History of the United States and Their Dependencies* (Washington, DC: Carnegie Institution of Washington, 1929), 194 (Treaty of Madrid and first quotation); "Mr. Carteret's Relation," 119–20; Lawrence S. Rowland, Alexander Moore, and George C. Rogers Jr., *The History of Beaufort County, South Carolina: Volume 1, 1514–1861* (Columbia: University of South Carolina Press, 1996), 62 (English settlement); Letter from Sir John Cochrane of Ochiltree to Mr. Mortone, governor at Ashley River, no date, GD158/847, NRS (second quotation).

9. *CSPC*, 11: 807 (quotation). On the Carolina Company, see especially Linda G. Fryer, "Documents Relating to the Formation of the Carolina Company in Scotland, 1682," *South Carolina Historical Magazine* 99, no. 2 (April 1998); and "The Covenanters' Lost Colony in South Carolina," *Scottish Archives: The Journal of the Scottish Records Association*, 2 (1996): 98–106.

10. Fryer's thesis is that the Carolina Company was primarily a business venture, and she minimizes the significance of religion as a motivating factor. See "Documents Relating to the Formation of the Carolina Company," 129; also see Allan I. Macinnes, M. D. Harper, and L. G. Fryer, eds., *Scotland and the Americas: A Documentary Source Book* (Edinburgh, Scotland: Scottish History Society, 2002), 72.

11. J. G. Dunlop, ed., *The Dunlop Papers: Volume II: The Dunlops of Dunlop: and of Auchenskait, Keppoch, and Gairbraid* (London: Butler and Tanner, 1932), 119–22 (Cochrane); Greaves, *Secrets of the Kingdom, 62* (Campbell).

12. On this dense network, see Fryer, "Covenanters' Lost Colony," 103. My own cursory analysis compared Fryer's list of investors, given in "Documents Relating to the Formation of the Carolina Company," 131–32, with Covenanters identified in John Erskine's *Journal* and elsewhere. One third is a minimum, as the list included many investors by last name only, whose identity could not be positively verified. For specific examples, see 35 (Hutcheson), 12 (Hallcraig), 11 (Craigends), 6 (Househill), and 32 (Loudons).

13. On Dunlop's life, see *Dunlop Papers*, II: 108–25; Anonymous letter, Edinburgh, to Sir George Campbell of Sesnock, Anent proposed settlement in America, 22 July 1682, Hume of Marchmont Muniments, NRS, GD158/846 (prayer).

14. Erskine, *Journal*, 71 (quotation).

15. *RPBRO*, I: 212–19, 261–62; *CSPC*, 11: 807, 808, 809, 1284, 1774, 1780. The theme of autonomy or "effective sovereignty" is prominent in Gingrich, 'To Erect a Collonie', 75–78.

16. Mattie Erma Edwards Parker, ed., *North Carolina Charters and Constitutions, 1578–1698* (Raleigh, NC: Carolina Charter Tercentenary Commission, 1963), 181–82, 202–3, 227–28.

17. John Crawford, *A New and Most Exact Account of the Fertiles and Famous Colony of Carolina* (Dublin, 1683), quotations on 3, 4, 7; *Dunlop Papers*, II: 29 (Margaret). Earlier in the century, the English in Virginia had also dreamed of an "Anglo-Indian Christian commonwealth." See Rebecca Anne Goetz, *The Baptism of Early Virginia: How Christianity Created Race* (Baltimore: Johns Hopkins University Press, 2012), 35–59.

18. On lost tribes theory, see Richard W. Cogley, "'Some Other Kinde of Being and Condition': The Controversy in Mid-Seventeenth-Century England over the Peopling of Ancient America," *Journal of the History of Ideas*, 68, no. 1 (January 2007), 35–56; and "The Fall of the Ottoman Empire and the Restoration of Israel in the 'Judeo-centric' Strand of Puritan Millenarianism," *Church History* 72 (2003): 304–332. I am indebted to Michael Winship for this insight connecting the lost tribes to Stuarts Town's prophetic role.

19. Richard Ashcraft, *Revolutionary Politics and Locke's Two Treatises of Government* (Princeton, NJ: Princeton University Press, 1986), 356.

20. For the argument that the company served as a cover for plotters, see Greaves, *Secrets of the Kingdom*, 163–65; Ashcraft, *Revolutionary Politics*, 367, 383–90, 426; Roper, *Conceiving Carolina*, 75–80; and Peter Karsten, "Plotters and Proprietors, 1682–83: The 'Council of Six' and the Colonies: Plan for Colonization or Front for Revolution?" *The Historian* 38 (1976) 476–77. Ashcraft's claim that Cochrane's and Campbell's visit to London in August 1682 was a "pretense" for plotting insurrection is without foundation, although evidence of this for 1683 is compelling; *Revolutionary Politics*, 354.

21. *RPCS*, 8: 211–15, 222, 268–69, 271, and 11: 87, 152.

22. Wodrow, *History of Sufferings*, IV: 1–6; Erskine, *Journal*, 5 (M'Quarrie), 36–37 (Kerr), 29 (Shaw), 33, 76–78, 81, 88–89, 72 (second quotation).

23. This is based mostly on Cardross's own account of his persecution, reprinted in Wodrow, *History of Sufferings*, III: 162, 192–93; and his 1675 indictment by the Privy Council, reprinted in Erskine, *Journal*, 223–6 (quotations on 223, 226). On John King, see Greaves, *Secrets*, 61–67.

24. Greaves, *Secrets*, 68 (first two quotations).

25. Erskine, *Journal*, 225–29; *The Last Speeches of the Two Ministers Mr. John King, and Mr. John Kid, at the Place of Execution at Edenburgh on the 14th day of August, 1679* (1680), 12. The relationship between the radicals and the so-called "moderate" Carolina colonizers has been examined in Mark Jardine, "United Societies: Militancy, Martyrdom, and the Presbyterian Movement in Late-Restoration Scotland, 1679–1688," (Doctoral dissertation, University of Edinburth, 2009), 59–60, 70–71, 130, 222. My own reading of the sources suggests that the theological and political differences between Cardross, Dunlop, and the radicals exiled to Carolina were not as pronounced as Jardine argues and, indeed, that the categories "radical" and "moderate" were highly fluid and complex. On the turn away from a bifurcated radical-conservative perspective on Covenanters, see McIntyre, "Preface," 333, and Macinnes, "Afterword."

26. J. G. Dunlop, ed., *The Dunlop Papers: Volume III, Letters and Journals, 1663–1889* (London: Butler and Tanner, 1953), 34, 20 (first two quotations); *Dunlop Papers*, II: 133 (remaining quotations).

27. Letter from Cochrane to Mortone (first quotation); David Dobson, *Scottish Emigration to Colonial America, 1607–1785* (Athens: University of Georgia Press, 1994), 65 (Ireland); George Pratt Insh, "The Carolina Merchant: Advice of Arrival," *Scottish Historical Review*, 25, 98 (January 1928): 102 (English, Antigua),

103 (reasonable and necessary); William Dunlop, "Project of a Settlement," Dunlop Papers, volume 9255, Special Collections, NLS (French, family indentures); *Dunlop Papers*, III: 24 (wives).

28. Dunlop, "Project of a Settlement."

29. Erskine, *Journal*, 72.

30. Erskine, *Journal*, 72; William Dunlop to Sir James Montgomery of Skelmorlie, [March?] 1686, GD3/5/772, NRS; Wodrow, *History of Sufferings*, IV: 9.

31. On Scotland's convict trade see Eric J. Graham, *A Maritime History of Scotland, 1650–1790* (Glasgow: Tuckwell Press, 2002), 44–48; Dobson, *Scottish Trade with Colonial Charleston*, 10; and Ian Adams and Meredyth Somerville, *Cargoes of Despair and Hope: Scottish Emigration to Colonial America, 1603–1803* (Edinburgh: Edinburgh University Press, 1993), 18–21.

32. For Gibson and Malloch, see *Bannatyne Miscellany*, vol. 3 (Edinburgh: Bannatyne Society, 1855), 383; Wodrow, *History of the Sufferings*, IV: 8–9; *RCPS* 7: 526–27; and Sir John Lauder Fountainhall, ed., *The Decisions of the Lords of Council and Session, from June 6th, 1678, to July 30th, 1712* (Edinburgh: G. Hamilton and J. Balfour, 1759).

33. Wodrow, *History of the Sufferings*, IV: 7 (first quotation), 8 (second quotation); Dobson, *Scottish Trade with Colonial Charleston*, 10 (three thousand); Adams and Somerville, *Cargoes of Despair*, 21 (eight hundred).

34. Murdoch, *Scotland and the Americas*, 23; "Wm. Marshall et. Al. to Wm. Dunlop," *Dunlop Papers* III: 15–18.

35. Adams and Somerville, *Cargoes of Despair*, 18–19 (drowned); Testimony of John Mathieson, MS 2832, NLS (quotation); Account of the voyage of transportees to Carolina, Wodrow Quarto XXXVI, 223–24, Wodrow Papers, NLS (Gibson).

36. Testimony of Mathieson; Account of the Voyage, Wodrow Quarto (Smith, Dick).

37. Historians have long recognized that, on the ground in the plantations, there was little distinction between indentured servitude and slavery until the population of enslaved Blacks increased in the later seventeenth or early eighteenth century. In South Carolina, unfree White laborers continued to outnumber Black slaves until the 1690s or later. I follow John Donoghue's lead in seeing indentured servitude and chattel slavery as two varieties of enslavement rather than two completely distinct labor systems, with two caveats: first, that conditions were evolving and colonial authorities were developing new, harsh slave laws in this period; and second, that the massive scale of forced migration and enslavement of Africans across the British Atlantic makes such equivalencies ring hollow (despite the equivalencies in local places such as Carolina). See "Out of the Land of Bondage: The English Revolution and the Atlantic Origins of Abolition," *American Historical Review* 115, no. 4 (October 2010): 943–74; Peter H. Wood, "The Changing Population of the Colonial South: An Overview by Race and Region, 1685," in *Powhatan's Mantle*, 38.

38. *RPCS*, 8: 710–11 (co-signer); Account of the Voyage, Wodrow Quarto (quotations); William Dunlop to Sir James Montgomery of Skelmorlie, July 13, 1687, GD3/5/777, NRS (seventeen servants).

39. Joseph S. Moore, "Covenanters and Antislavery in the Atlantic World," *Slavery & Abolition* 34, no. 4 (2013): 540–42.

40. Alexander Shields, *A Hind Let Loose, or, an Historical Representation of the Testimonies of the Church of Scotland, for the Interest of Christ* ... 1687, 181, 190, 197, https://quod.lib.umich.edu/e/eebo/A59963.0001.001?view=toc, accessed May 6, 2022.

41. Account of the Voyage, Wodrow Quarto; James McClintock to Thomas Linning, June 1684, Wodrow Quarto, XXXVI, 204–6 (quotation).

CHAPTER 3: 1684

1. Thomas Ashe, "Carolina, or a Description of the Present State of that Country," in *Narratives of Early Carolina*, 157 (first quotation); William Dunlop to the Governor, July 17, 1685, in *RBPRO*, 80 (second quotation). On the Yamasee migration, see John E. Worth, "Yamasee," in *Handbook of North American Indians*, 247–48, 251–52. On Yamasee towns in Port Royal, see William Green, Chester B. DePratter, and Bobby Southerlin, "The Yamasee in South Carolina: Native American Adaptation and Interaction along the Carolina Frontier," in *Another's Country: Archaeological and Historical Perspectives on Cultural Interactions in the Southern Colonies*, eds. J. W. Joseph and Martha Zierden (Tuscaloosa: University of Alabama Press, 2009), 13–29.

2. *CSPC* 11: 808 (Scots); Register of the Province Conveyance Books, Volume A, 1682–1693, 104-4, 107–8, 115–17, 132–37, South Carolina Department of Archives and History, Columbia, SC [hereinafter SCDAH] (quotation on 107); 1675–1705, Proprietary Grants, volume 38, no. 1, 193–97, 200–206, SCDAH (cessions); David H. DeJong, *American Indian Treaties: A Guide to Ratified and Unratified Colonial, United States, Foreign, and Intertribal Treaties and Agreements, 1607–1911* (Salt Lake City: University of Utah Press, 2015), 3, 12 (Native forms).

3. Samuel Wilson, "An Account of the Province of Carolina . . . 1682," in *Narratives of Early Carolina*, 172 (first quotation); Maurice Mathews, "A Contemporary View of South Carolina in 1680," *South Carolina Historical Magazine*, 55, no. 3 (July 1954), 158 (second and fifth quotations) [hereinafter *SCHM*]; Ashe, "Carolina," 157 (third quotation); Crawford, *New and Most Exact Account*, 7 (fourth quotation); R. F., *Present State of Carolina*, 13–15; "Letters of Thomas Newe, 1682," in *Narratives of Early Carolina*, 182. For the interventions, see *BPRO*, I: 55–56, 97–102, 142 (sixth quotation), 174; *CSPC*, 10:1357, 11: 498.

4. Wilson, "Account of the Province," 173 (all quotations); R. F., *Present State*, 14 (population). Crawford, *New and Most Exact Account*, 6, estimated no more than one hundred sixty Natives living in the Port Royal area in 1682.

5. The coastal peoples' territory extended only about fifty miles into the coastal plain, not all the way to the Appalachian Mountains as the cession records stated. This comprised about two million acres.

6. Waddell, an expert on the locations of the coastal towns, argued that the towns on St. Helena moved to the north side of Port Royal after 1684. This is a logical inference, given the plans of the Scots to occupy Wimbee and St. Helena islands. See *Indians of the South Carolina Lowcountry*, 5.

7. In 1680, Mathews claimed that "those who live toward the Indian parts of the settlements have brought them by ane Indian in one year 100 sometimes 200 deer." Allowing for the exaggeration typical of promotional materials, this indicates a thriving trade in deer skins that engaged the coastal towns south of Charles Town. Mathews, "Contemporary View," 157.

8. *CSPC* 11: 1284 (first three quotations), 1364 (fourth quotation), 1722 (surveyor general).

9. *CSPC* 11: 807 (first quotation), 1722, 1733; *BPRO*, I: 287, 289, 291, 296, 298–306 (second quotation on 301, third quotation on 300), and II: 31–34.

10. *CSPC*, 11: 1733 (first quotation); Rowland, Moore, and Rogers Jr., *History of Beaufort County*, 70 (counterbalance). As late as 1688, South Carolina's Governor Colleton wrote that he was powerless to force the Yamasee out of his province without a full-scale war authorized by the crown; see Bushnell, "Living at Liberty," 39.

11. Autonomy, adaptability, and networking are major themes in recent scholarship on the Yamasees; see Bossy, "Yamasee Mobility" and "Spiritual Diplomacy," and the many excellent essays in Bossy, ed., *Yamasee Indians*, especially Bushnell, "Living at Liberty," and Alexander Y. Sweeney, "Cultural Continuity and Change: Archaeological Research at Yamasee Primary Towns in South Carolina," 99–127. On the challenges facing coalescing groups in general, see Hahn, *Invention of the Creek Nation*, 19.

12. Worth, "Yamasee," 245 (origins); Bossy, "Yamasee Mobility," 206–208 (polities); Bushnell, "Living at Liberty," 28 (quotation), 29–33; Hall, *Zamumo's Gifts*, 87–88 (trade).

13. Bossy, "Yamasee Mobility," 209–11; Hall, *Zamumo's Gifts*, 93.

14. Bushnell, "Living at Liberty," 30, 31, 36, 50n52; Hahn, *Invention of the Creek Nation*, 42 (Niquisalla). Altamaha's people initially settled on another island closer to the Scottish colony. This may have been St. Helena, the former site of the Escamaçu town. As more migrants arrived, they were sent to Hilton Head. See Caleb Westbrooke's letter in *RBPRO*, 8–9.

15. *CSPC*, 11: 1284; Warren, *Worlds the Shawnees Made*, 93.

16. *RBPRO*, 8–9 (Altamaha, Westbrooke quotations); Worth, *Struggle,* 54 n. 45 (Niquisalla); George Pratt Insh, "Arrival of the Cardross Settlers," *SCHGM* 30, no. 2 (April 1929), 76 (Cardross); Mathews, "Contemporary View," 158 (Charles Town population).

17. Bushnell, "Living at Liberty," 27 (first quotation); Eric C. Poplin and Jon Bernard Marcoux, "Yamasee Material Culture and Identity: Altamaha/San Marcos Ceramics in Seventeenth- and Eighteenth-Century Yamasee Indian Settlements, Georgia and South Carolina," in Bossy, *Yamasee Indians*, 84–91 (ceramics); William Dunlop, "Capt. Dunlop's Voyage to the Southward, 1687," eds. J. G. Dunlop and Mabel L. Webber, *SCHGM* 30, no. 3 (April 1929), 131, 133 (remaining quotations).

18. Hahn, *Invention of the Creek Nation*, 21; Bossy, "Spiritual Diplomacy," 375–76; Hudson, *Southeastern Indians*, 224–25, 234–35; Worth, *Struggle*, 168n56.

19. "Letter from Cardross to the Governor and Grand Council at Charles Town, 25 March, 1684," in William James Rivers, *A Sketch of the History of South Carolina to the Close of the Proprietary Government* (Charleston: MacArthur and Co., 1856),

408. On Wina's earlier exploits, see "Depositions of Ynna, Sthiaco, and Huannucase, Aug. 1, 1671," Childs Family Papers, 7–8; and Register of the Province Conveyance Books, Volume A, 1682–1693, 107–8.

20. "Account of the Carolina Voyage," Wodrow Quarto, 223–24. One significant exception was the prisoner, George Smith; see the Epilogue.

21. Cardross, "Arrival of the Cardross Settlers," 72–73 (first, second, and fifth quotations); Erskine, *Journal*, 159 (third and fourth quotations); St. Julien Ravenel Childs, *Malaria and Colonization in the Carolina Low Country, 1526–1696* (Baltimore: Johns Hopkins, 1940), 225 (malaria); Eric J. Graham, *A Maritime History of Scotland, 1650–1790* (Glasgow: Tuckwell Press, 2002), 41n94 (*James of Ayr*); RBPRO, I: 307–8 (sixth quotation).

22. "Arrival of Cardross Settlers," 73 (quotation). The precise location of Stuarts Town is unknown. Cardross, "Arrival," 73, placed it twenty miles from the mouth of the Broad River, but later references to its location by Dunlop suggest that it was fifteen miles from the mouth in the present-day city of Beaufort. See "Capt. Dunlop's Voyage to the Southward," 130, where Dunlop locates Stuarts Town five miles from the "lower end of Wimbee isle;" and William Dunlop to Sir James Montgomery of Skelmorlie, 1686, GD3/5/773, NRS, where he situates the town eight miles above the cleared land on St. Helena (now Parris) Island.

23. "Arrival of the Cardross Settlers," 73–74; "Cardross to the Governor," 408 (great guns).

24. "Arrival of the Cardross Settlers," 75–76; RBPRO, 63.

25. "Arrival of the Cardross Settlers," 75–76; Hudson, *Juan Pardo*, 169–71; Shaftesbury to William Sayle, May 13, 1771, *Shaftesbury Papers*, 327 (Woodward).

26. "Arrival of the Cardross Settlers," 75–76; "Cardross to the Governor," 408.

27. "Cardross to the Governor," 408.

28. Juan Marquez Cabrera to the King, June 14, 1681, Matheos Documents: Phase VI, p. 39 (quotations); Grady, *Anglo-Spanish Rivalry*, 56 (treaty); Jane Landers, "The Geopolitics of Seventeenth-Century Florida," *Florida Historical Quarterly*, 92, no. 3 (Winter 2014), 486–87 (militias).

29. Worth, *Struggle*, 36–37, 41–42, 151, 157n30.

30. William Edward Dunn, *Spanish and French Rivalry in the Gulf Region of the United States, 1678–1702: The Beginnings of Texas and Pensacola* (Austin: The University of Texas Bulletin, 1917), 13–22.

31. Grady, *Anglo-Spanish Rivalry*, 51 (population).

32. On the usefulness of "lived experience" rather than societal frameworks for understanding slavery in colonial borderlands, see Brooks, "Intersections," 434.

33. Wood, "Changing Population of the Colonial South," 38 (overall figures); Russell Menard, *Migrants, Servants, and Slaves: Unfree Labor in Colonial British America* (Farnham, UK: Ashgate Publishing, 2001), 105 (proportions). Wood probably underestimates the number of slaves. Two escaped servants claimed in early 1686 that Carolina had between six hundred and eight hundred slaves. This number included at least two hundred who had been taken in Vera Cruz by pirates and sold in Charles Town in 1685. See Testimony of 2 Savoyards from Carolina, January 1686, Child Family Papers. By one estimate, the number of enslaved Indians was small, numbering

only one hundred in 1690; most were exported to the West Indies. See Russell Menard, "Slave Demography in the Lowcountry, 1670–1740: From Frontier Society to Plantation Regime," *SCHM* 101, no. 3 (July 2000), 190–213.

34. "Account of the Carolina Voyage," 223–24 (Paton and Smith); "Declaration of Catalina, English," in Worth, *Struggle*, 151; J. G. Dunlop, ed., "Paul Grimball's Losses by the Spanish Invasion in 1686," *SCHGM* 29 (July 1928): 231–37 (Oats). On spiriting and the blurred lines between slavery and servitude, see John Donoghue, "Indentured Servitude in the 17th Century English Atlantic: A Brief Survey of the Literature," *History Compass* 11, no. 10 (Oct. 2013), 894–902.

35. "Declaration of Juan Clar," Worth, *Struggle*, 149–51.

36. "Declaration of Juan Clar," 150; Testimony of 2 Savoyards, Childs Family Papers; *RBPRO*, 2: 80 (Dunlop); Testimony of John Mathieson.

37. Testimony of 2 Savoyards (Vera Cruz, Patrick); William Dunlop, "William Dunlop's Mission to St. Augustine in 1688," ed. J. G. Dunlop, *SCHGM*, 34, no. 1 (January 1933), 5 (DuBourdieu), 25 (murder), 26 (names), 29 (daughter); Nicolas Ponce de Leon relative to the arrival of four Englishmen from San Jorge, May 8, 1674, AI 58-1-35, Stetson Papers, reel 14, P.K. Yonge Library (Robson).

38. The Questioning of a Guale Indian Returned from English Territory to his Native Guale, December 29, 1685, Matheos Documents, Phase III, 37–9 (Nicolás); "Declaration," Worth, *Struggle*, 154 (Matheo); *RBPRO*, II: 80 (rascals).

39. "Declaration of Juan Clar" (Spanish slaves); Joseph Morton to William Dunlop, May 4, 1693, accession number 9251, Dunlop Papers, NLS (girl); Worth, *Struggle*, 164, 170–71 (Torre).

CHAPTER 4: CONSUMING FIRE

1. *RPBRO*, I: 255–60 (quotation on 259); *CSPC*, 11: 1284 and 1722; 12: 172.

2. Bushnell, "Living at Liberty;" Moore, "Covenanters and Antislavery," 540–42.

3. Snyder, *Slavery in Indian Country*, 5–6; T. M. Devine, ed., *Recovering Scotland's Slavery Past: The Caribbean Connection* (Edinburgh: Edinburgh University Press, 2015), 28, 247.

4. Dr. Henry Woodward to Deputy Governor John Godfrey, *CSPC*, 12: 83 (Woodward, Antonio, Yamacraw), 28 (Spanish plot); Bushnell, "Living at Liberty," 36 (guns); "Peter Colleton to Lord Cardross, 1687," in *Dunlop Papers*, III: 47–8 (Mathews); Apalachee Chiefs' Complaints to Governor Márquez Cabrera about Their Treatment by Antonio Matheos and the Governor's Ignoring of the Same and His Role in the Flight of Santa Maria's Yamasee from Amelia Island Florida, 4 of October of 1686, in Hann, Matheos Documents, Phase IV, 94–5; "Examacon of several Yamasse Indians," *RBPRO*, 2: 66.

5. Bushnell, "Living at Liberty," 35 (beacons); *CSPC*, 12: 28 (Westbrooke quotation); "Examacon of several Yamasse Indians," 66 (chieftain); Worth, *Struggle*, 54n45; Carte del Theniente de la provincia de Timucua, Sect. V: Aud. de Santo Domingo, Legajo 839, John Tate Lanning Papers, no. 251, pp. 4–5, St. Louis Mercantile Library, St. Louis, Missouri (Niquisalla); Hann, *History of the Timucua Indians*, 273 (six hours).

6. Hann, *History of the Timucua Indians*, 228, 247, 252, 254–55.

7. Hann, *History of the Timucua Indians*, 273; Bushnell, "Living at Liberty," 36; "Examacon of several Yamasse Indians," 66; Woodward to John Godfrey; Questioning of a Guale Indian, Matheos Documents; Antonio Matheos to Márquez Cabrera, San Luis, May 21, 1686, in Matheos Documents, Phase III, 71 (quotation); Worth, *Struggle*, 45–46.

8. Carte del Theniente de la provincia de Timucua, 1–3; Questioning of a Guale Indian (quotation).

9. Sources differ only slightly on the number of captives. Most agree that twenty-two women were given to the Scots, and three boys were kept by the raiders. Two women escaped, and one was either killed or refused to eat and died of grief, bringing the total taken from Santa Catalina to twenty-eight. They also agree on the disposal of the captives by the Scots, although some are more precise than others. See "Woodward to Godfrey" (quotation); "Examacon of several Yamasse Indians;" Testimony of 2 Savoyards, Childs Family Papers; Matheos to Márquez Cabrera, May 21, 1686, 71; and, for the most detailed account, Questioning of a Guale Indian, Matheos Documents. On Dunlop's Indian slave, see Morton to William Dunlop, May 4, 1693.

10. "Arrival of the Cardross Settlers," 75–76; "Capt. Dunlop's Voyage to the Southward," 131 (first quotation, Yamacraw, Sapala); Apalachee Chiefs' Complaints, 94 (second quotation); Manuel Gómez, Lieutenant of Timucua, to Márquez Cabrera, Santa Fée, November 12, 1685, Matheos Documents, Phase III, 31–32 (rumors).

11. On Woodward's commission and his struggles with the Goose Creek men, see Bowne, "Henry Woodward's Role," 85–87.

12. *RBPRO*, 2: 63, 64 (first quotation); Lord Cardross to the Governor and Grand Council, March 25, 1685, *CSPC*, 12: 92 (remaining quotations).

13. *RBPRO*, 2: 61–2.

14. *CSPC*, 12: 286 (first quotation), 287 (second quotation); *RBPRO*, 2: 65, 69, 75–6, 79–80, 193 (remaining quotations).

15. "Arrival of the Cardross Settlers," 76 (quotation). On the role of the Yamasees in brokering the trade deal between Apalachicola and Charles Town, see Joseph Hall, "Anxious Alliances: Apalachicola Efforts to Survive the Slave Trade, 1698–1705," in *Indian Slavery in Colonial America*, 163–64.

16. Matheos to Márquez Cabrera, San Luis, May 21, 1686, 69–71 (quotations); and the same from Caueta, January 12, 1686, 44, 46 [block house]; Worth, *Struggle*, 155–56. Denise I. Bossy has noted that the raid on Timucua was partly a recruiting push to attract more people to Yamasee and make it a regional power. The raiders' behavior in Apalachicola seems to confirm that claim. See "Yamasee Mobility," 212–13.

17. University of St. Andrews, *Records of the Parliaments of Scotland to 1707*, 1685/4/22 and 1685/4/28, online at www.rps.ac.uk [accessed January 28, 2021]; Erskine, *Journal*, xxii; *RPCS*, 11:79, 152, 550; *RBPRO*, 2:2.

18. "Arrival of Cardross Settlers," 72 (first quotation); Dunlop to Skelmorlie, [March?] 1686, GD3/5/772, 2, 3 (second quotation, servants); Testimony of Two Savoyards (eighty settlers); Childs, *Malaria and Colonization*, 29, 231 (Abercorne); William Dunlop to Sir James Montgomery of Skelmorlie, July 15, 1686, GD3/5/774, NRS (death rate), and October 1, 1685, GD3/5/775 (thirty men).

19. Dunlop to Skelmorlie, GD3/5/773 (all quotations) and 774.

20. Dunlop to Skelmorlie, GD3/5/772, 774, 775, 776.

21. Dunlop to Skelmorlie, GD3/5/772, 773, 775.

22. Dunlop to Skelmorlie, GD3/5/772; Dunlop Papers, Special Collections, NLS, vol. 9257 (commissions for escheator, canal); "Letters from John Stewart to William Dunlop," eds. J. G. Dunlop and Mabel L. Webber, *SCHGM*, 32, 1 (January 1931), 2.

23. Sarah Carstares to William Dunlop, February 24, 1686, pp. 20–21; June 29, 1686, p. 24; July 20, 1686, p. 27, in *Dunlop Papers*, vol. II.

24. Ibid., 20, 21, 25–28, 33, 35.

25. Dunlop to Skelmorlie, GD3/5/772, 773, 775.

26. Hann, *History of the Timucua*, 273; Manuel Gómez, Lieutenant of Timucua, to Márquez Cabrera, November 12, 1685, in Hann, Matheos Documents, Phase III, 32.

27. On Spanish ignorance of the peoples and lands beyond the mission settlements, see Hall, *Zamumo's Gift*, 71.

28. Matheos to Márquez Cabrera, September 21, 1685; October 4, 1685; and November 27, 1685, in Hann, Matheos Documents, III, 14, 20, 21, 24.

29. Domingo de Leturiondo to Márquez Cabrera, November 28, 1865; Márquez Cabrera to Matheos, no date; in Hann, Matheos Documents, III, 26, 33–34.

30. Matheos to Márquez Cabrera, January 12, 1686, and February 8, 1686, in Hann, Matheos Documents, III, 45, 46, 50.

31. On the significance of Matheos's scorched earth tactics in Apalachicola, see Steven J. Oatis, *A Colonial Complex: South Carolina's Frontiers in the Era of the Yamasee War, 1680–1730* (Lincoln: University of Nebraska Press, 2004), 29–33; Hahn, *Invention of the Creek Nation*, 42–5; Hall, *Zamumo's Gift*, 96–98.

32. Questioning of a Guale Indian, 37–39; Testimony of Two Savoyards; Matheos to Márquez Cabrera, May 21, 1686; and Thomás Menéndez Márquez and Francisco de la Rocha to the King, October 4, 1686, in Hann, Matheos Documents, III, 70, 95.

33. Worth, *Struggle*, 147 (quotation).

34. J. G. Dunlop, ed., "Spanish Depredations, 1686," *SCHGM* 30 (April 1929), 82 (two bodies, guides, second quotation); Dunlop to Skelmorlie, October 21, 1686, GD3/5/775 (first quotation, destruction). On John Livingstone, see "Declaration of John Livingstone," in Worth, *Struggle*, 152; and Sarah Carstares to Dunlop, July 20, 1686, in *Dunlop Papers*, III:27.

35. Dunlop to Skelmorlie, October 21, 1686, and "Spanish Depredations," 84 (slaves); Worth, *Struggle*, 153 (Yankey), 151 (Oats); J. G. Dunlop, ed., "Paul Grimball's Losses by the Spanish Invasion in 1686," *SCHGM* 29 (July 1928), 231–37.

36. "Spanish Depredations," 82–85.

37. Worth, *Struggle*, 155–56.

38. Worth, *Struggle*, 162 63; "Dunlop's Voyage to the Southward," 131

39. Dunlop to Skelmorlie, October 21, 1686; Memorial to the King of the Hostilities committed in the province of Carolina by the Spaniards, Dunlop Papers, accession number 9255, NLS.

40. "Spanish Depredations," 85; Dunlop to Skelmorlie, GD3/5/775.

41. "Spanish Depredations," 86; Dunlop to Skelmorlie, GD3/5/775 (quotations);

"An Act to Levy and Impresse Men, Arms etc. for the Defence of the Government," in *The Statutes at Large of South Carolina* (Volume 2), eds. Thomas Cooper and David J. McCord, (Columbia, SC: A. S. Johnston, 1837), 15–18.

42. *RBPRO*, II: 184–88, 221–28 (quotations on 184 and 185).

43. James Colleton to Captain William Dunlop, Carolina, March 25, 1687, accession number 9255, p. 40, Dunlop Papers, NLS (commission, second quotation); "Dunlop's Voyage to the Southward," 129 (first quotation).

44. "Dunlop's Voyage to the Southward," 127–30.

45. "Dunlop's Voyage to the Southward," 130–32; Worth, *Struggle*, 53–4.

46. "Dunlop's Voyage to the Southward," 132–33; Dunlop to Skelmorlie, July 13, 1687, GD3/5/777.

47. J. G. Dunlop, ed., "William Dunlop's Mission to St. Augustine," *SCHGM* 34, 1 (January 1933), 20–2 (quotations), 23–4; Louis Jordan, "The Value of Money in Colonial America," *Colonial Currency* (website of University of Notre Dame Special Collections), https://coins.nd.edu/ColCurrency/index.html (accessed May 5, 2022).

48. "Dunlop's Mission," 24–26.

49. For the letters from Torres y Ayala, see St. Julien Ravenel Childs Papers, box 313, folder 7, South Carolina Historical Society, Charleston. On the importance of runaway slaves to Carolina and Florida in this period, see Dubcovsky, *Informed Power*, 114–17; and Jane Landers, *Black Society in Spanish Florida* (Urbana: University of Illinois Press, 1999), 24–5.

EPILOGUE: UNFINISHED BUSINESS

1. Dunlop to Skelmorlie, October 21, 1686; November 21, 1686; July 13, 1687 (quotations); and March 26, 1688; *Dunlop Papers*, III: 24 and 37 (Sarah), 39 (Bessi). The date of Cardross's return is based on Dunlop's July 1687 letter, which Cardross delivered.

2. *Dunlop Papers*, III: 43 (mother), 49–50 (ministers); Sarah Carstares to William Dunlop, 6 Feb. 1688, Dunlop Papers, no. 9250, NLS.

3. *Dunlop Papers*, II: 133–34.

4. "Why Stuarts Town failed" is a theme in the historical literature. See Insh, *Scottish Colonial Schemes*, 187 (debatable land) and 210 (border feuds); Gingrich, "That Will Make Carolina Powerful," 22 (poor leadership); and Roper, *Conceiving Carolina*, 92 (envy, political machinations). Also see Devine, *Scotland's Empire*, 38–39, who cites several of these factors; and Gallay, *Indian Slave Trade*, 88, who points to diplomatic problems and cultural gaps between Scots and Yamasee.

5. With apologies to Perry Miller, "Errand Into the Wilderness," *WMQ* 10, 1 (January 1953): 3–32.

6. *Dunlop Papers*, II: 132–33 (first quotation); Dunlop to Skelmorlie, July 13, 1687 (second quotation). The third quotation is from Robert Wodrow, quoted in *Dunlop Papers* II: 141. On the Darien Venture, see Douglass Watt, *The Price of Scotland: Darien, Union and the Wealth of Nations* (Edinburgh: Luath Press, 2007); and Ignacio Gallup-Diaz, *The Door of the Seas and Key to the Universe: Indian Politics and Imperial Rivalry in the Darien, 1640–1750* (New York: Columbia University Press, 2004). On Archibald Stobo, see Peter N. Moore, *Archibald Simpson's Unpeaceable Kingdom:*

The Ordeal of Evangelicalism in the Colonial South (Lanham, MD: Lexington Books, 2018), 66–68.

7. Proposalls for the propagating of the Christian Religion, and Converting of Slaves whether Negroes or Indians in the English plantations, accession number 9255, Dunlop Papers, NLS. The Boyle version has been reprinted and analyzed by Ruth Paley, Christina Malcolmson, and Michael Hunter, "Parliament and Slavery, 1660–c. 1710," *Slavery & Abolition*, 31, no. 2 (June 2010): 257–81. For a full treatment of this document, its provenance, and its significance, see Peter N. Moore, "An Enslaver's Guide to Slavery Reform: William Dunlop's 1690 Proposals to Christianize Slaves in the British Atlantic," *Church History*, 91, no. 2 (June 2022), 264–85.

8. *Dunlop Papers*, II: 135.

9. *RPCS*, 13: 379, 508, 539; Wodrow Letters Quarto V, nos. 10 and 16, letters from Lord Cardross to Robert Wodrow, Wodrow Papers, NLS.

10. "Letters from John Stuart to William Dunlop," *SCHGM*, 32, 1 (January 1931), no. 1 (first two quotations), 32, no. 2 (April 1931), 110 (third quotation), 32, no. 3 (July 1931), 172; Weir, *Colonial South Carolina*, 69–71; Bowne, "Woodward's Role," 88–9; *RBPRO*, 3: 109–12 (Westbrooke). Land grants in Port Royal resumed in 1700; see Abstracts of Land Grants, vol. 38, pp. 387, 389–90, S213019, SCDAH.

11. Cooper and McCord, *Statutes at Large of South Carolina*, 1: 109, 309. Of all the Indigenous coastal peoples, only the Kusso have survived as a tribe. They continue to live in the South Carolina lowcountry.

12. Hahn, *Invention of the Creek Nation*, 49–52; Hall, "Anxious Alliances," 171; Charles R. Cobb and Chester B. DePratter, "Carolina's Southern Frontier: Edge of a New World Order," in *Archaeology in South Carolina*, 45–61.

13. Sweeney, "Cultural Continuity and Change," 103–4 (settlement); "Letters from John Stuart to William Dunlop," 32, no. 2, p. 94 (contract); Bartholomew Rivers Carroll, *Historical Collections of South Carolina* (New York: Harper and Brothers, 1836), II: 424 (retreat); Bossy, "Spiritual Diplomacy," 375–6 (white chief).

14. Sweeney, "Cultural Continuity and Change," 105–20.

15. Sweeney, "Cultural Continuity and Change," 105–20; Sweeney and Poplin, "Yamasee Indians of Early South Carolina," 72–8. Hall, "Anxious Alliances," 164, gives a much higher figure (four thousand) for the Yamasees in 1703.

16. Adaptability and autonomy are major themes in Bossy (ed.), *Yamasee Indians*. On the Euhaw prince, see Bossy, "Spiritual Diplomacy."

17. John E. Worth, "Razing Florida: The Indian Slave Trade and the Devastation of Spanish Florida, 1659–1715," in *Mapping the Mississippian Shatter Zone*, 300–1; Denise I. Bossy, "Indian Slavery in Southeastern Indian and British Societies, 1670–1730," in *Indian Slavery in Colonial America*, 220–21; Hall, "Anxious Alliances," 171; *RBPRO*, 2: 293 (quotation).

18. Weir, *Colonial South Carolina*, 81–2; Worth, "Razing Florida," 300–5; Matthew Jennings, "'Cutting One Another's Throats': British, Native, and African Violence in Early Carolina," in *Creating and Contesting Carolina*, 126.

19. Denise I. Bossy, "Introduction: Recovering Yamasee History," in *Yamasee Indians*, 1–6.

Bibliography

PRIMARY SOURCES: MANUSCRIPTS AND
ARCHIVAL COLLECTIONS

Abstracts of Land Grants. Vol. 38. South Carolina Department of Archives and History, Columbia, SC.

Bundle A20. Bute Archives at Mount Stuart, Rothesay, Isle of Bute, Scotland.

Cardross Family History and Genealogy Research Files. Manuscripts, South Carolina Historical Society, Charleston, SC.

Childs Family Papers. South Carolina Historical Society, Charleston, SC.

Dunlop, Alexander. Memorandum Book. Manuscripts Division, William L. Clements Library, University of Michigan. Ann Arbor, MI.

Dunlop Papers. Special Collections, National Library of Scotland, Edinburgh, UK.

Hume of Marchmont Muniments. National Records of Scotland, Edinburgh, UK.

John B. Stetson Collection. P.K. Yonge Library, University of Florida, Gainesville, FL.

John F. Morrall Research Papers. Manuscripts, South Carolina Historical Society, Charleston, SC.

John Tate Lanning Papers. St. Louis Mercantile Library, St. Louis, MO.

Mathews, Maurice, and Joel Gascoyne. A Plat of the Province of Carolina in North America. The British Library, London, UK.

Papers of the Baird Family of Saughtonhall. National Records of Scotland, Edinburgh, UK.

Papers of the Family of Hume of Polwarth, Berwickshire, Earls of Marchmont. National Records of Scotland, Edinburgh, UK.

Papers of Montgomerie Family, Earls of Eglinton. National Records of Scotland, Edinburgh, UK.

Papers of William Dunlop. Centre for Research Collections, Edinburgh University Library, Edinburgh, UK.

Papers of William Dunlop. Special Collections, University of Glasgow Library, Glasgow, UK.

Proprietary Grants, 1675–1705. Volume 38. South Carolina Department of Archives and History, Columbia, SC.

Quarry, Robert. Letter, ca. 1685. Manuscripts, South Carolina Historical Society, Charleston, SC.

Register of the Province Conveyance Books. Volume A, 1682–1693. South Carolina Department of Archives and History, Columbia, SC.

Research on Henry Woodward, ca. 1960–1986. Manuscripts, South Carolina Historical Society, Charleston, SC.
Wodrow Manuscripts. National Library of Scotland, Edinburgh, UK.
Woodward, Henry. Accounts as Indian agent of the first Earl of Shaftesbury 1674–
   1678. Personal Papers, South Carolina Department of Archives and History, Columbia, SC.

PRINTED PRIMARY SOURCES

Bannatyne Miscellany, Vol. 3. Edinburgh, UK: Bannatyne Society, 1855.
Bolton, Herbert E., ed. *Arredondo's Historical Proof of Spain's Title to Georgia.*
   Berkeley: University of California Press, 1925.
Burnet, Gilbert. *Bishop Burnet's History of His Own Time, Volume I.* London:
   Thomas Ward, 1724.
Carroll, Bartholomew Rivers. *Historical Collections of South Carolina.* New York:
   Harper and Brothers, 1836.
Cheeves, Langdon, ed. *The Shaftesbury Papers and Other Records Relating to Caro-
   lina.* Charleston: South Carolina Historical Society, 1897, reprint 2010.
Cooper, Thomas, and David J. McCord, eds. *The Statutes at Large of South Carolina,*
   Vol. 1 Acts, records, and documents of a constitutional character. Columbia, SC:
   A.S. Johnston, 1837.
———. *The Statutes at Large of South Carolina,* Vol. 2 [Acts, 1682–1716]. Columbia,
   SC: A.S. Johnston, 1837.
Crawford, John. *A New and Most Exact Account of the Fertiles and Famous Colony
   of Carolina.* Dublin, 1683.
DeBeer, E. S., ed. *The Correspondence of John Locke: Volume One: Introduction,
   Letters Nos. 1–461.* Oxford: Oxford University Press, 1976.
Diaz Vara Calderon, Gabriel. "A 17th Century Letter of Gabriel Diaz Vara Calderon,
   Bishop of Cuba, Describing the Indians and Indian Missions of Florida." Trans-
   lated by L. L. Wenhold. *Smithsonian Miscellaneous Collections* 95, no. 16 (1937):
   1–14.
Dunlop, J. G., ed. *The Dunlop Papers.* [3 vols.] Frome: Butler and Tanner Ltd.,
   1932–53.
———. "Spanish Depredations, 1686." *South Carolina Historical and Genealogical
   Magazine* 30, no. 2 (April 1929): 81–89.
Dunlop, William. "Capt. Dunlop's Voyage to the Southward, 1687," edited by J. G.
   Dunlop and Mabel L. Webber, *South Carolina Historical and Genealogical Maga-
   zine* 30, no. 3 (July 1929): 127–33.
———. "William Dunlop's Mission to St. Augustine in 1688," edited by J.G. Dunlop.
   South Carolina Historical and Genealogical Magazine 34, no. 1 (January 1933):
   1–30.
Erskine, John. *Journal of the Hon. John Erskine of Carnock, 1683–1687.* Edinburgh,
   UK: Scottish History Society, 1893.
F[erguson], R[obert]. *The Present State of Carolina, with Advice to Settlers.* Lon-
   don: Printed by John Bringhurst, at the Sign of the Book in Grace-Church-Street,
   1682.

Fountainhall, Sir John Lauder, ed. *The Decisions of the Lords of Council and Session, from June 6th, 1678, to July 30th, 1712*. Edinburgh, UK: G. Hamilton and J. Balfour, 1759.

Fortescue, J. W., ed. *Calendar of State Papers, Colonial Series, America and the West Indies, Volume 11, 1681–1685*. London: HMSO, 1898.

———. *Calendar of State Papers, Colonial Series, America and the West Indies, Volume 12, 1685–1688*. London: HMSO, 1898.

Gallardo, José Miguel, ed. "The Spaniards and the English Settlement in Charles Town." *South Carolina Historical and Genealogical Magazine* 37, no. 2 (April 1936): 49–64; 37, no. 3 (July 1936): 91–99.

Grimball, Paul. "Paul Grimball's Losses by the Spanish Invasion in 1686." *South Carolina Historical and Genealogical Magazine* 29, no. 3 (July 1928): 231–37.

Hakluyt, Richard. *Hakluyt's Collection of the Early Voyages, Travels, and Discoveries of the English Nation*. London: R. H. Evans, 1810.

Hann, John H., ed. *Antonio Matheos Documents, Phases III and IV*. Gainesville: John H. Hann Collection of Colonial Records, P.K. Yonge Library, University of Florida.

———. *Holy Spirit Bay Expedition*. Gainesville: John H. Hann Collection of Colonial Records. P.K. Yonge Library, University of Florida.

Insh, George Pratt, ed. "Arrival of the Cardross Settlers." *South Carolina Historical and Genealogical Magazine* 30, no. 2 (April 1929): 69–80.

———. "The Carolina Merchant: Advice of Arrival." *Scottish Historical Review* 25, no. 98 (January 1928): 98–108.

King, John, and John Kid. *The Last Speeches of the Two Ministers Mr. John King, and Mr. John Kid, at the Place of Execution at Edenburgh on the 14th day of August, 1679*. Place and publisher not given, 1680. Available at http://name.umdl.umich.edu/A47415.0001.001.

Macinnes, Allan I., M. D. Harper, and L. G. Fryer, eds. *Scotland and the Americas: A Documentary Source Book*. Edinburgh, UK: Scottish History Society, 2002.

Mathews, Maurice. "A Contemporary View of South Carolina in 1680." *South Carolina Historical Magazine* 55, no. 3 (July 1954): 153–59.

Parker, Mattie Erma Edwards, ed. *North Carolina Charters and Constitutions, 1578–1698*. Raleigh, NC: Carolina Charter Tercentenary Commission, 1963.

Register of the Privy Council of Scotland, third series, Vols. 7, 8, and 9. Edinburgh, UK: General Register House, 1915–1924.

Rogel, Juan. "Rogel's Account of the Florida Mission." *The Historical Magazine, and Notes and Queries Concerning the Antiquities, History and Biography of America* V, no. 11 (November 1861): 327–30.

Sainsbury, W. Noel, ed. *Calendar of State Papers Colonial, America and West Indies: Volume 7, 1669–1674*. London: Her Majesty's Stationery Office, 1889.

———. *Calendar of State Papers Colonial, America and West Indies: Volume 10: 1677–1680*. London: Her Majesty's Stationery Office, 1896.

Salley, Alexander S., Jr., ed. *Journal of the Grand Council of South Carolina*. Columbia: Historical Commission of South Carolina, 1907.

———. *Narratives of Early Carolina, 1650–1708*. New York: Charles Scribner's Sons, 1911.

BLIOGRAPHY

———. *Records in the British Public Record Office Relating to South Carolina, 1685–1690.* Atlanta: Historical Commission of South Carolina, 1929.

———. *Warrants for Lands in South Carolina, 1680–1692.* Columbia: Historical Commission of South Carolina, 1911.

Serrano y Sanz, M. ed. *Documentos Historicos de la Florida y la Luisiana, Siglos XVI al XVIII.* Madrid: V. Suarez, 1912.

Shields, Alexander. *A Hind Let Loose, or, an Historical Representation of the Testimonies of the Church of Scotland, for the Interest of Christ* [No publisher name or location], 1687. Accessed May 6, 2022. https://quod.lib.umich.edu/e/eebo /A59963.0001.001?view=toc.

Solis de Merás, Gonzalo. *Pedro Menéndez de Avilés: Adelantado, Governor and Captain-general of Florida.* Translated by Jeanette Thurber Connor. Deland: The Florida State Historical Society, 1923.

———. *Pedro Menéndez de Avilés and the Conquest of Florida: A New Manuscript.* Translated by David Arbesu-Fernandez. Gainesville: University of Florida Press, 2017.

Stewart, John. "Letters from John Stewart to William Dunlop," edited by J.G. Dunlop and Mabel L. Webber. *South Carolina Historical and Genealogical Magazine* 32, no. 1 (January 1931): 1–33; 32, no. 2 (April 1931): 81–114; and no. 3 (July 1931): 170–74.

Thurber Connor, Jeannette M., ed. *Colonial Records of Spanish Florida: Letters and Reports of Governors and Secular Persons.* Deland: Florida Historical Society, 1925–1930.

True, David O., ed. *Memoir of Do. D'Escalente Fontaneda Respecting Florida, Written in Spain about the Year 1575.* Miami: Florida Historical Association, 1944.

Ugarte, Ruben Vargas. "The First Jesuit Mission in Florida." *Historical Records and Studies* 25 (1935): 59–148.

University of St. Andrews. *Records of the Parliaments of Scotland to 1707* [website]. Accessed May 6, 2022. www.rps.ac.uk.

Woory, Joseph. "Joseph Woory (1666): Discovery." In *The Travelers' Charleston: Accounts of Charleston and Lowcountry, South Carolina, 1666–1861,* edited by Jennie Holton Fant, 1–7. Columbia: University of South Carolina Press, 2013.

Zubillaga, Félix, ed. *Monumenta antiquae Floridae (1566–1572).* Rome: Monumenta Historica Soc. Iesu, 1946.

SECONDARY SOURCES

Adams, Ian, and Meredyth Somerville. *Cargoes of Despair and Hope: Scottish Emigration to Colonial America, 1603–1803.* Edinburgh, UK: Edinburgh University Press, 1993.

Anderson, David G. *The Savannah River Chiefdoms: Political Change in the Late Prehistoric Southeast.* Tuscaloosa: University of Alabama Press, 1994.

Ashcraft, Richard. *Revolutionary Politics and Locke's Two Treatises of Government.* Princeton, NJ: Princeton University Press, 1986.

Barr, Juliana. *Peace Came in the Form of a Woman: Indians and Spaniards in the Texas Borderlands.* Chapel Hill: University of North Carolina Press, 2007.

Beck, Robin. *Chiefdoms, Collapse, and Coalescence in the Early American South.* New York: Cambridge University Press, 2013.

Beck, Robin A. "Catawba Coalescence and the Shattering of the Carolina Piedmont, 1540–1675." In *Mapping the Mississippian Shatter Zone: The Colonial Indian Slave Trade and Regional Instability in the American South,* edited by Robbie Ethridge and Sheri M. Shuck-Hall, 115–41. Lincoln: University of Nebraska Press, 2009.

Beck, Robin A., Jr., Christopher B. Rodning, and David G. Moore. "Limiting Resistance: Juan Pardo and the Shrinking of Spanish Florida." In *Enduring Conquests: Rethinking the Archaeology of Resistance to Spanish Colonialism in the Americas,* edited by Matthew Liebmann and Melissa S. Murphy, 19–39. Santa Fe, NM: School for Advanced Research Press, 2011.

Blanton, Denise B. "The Factors of Climate and Weather in Sixteenth-Century La Florida." In *Native and Spanish New Worlds: Sixteenth-Century Entradas in the American Southwest and Southeast,* edited by Clay Mathers, Jeffrey M. Mitchem, and Charles M. Haecker, 99–122. Tucson: University of Arizona Press, 2013.

Booker, Karen M., Charles M. Hudson and Robert L. Rankin. "Place Name Identification and Multilingualism in the Sixteenth-Century Southeast." *Ethnohistory* 39, no. 4 (Autumn 1992): 399–451.

Bossy, Denise I., ed. *The Yamasee Indians: From Florida to South Carolina.* Lincoln: University of Nebraska Press, 2018.

———. "Indian Slavery in Southeastern Indian and British Societies, 1670–1730." In *Indian Slavery in Colonial America,* edited by Alan Gallay, 207–50. Lincoln: University of Nebraska Press, 2009.

———. "Spiritual Diplomacy, the Yamasees, and the Society for the Propagation of the Gospel." *Early American Studies* 12, no. 2 (Spring 2014): 366–401.

———. "Yamasee Mobility: Mississippian Roots, Seventeenth-Century Strategies." In *Contact, Colonialism and Native Communities in the Southeastern United States,* edited by Edmond A. Boudreaux III, Maureen Meyers, and Jay K. Johnson, 204–15. Gainesville: University of Florida Press, 2020.

Botwick, Brad. "Prehistoric Settlement and Land Use in the Sea Islands: Archaeological Investigations at a Multi-Component Interior Site on Port Royal Island, South Carolina." *South Carolina Antiquities* 40 (2008): 1–21.

Bowne, Eric E. "'Carryinge awaye their Corne and Children': The Effects of Westo Slave Raids on the Indians of the Lower South." In *Mapping the Mississippian Shatter Zone: The Colonial Indian Slave Trade and Regional Instability in the American South,* edited by Robbie Ethridge and Sheri M. Shuck-Hall, 104–14. Lincoln: University of Nebraska Press, 2009.

———. "Dr. Henry Woodward's Role in Early Carolina Indian Relations." In *Creating and Contesting Carolina: Proprietary Era Histories,* edited by Michelle LeMaster and Bradford J. Wood, 73–93. Columbia: University of South Carolina Press, 2013.

———. "From Westo to Comanche: The Role of Commercial Indian Slaving in the Development of Colonial North America." In *Linking the Histories of Slavery: North America and Its Borderlands,* edited by Bonnie Martin and James F. Brooks, 35–62. Santa Fe, NM: School for Advanced Research, 2015.

———. *The Westo Indians: Slave Traders of the Early Colonial South*. Tuscaloosa: University of Alabama Press, 2005.

Brooks, James. "Conclusion: Intersections: Slavery, Borderlands, Edges." In *What Is a Slave Society? The Practice of Slavery in Global Perspective*, edited by Noel Lenski and Catherine N. Cameron, 429–38. Cambridge, UK: Cambridge University Press, 2018.

Brooks, Mark J., Veletta Canouts, Keith M. Derting, Helen W. Haskell, William H. Marquart, and JoLee A. Pearson. "Modeling Subsistence Change in the Late Prehistoric Period in the Interior Lower Coastal Plain of South Carolina." In *Anthropological Studies: Volume 6*, edited by Mark J. Brooks and Veletta Canouts. Columbia: South Carolina Institute of Archaeology and Anthropology, 1984.

Bushnell, Amy Turner. "Living at Liberty: The Ungovernable Yamasees of Spanish Florida." In *The Yamasee Indians: From Florida to South Carolina*, edited by Denise I. Bossy, 27–54. Lincoln: University of Nebraska Press, 2018.

———. "Ruling 'the Republic of Indians' in Seventeenth-Century Florida." In *Powhatan's Mantle: Indians in the Colonial Southeast*, edited by Gregory A. Waselkov, Peter H. Wood, and Tom Hatley, 195–214. Lincoln: University of Nebraska Press, 2006.

———. *Situado and Sabana: Spain's Support System for the Presidio and Mission Provinces of Florida*. New York: Anthropological Papers of the American Museum of Natural History, 1994.

Childs, St. Julien Ravenel. *Malaria and Colonization in the Carolina Low Country, 1526–1696*. Baltimore: Johns Hopkins University Press, 1940.

Cobb, Charles R., and Chester B. DePratter. "Carolina's Southern Frontier: Edge of a New World Order." In *Archaeology in South Carolina: Exploring the Hidden Heritage of the Palmetto State*, edited by Adam King, 45–61. Columbia: University of South Carolina Press, 2016.

Cogley, Richard W. "The Fall of the Ottoman Empire and the Restoration of Israel in the 'Judeo-centric' Strand of Puritan Millenarianism." *Church History* 72, no. 2 (June 2003): 304–32.

———. "'Some Other Kinde of Being and Condition': The Controversy in Mid-Seventeenth-Century England over the Peopling of Ancient America." *Journal of the History of Ideas* 68, no. 1 (January 2007): 35–56.

Covington, James W. "Stuart's Town, the Yamasee Indians, and Spanish Florida." *Florida Anthropologist* 21 (March 1968): 8–13.

Davenport, Frances Gardiner, ed. *European Treaties Bearing on the History of the United States and Their Dependencies*. Washington, DC: Carnegie Institution of Washington, 1929.

DeJong, David H. *American Indian Treaties: A Guide to Ratified and Unratified Colonial, United States, Foreign, and Intertribal Treaties and Agreements, 1607–1911*. Salt Lake City: University of Utah Press, 2015.

DePratter, Chester B. "Cofitachequi: Ethnohistorical and Archaeological Evidence." *Anthropological Studies* 9 (1989), 133–156.

———. "Irene and Altamaha Pottery from the Charlesfort/Santa Elena Site, Parris Island, South Carolina." In *From Santa Elena to St. Augustine: Indigenous Ceramic*

Variability, A.D. 1400–1700, edited by Kathleen Deagan and David Hurst Thomas, 19–47. New York: Anthropological Papers of the American Museum of Natural History, 90, August 26, 2009.

Devine, T. M. "The Modern Economy: Scotland and the Act of Union." In *The Transformation of Scotland: The Economy since 1700,* edited by T. M Devine, C. H. Lee, and G. C. Peden, 13–33. Edinburgh, UK: Edinburgh University Press, 2005.

Devine, T. M., ed. *Recovering Scotland's Slavery Past: The Caribbean Connection.* Edinburgh, UK: Edinburgh University Press, 2015.

Dobson, David. *Scottish Emigration to Colonial America, 1607–1785.* Athens: University of Georgia Press, 1994.

———. *Scottish Trade with Colonial Charleston, 1683–1783.* Glasgow, UK: Humming Earth, 2009.

———. "Seventeenth-Century Scottish Communities in the Americas." In *Scottish Communities Abroad in the Early Modern Period,* edited by Alexia Grosjean and Steve Murdoch, 105–32. Boston: Brill, 2005.

Donoghue, John. "Indentured Servitude in the 17th Century English Atlantic: A Brief Survey of the Literature." *History Compass* 11, no. 10 (October 2013): 894–902.

———. "Out of the Land of Bondage: The English Revolution and the Atlantic Origins of Abolition." *American Historical Review* 115, no. 4 (October 2010): 943–74.

Dubcovsky, Alejandra. *Informed Power: Communication in the Early American South.* Cambridge, MA: Harvard University Press, 2016.

Dunn, William Edward. *Spanish and French Rivalry in the Gulf Region of the United States, 1678–1702: The Beginnings of Texas and Pensacola.* Austin: The University of Texas Bulletin, 1917.

Edwards, Tai S., and Paul Kelton. "Germs, Genocides, and America's Indigenous Peoples." *Journal of American History,* 107, no. 1 (June 2020): 52–76.

Ethridge, Robbie. "Contact Era Studies and the Southeastern Indians." In *Native and Spanish New Worlds: Sixteenth-Century Entradas in the American Southwest and Southeast,* edited by Clay Mathers, Jeffrey M. Mitchem, and Charles M. Haecker, 63–80. Tucson: University of Arizona Press, 2013.

———. *From Chicaza to Chickasaw: The European Invasion and the Transformation of the Mississippian World, 1540–1715.* Chapel Hill: University of North Carolina Press, 2010.

Ethridge, Robbie, and Charles M. Hudson, eds. *The Transformation of the Southeastern Indians, 1540–1760.* Jackson: University Press of Mississippi, 2002.

Ethridge, Robbie, and Sheri M. Shuck-Hall, eds. *Mapping the Mississippian Shatter Zone: The Colonial Indian Slave Trade and Regional Instability in the American South.* Lincoln: University of Nebraska Press, 2009.

Francis, J. Michael, and Kathleen Kole. *Murder and Martyrdom in Spanish Florida: Don Juan and the Guale Uprising of 1597.* Washington, DC: American Museum of Natural History, 2011.

Frank, Andrew K., and A. Glenn Crothers, eds. *Borderland Narratives: Negotiation and Accommodation in North America's Contested Spaces, 1500–1850.* Gainesville: University of Florida Press, 2017.

Fryer, Linda G. "The Covenanters' Lost Colony in South Carolina." *Scottish Archives: The Journal of the Scottish Records Association* 2 (1996): 98–106.

———. "Documents Relating to the Formation of the Carolina Company in Scotland, 1682." *South Carolina Historical Magazine* 99, no. 2 (April 1998): 110–34.

Gallagher, Craig. "'Them that are Dispersed Abroad': the Covenanters and their Legacy in North America, 1650–1776." *The Scottish Historical Review* 99, no. 3 (December 2020): 454–72.

Gallay, Alan. *The Indian Slave Trade: The Rise of the English Empire in the American South, 1670–1717*. New Haven, CT: Yale University Press, 2002.

Gallup-Diaz, Ignacio. *The Door of the Seas and Key to the Universe: Indian Politics and Imperial Rivalry in Darién, 1640–1750*. New York: Columbia University Press, 2004.

Gingrich, Kurt. "'That Will Make Carolina Powerful and Flourishing': Scots and Huguenots in Carolina in the 1680s." *South Carolina Historical Magazine* 110, no. 1/2 (January/April 2009): 6–34.

———. "'To Erect a Collonie of Scottish Subjects in Aney Pairt of America': The Quest for a Scottish Colony in North America in the 1680s." *Journal of Early American History* 2 (2012): 68–98.

Goetz, Rebecca Anne. *The Baptism of Early Virginia: How Christianity Created Race.* Baltimore: Johns Hopkins University Press, 2012.

Grady, Timothy Paul. *Anglo-Spanish Rivalry in Colonial South-East America, 1650–1725*. London: Pickering and Chatto, 2010.

Graham, Eric J. *A Maritime History of Scotland, 1650–1790.* Glasgow, UK: Tuckwell Press, 2002.

Greaves, Richard L. *Secrets of the Kingdom: British Radicals from the Popish Plot to the Revolution of 1688–89.* Stanford, CA: Stanford University Press, 1992.

Green, William, Chester B. DePratter, and Bobby Southerlin. "The Yamasee in South Carolina: Native American Adaptation and Interaction along the Carolina Frontier." In *Another's Country: Archaeological and Historical Perspectives on Cultural Interactions in the Southern Colonies,* edited J. W. Joseph and Martha Zierden, 13–29. Tuscaloosa: University of Alabama Press, 2009.

Hahn, Steven C. *The Invention of the Creek Nation, 1670–1763.* Lincoln: University of Nebraska Press, 2014.

Hall, Joseph. "Anxious Alliances: Apalachicola Efforts to Survive the Slave Trade, 1698–1705." In *Indian Slavery in Colonial America,* edited by Alan Gallay, 147–84. Lincoln: University of Nebraska Press, 2009.

———. *Zamumo's Gift: Indian-European Exchange in the Colonial Southeast.* Philadelphia: University of Pennsylvania Press, 2012.

Hämäläinen, Pekka. "Shapes of Power: Indians, Europeans, and North American Worlds from the Seventeenth to the Nineteenth Century." In *Contested Spaces of Early America,* edited by Juliana Barr and Edward Countryman, 31–68. Philadelphia: University of Pennsylvania Press, 2014.

Hämäläinen, Pekka, and Samuel Truett. "On Borderlands." *Journal of American History* 98, no. 2 (September 2011): 338–61.

Hann, John H. *The History of the Timucua Indians and Missions*. Gainesville: University of Florida Press, 1996.

———. *Translation of the Ecija Voyages of 1605 and 1609 and the González Derrotero of 1609* [Florida Archaeology, no. 2]. Tallahassee: Florida Bureau of Archaeological Research, 1986.

Heard, J. Norman. *Handbook of the American Frontier: Four Centuries of Indian-White Relationships: Volume 1, Southeastern Woodlands*. Metuchin, NJ: Scarecrow Press, 1987.

Howe, George. *History of the Presbyterian Church in South Carolina, Volume I*. Columbia, SC: Duffie and Chapman, 1870.

Hudson, Charles M. *The Juan Pardo Expeditions: Explorations of the Carolinas and Tennessee, 1566–1568*. Tuscaloosa: University of Alabama Press, 2005.

———. *The Southeastern Indians*. Knoxville: University of Tennessee Press, 1976.

Hyman, Elizabeth Hannan. "A Church Militant: Scotland, 1661–1690." *Sixteenth Century Journal*, XXVI, no. 1 (1995): 49–74.

Insh, George Pratt. *Scottish Colonial Schemes, 1620–1686*. Glasgow, UK: Maclehose, Jackson & Co., 1922.

Jackson, Jason Baird. "Yuchi." In *Handbook of North American Indians: Volume 14: Southeast*, edited by Raymond J. Fogelson, 415–28. Washington, DC: Smithsonian Institution, 2004.

Jardine, Mark. "United Societies: Militancy, Martyrdom, and the Presbyterian Movement in Late-Restoration Scotland, 1679–1688." PhD diss., University of Edinburgh, 2009.

Jennings, Matthew. "'Cutting one anothers Throats': British, Native, and African Violence in Early Carolina." In *Creating and Contesting Carolina: Proprietary Era Histories*, edited by Michelle LeMaster and Bradford J. Wood, 118–39. Columbia: University of South Carolina Press, 2013.

Jordan, Louis. "The Value of Money in Colonial America." *Colonial Currency* (website of University of Notre Dame Special Collections). Accessed April 15, 2021. https://coins.nd.edu/ColCurrency/index.html.

Karsten, Peter. "Plotters and Proprietors, 1682–83: The 'Council of Six' and the Colonies: Plan for Colonization or Front for Revolution?" *The Historian* 38 (1976): 474–84.

Kelton, Paul. *Epidemics and Enslavement: Biological Catastrophes in the Native Southeast, 1492–1715*. Lincoln: University of Nebraska Press, 2007.

King, Adam, and Keith Stephenson. "Foragers, Farmers, and Chiefs: The Woodland and Mississippian Periods in the Middle Savannah River Valley." In *Archaeology in South Carolina: Exploring the Hidden Heritage of the Palmetto State*, edited by Adam King, 34–44. Columbia: University of South Carolina Press, 2016.

Landers, Jane. *Black Society in Spanish Florida*. Urbana: University of Illinois Press, 1999.

———. "The Geopolitics of Seventeenth-Century Florida." *Florida Historical Quarterly*, 92, no. 3 (Winter 2014): 480–90.

LeMaster, Michelle, and Bradford J. Wood, eds. *Creating and Contesting Carolina: Proprietary Era Histories*. Columbia: University of South Carolina Press, 2013.

Lenman, Bruce. "Scots and Access to Spanish America from before Union to 1748." *Journal of Scottish Historical Studies* 38, no. 1 (May 2018): 73–87.

Lesser, Charles H., ed. *South Carolina Begins: The Records of a Proprietary Colony, 1663–1721.* Columbia: South Carolina Department of Archives and History, 1995.

Macinnes, Allan I. "Afterword: Radicalism Reasserted: Covenanting in the Seventeenth Century," *Scottish Historical Review* 99 (December 2020): 473–90.

Martin, Bonnie, and James F. Brooks, eds. *Linking the Histories of Slavery: North America and Its Borderlands.* Santa Fe, NM: School for Advanced Research, 2015.

McIntyre, Neil. "Preface: Experiencing the Covenant at Home and Abroad." *Scottish Historical Review* 99 (December 2020): 331–35.

Menard, Russell R. *Migrants, Servants, and Slaves: Unfree Labor in Colonial British America.* Farnham, UK: Ashgate Publishing, 2001.

———. "Slave Demography in the Lowcountry, 1670–1740: From Frontier Society to Plantation Regime." *South Carolina Historical Magazine* 101, no. 3 (July 2000): 190–213.

Meyers, Maureen. "From Refugees to Slave Traders: The Transformation of the Westo Indians." In *Mapping the Mississippian Shatter Zone: The Colonial Indian Slave Trade and Regional Instability in the American South,* edited by Robbie Ethridge and Sheri M. Shuck-Hall, 81–103. Lincoln: University of Nebraska Press, 2009.

Michie, James L. "The Daws Island Shell Midden: Cultural Diversity on the Lower South Carolina Coast During the Late Archaic Period." *South Carolina Antiquities* 32 (2000): 3–48.

Milanich, Jerald T. "Prehistory of the Lower Atlantic Coast after 500 B.C." In *Handbook of North American Indians: Volume 14: Southeast,* edited by Raymond J. Fogelson, 229–37. Washington, DC: Smithsonian Institution, 2004.

Miller, Perry. "Errand Into the Wilderness." *William & Mary Quarterly* 10, no. 1 (January 1953): 3–32.

Moore, Joseph S. "Covenanters and Antislavery in the Atlantic World." *Slavery & Abolition* 34, no. 4 (2013): 539–61.

Moore, Peter N. "An Enslaver's Guide to Slavery Reform: William Dunlop's 1690 Proposals to Christianize Slaves in the British Atlantic." *Church History,* 91, no. 2 (June 2022), 264–85.

———. *Archibald Simpson's Unpeaceable Kingdom: The Ordeal of Evangelicalism in the Colonial South.* Lanham, MD: Lexington Books, 2018.

———. "Scotland's Lost Colony Found: Rediscovering Stuarts Town, 1682–88." *Scottish Historical Review,* 99, no. 1 (April 2020): 26–50.

Murdoch, Alexander. *Scotland and America, c. 1600–c. 1800.* New York: Palgrave Macmillan, 2010.

Navin, John J. *The Grim Years: Settling South Carolina, 1670–1720.* Columbia: University of South Carolina Press, 2020.

Oatis, Steven J. *A Colonial Complex: South Carolina's Frontiers in the Era of the Yamasee War, 1680–1730.* Lincoln: University of Nebraska Press, 2004.

Paar, Karen L. "Climate in the Historical Record of Sixteenth-Century Spanish Florida: The Case of Santa Elena Re-examined." In *Historical Climate Variability and Impacts in North America,* edited by Lesley-Ann Dupigny-Giroux and Cary J. Mock, 47–58. Dordrecht, the Netherlands: Springer, 2009.

———. "'To Settle Is to Conquer': Spaniards, Native Americans, and the Colonization of Santa Elena in Sixteenth Century Florida." PhD diss., University of North Carolina at Chapel Hill, 1999.

Paley, Ruth, Christina Malcolmson, and Michael Hunter. "Parliament and Slavery, 1660–c. 1710." *Slavery & Abolition,* 31, no. 2 (June 2010): 257–81.

Panich, Lee M., and Tsim D. Schneider, eds. *Indigenous Landscapes and Spanish Missions: New Perspectives from Archaeology and Ethnohistory.* Tucson: University of Arizona Press, 2014.

Piker, Joshua. *Okfuskee: A Creek Indian Town in Colonial America.* Cambridge, MA: Harvard University Press, 2006.

Poplin, Eric C., and Jon Bernard Marcoux. "Yamasee Material Culture and Identity: Altamaha/San Marcos Ceramics in Seventeenth- and Eighteenth-Century Yamasee Indian Settlements, Georgia and South Carolina." In *The Yamasee Indians: From Florida to South Carolina,* edited by Denise I. Bossy, 84–91. Lincoln: University of Nebraska Press, 2018.

Quattlebaum, Paul. *The Land Called Chicora: The Carolinas under Spanish Rule with French Intrusions, 1520–1670.* Gainesville: University of Florida Press, 1956.

Reid, Dawn. "The Causal Relationship Between Population Increases and the Domination of Maize in the Late Prehistoric Diet and the Demographic Consequences of this Change in Subsistence Strategy in the Eastern United States." *South Carolina Antiquities* 30 (1998): 24–36.

Richter, Daniel K. *The Ordeal of the Longhouse: The Peoples of the Iroquois League in the Era of European Colonization.* Williamsburg, VA: Omohundro Institute of Early American History and Culture, 1992.

Rivers, William James. *A Sketch of the History of South Carolina to the Close of the Proprietary Government.* Charleston, SC: MacArthur and Co., 1856.

Robinson, Emily Moberg. "Sacred Memory: The Covenanter Use of History in Scotland and America." *Journal of Transatlantic Studies,* 11, no. 2 (Summer 2013): 135–57.

Roper, L. H. *Conceiving Carolina: Proprietors, Planters, and Plots, 1662–1719.* New York: Palgrave-Macmillan, 2004.

Rowland, Lawrence S., Alexander Moore, and George C. Rogers Jr. *The History of Beaufort County, South Carolina: Volume 1, 1514–1861.* Columbia: University of South Carolina Press, 1996.

Rudes, Blair A. "Pre-Columbian Links to the Caribbean: Evidence Connecting Cusabo to Taino." In *New Perspectives on Language Variety in the South: Historical and Contemporary Approaches,* edited by Michael D. Picone and Catherine Evans Davies, 82–93. Tuscaloosa: University of Alabama Press, 2015.

Shefveland, Kristalyn Marie. *Anglo-Native Virginia: Trade, Conversion, and Indian Slavery in the Old Dominion, 1646–1722.* Lincoln: University of Nebraska Press, 2016.

Smith, Marvin T. "Aboriginal Population Movements in the Postcontact Southeast." In *Transformation of the Southeastern Indians, 1540–1760,* edited by Robbie

Ethridge and Charles M. Hudson, 3–20. Jackson: University Press of Mississippi, 2002.

———. *Coosa: The Rise and Fall of a Mississippian Chiefdom.* Gainesville: University of Florida Press, 2000.

Snyder, Christina. "Native American Slavery in Global Context." In *What Is a Slave Society? The Practice of Slavery in Global Perspective,* edited by Noel Lenski and Catherine N. Cameron, 169–90. Cambridge, UK: Cambridge University Press, 2018.

———. *Slavery in Indian Country: The Changing Face of Captivity in Early America.* Cambridge, MA: Harvard University Press, 2010.

Story, Robert Herbert. *William Carstares: A Character and Career of the Revolutionary Epoch, 1649–1715.* London: Macmillan, 1874.

Swanton, John R. *The Indians of the Southeastern United States.* Washington, DC: Government Printing Office, 1946.

———. *Smithsonian Institution Bureau of Ethnology Bulletin of the Indians of the Southeastern United States.* Washington, DC: Government Printing Office, 1946.

Sweeney, Alexander Y. "Cultural Continuity and Change: Archaeological Research at Yamasee Primary Towns in South Carolina." In *The Yamasee Indians: From Florida to South Carolina,* edited by Denise I. Bossy, 99–127. Lincoln: University of Nebraska Press, 2018.

Sweeney, Alexander Y., and Eric C. Poplin. "The Yamasee Indians of Early South Carolina." In *Archaeology in South Carolina: Exploring the Hidden Heritage of the Palmetto State,* edited by Adam King, 62–81. Columbia: University of South Carolina Press, 2016.

Taylor, Alan. *American Colonies: The Settling of North America.* New York: Penguin Books, 2001.

Thompson, Victor D., Chester B. DePratter, Jacob Lulewicz, Isabelle Lulewicz, Amanda D. Roberts Thompson, Justin Cramb, Brandon D. Ritchison, and Mathew H. Colvin. "The Archaeology and Remote Sensing of Santa Elena's Four Millennia of Occupation." *Remote Sensing* 10, no. 2 (February 2018): 1–30.

Trinkley, Michael. *Further Investigations of Prehistoric and Historic Lifeways on Callawassie and Spring Islands, Beaufort County, South Carolina.* Columbia, SC: Chicora Foundation, 1991.

Trocolli, Ruth. "Elite Status and Gender: Women Leaders in Chiefdom Societies of the Southeastern United States." PhD diss., University of Florida, 2006.

Waddell, Gene. "Cusabo." In *Handbook of North American Indians: Volume 14: Southeast,* edited by Raymond J. Fogelson, 254–64. Washington, DC: Smithsonian Institution, 2004.

———. *Indians of the South Carolina Lowcountry, 1562–1751.* Columbia: University of South Carolina Southern Studies Program, 1980.

Warren, Stephen. *The Worlds the Shawnees Made: Migration and Violence in Early America.* Chapel Hill: University of North Carolina Press, 2014.

Watt, Douglas. *The Price of Scotland: Darien, Union and the Wealth of Nations.* Edinburgh, UK: Luath Press, 2007.

Weir, Robert M. *Colonial South Carolina: A History*. Columbia: University of South Carolina Press, 1997.

———. "'Shaftesbury's Darling': British Settlement in the Carolinas at the Close of the Seventeenth Century." In *The Origins of Empire: British Overseas Enterprise to the Close of the Seventeenth Century*, edited by Nicholas P. Canny, 375–97. New York: Oxford University Press, 1998.

Wodrow, Robert. *History of the Sufferings of the Church of Scotland, from the Restoration to the Revolution* [4 vols.]. Glasgow, UK: Blackie and Son, 1832.

Wood, Peter H. *Black Majority: Negroes in Colonial South Carolina from 1670 through the Stono Rebellion*. New York: W. W. Norton, 1974.

———. "The Changing Population of the Colonial South: An Overview by Race and Region, 1685–1790." In *Powhatan's Mantle: Indians in the Colonial Southeast*, edited by Gregory A. Waselkov, Peter H. Wood, and Tom Hatley, 57–132. Lincoln: University of Nebraska Press, 2006.

Worth, John E. "Razing Florida: The Indian Slave Trade and the Devastation of Spanish Florida, 1659–1715." In *Mapping the Mississippian Shatter Zone: The Colonial Indian Slave Trade and Regional Instability in the American South*, edited by Robbie Ethridge and Sheri M. Shuck-Hall, 295–311. Lincoln: University of Nebraska Press, 2009.

———. "Spanish Missions and the Persistence of Chiefly Power." In *Transformation of the Southeastern Indians, 1540–1760*, edited by Robbie Ethridge and Charles M. Hudson, 53–59. Jackson: University Press of Mississippi, 2002.

———. *The Struggle for the Georgia Coast*. Tuscaloosa: University of Alabama Press, 2007.

———. *The Timucuan Chiefdoms of Spanish Florida, Volume 2: Resistance and Destruction*. Gainesville: University of Florida Press, 1999.

———. "Yamasee." In *Handbook of North American Indians: Volume 14: Southeast*, edited by Raymond J. Fogelson, 245–59. Washington, DC: Smithsonian Institution, 2004.

Index